MANANNAN'S ISLE

DOUGLAS BRIDGE, 1795

With the Nunnery in the background

MANANNAN'S ISLE

by

DAVID CRAINE
M.A., C.P.

THE MANX MUSEUM AND NATIONAL TRUST
1955

PRINTED AND BOUND FOR
THE MANX MUSEUM AND NATIONAL TRUST
BY ROBERT MACLEHOSE AND COMPANY LIMITED
AT THE UNIVERSITY PRESS, GLASGOW

*The cost of publishing this book has been met by the
Trust from the F. M. Cubbon Publication Fund.*

CONTENTS

CHAPTER

FOREWORD *page* 9

INTRODUCTION 11

I. SORCERY AND WITCHCRAFT 13

II. EARLY MANX DOCTORS 31

III. THE LORD OF THE ISLE 36

IV. EARLY MANX SETTLERS IN AMERICA 49

V. CORONER AND MOAR 57

VI. CAPTAIN OF THE PARISH 63

VII. CAPTAIN OF THE TOWN 84

VIII. MILNTOWN 94

IX. THE KILLING OF WILLIAM MAC A FAILLE 100

X. CHURCH AND CLERGY, 1600-1800 104

XI. THE DUNGEON OF ST. GERMAN'S 129

XII. THE GREAT ENQUEST 149

XIII. A MANX MERCHANT OF THE EIGHTEENTH CENTURY 174

XIV. THE POTATO RIOTS, 1825 197

XV. BALLAUGH 210

XVI. KIRK PATRICK OF JURBY 230

XVII. P. M. C. KERMODE 248

INDEX 251

LIST OF ILLUSTRATIONS

DOUGLAS BRIDGE, 1795   *Frontispiece*

PLATE   FACING PAGE

I. CASTLE RUSHEN, 1795   48

II. TYNWALD DAY, 1795   65

III. RAMSEY HARBOUR FROM THE NORTH, 1795   88

IV. PEEL CASTLE AND CATHEDRAL, 1795   144

V. GROUDLE MILL, 1875   161

VI. DOUGLAS 1795   208

VII. RAMSEY BAY FROM BALLURE GLEN, 1795   225

MAP: ADMINISTRATIVE DIVISIONS OF THE ISLE OF
     MAN   104

With the exception of Plate V and the map, the illustrations are from original watercolours by John 'Warwick' Smith, lately presented to the Manx Museum by Major F. C. Harris. Plate V is from a watercolour by J. M. Nicholson, also in the Manx Museum collection.

FOREWORD

By Ramsey B. Moore

Chairman, Manx Museum and National Trust

*I*t is a great personal pleasure to introduce this work by my colleague and Vice-Chairman, Mr. David Craine, M.A., Captain of the Parish of Ballaugh. Mr. Craine belongs to an old Manx family, whose patrimony from earliest days has been in the parish of Ballaugh, where he was born. Like so many of our best youth he left the Island to follow the scholastic profession, but in his case absence made the heart grow fonder and for years he has devoted his spare time to delving among our records, in Man, in London, and elsewhere and he has built up a knowledge of the life of the Manx people which is quite outstanding. In his researches he has combined a fine gift of patient industry with a sympathetic understanding, and established a humorous fellowship with his own folk over the centuries.

On his retirement, it was inevitable that Mr. Craine should return to the Island and, of course, take up his residence in his beloved Ballaugh. His gift of presenting the product of his research in an interesting and entertaining way, clothed in choice English, caused him to be in request up and down the Island. The Isle of Man Natural History and Antiquarian Society made him its President, as did the Manx branch of the Celtic Congress of which he has been for some years the International President. He was early elected a Trustee of the Manx Museum, and he is now Vice-Chairman of the Trust. His fellow-Trustees, appreciating the value of his work, felt that the fruits of his research should be put into permanent form and made available to a wider public. Accordingly, when the endowment established by the Rev. F. M. Cubbon for the publication of original works by Manx authors was able to provide the funds, they invited Mr. Craine to compile a book based on his researches, and it is with the greatest pleasure that the Trustees are now able to place this book before the public with their hearty commendation. Not only in the Isle of Man but to Manx people scattered over the whole world this book will afford interest and give pleasure. Perhaps I may be allowed to add that the proceeds of the sale of this book will go back again into the F. M. Cubbon Fund, and in that

9

way the endowment will be restored to continue the good work for which it was established.

The illustrations in this book are from original pictures here published for the first time. With one exception, they are from the fine collection of twenty-six Manx landscapes painted by John 'Warwick' Smith in 1795, and are not far removed in time from some of the events dealt with in the book. Formerly housed at Blair Castle, these watercolours were lately presented by Major F. C. Harris to the Manx Museum.

RAMSEY B. MOORE
Chairman,

March 1955   *The Manx Museum and National Trust*

INTRODUCTION

*M*ANANNAN'S ISLE is chiefly concerned with some of the aspects and episodes of Manx life and history during the seventeenth and eighteenth centuries.

There are two exceptions—the account of the Potato Riots of 1825, drawn from Home Office correspondence in the Public Record Office, London; and an address on the Manx archaeologist, Philip Kermode, which has been included at the special request of the Chairman of the Manx Museum and National Trust.

The rest of the subject matter is derived from sworn evidences and other historical material found in the Manx national archives, and collected here with much that has already appeared under the writer's name in the Manx Museum Journal and the Proceedings of the Natural History and Antiquarian Society.

Three hundred years ago there was no leisured class in the Isle of Man, with time for the cultivation of the arts and an urge to set down in letters and diaries some account of the life of their day.

Even in the eighteenth century, when increasing Insular trade had brought prosperity to the town merchants and raised the standard of living in the country parishes, the most cultured members of the community, the clergy, were still too much occupied with the struggle for a livelihood to indulge any literary talent they might possess; and with one exception, the celebrated Philip Moore, have left little remains of literary or historical significance, save in chance letters or statements in the Diocesan Registry.

In this and the records of the Civil Administration the searcher is rewarded with brief but vivid glimpses of by-gone days, and forgotten customs and attitudes of mind. In 1737, for instance, there was a robbery at Castletown. The victim, Ann Bell, found that the thief had carried off her money from a 'chist' where it had been hidden in her 'designed winding sheet'—a normal personal possession in an age when death came suddenly, and the average expectation of life was between twenty and thirty years.

She pursued the suspected culprit to Ballasalla, and found him before the door of Deemster Moore, who was holding a Court. Acting in accordance with the customary law she immediately took the surprised and unresisting offender by the arm, led him before the judge, ceremonially set her foot on the the foot of the accused, and, without any other preliminaries, made her complaint and asked for justice. The thief was thereupon searched on the Deemster's 'street', and his guilt confirmed.

Again, in 1722, a case involving the ownership of a horse recalls Bishop Wilson's imprisonment in Castle Rushen; for the animal in dispute was said to have taken part in, and died at the end of, the Bishop's triumphal ride after his release, when three hundred mounted countrymen, playing joyful music on flutes of *trammon* (elder) wood, escorted him home to Bishopscourt.

The prominence which departures from the normal in human behaviour assume in the reports of the disciplinary courts tends to exaggerate their importance as indications of national morale, and tempts the reader to base sweeping statements on special cases. As a corrective one may recall the judgments of other than native observers of the Island scene in the period under consideration—from Archdeacon Rutter who sang the praises of 'this little quiet nation', to Bishop Wilson, a hundred years later, declaring that 'The inhabitants are an orderly civilised people, and courteous enough to strangers; and if they have been otherwise represented it has been by those that knew them not'.

And in the last half of the eighteenth century Governor Smith was able to speak in sympathetic and, indeed, flattering terms of the Manx people when in 1784, he urged the British Admiralty to establish a naval school at Peel; where, with other students, promising youths of the Island should be trained and instructed—'youths', he said, 'with Principles and Constitution equally uncorrupt, in consequence of the Temper and Moral Decency of this unfrequented and retired Island.'

ACKNOWLEDGMENTS

The author would like to express his grateful thanks to His Honour the Clerk of the Rolls and officials of the Rolls and Registry Offices for their unvarying courtesy and helpfulness; to Mr. T. G. Hodgson —by courtesy of the Rev. F. M. Cubbon—for typing; to Major T. E. Brownsdon, Mr. P. W. Caine and Mr. W. T. Quayle; to Mr. Ramsey B. Moore for kindly writing the Foreword of the book, and for his very active and sympathetic interest in its inception; and to Mr. B. R. S. Megaw and Mr. Marshall Cubbon, Director and Assistant Director, respectively, of the Manx Museum, for their invaluable advice and assistance in the provision of illustrations and in the general business arrangements.

Ballaugh, 1955   DAVID CRAINE

I

SORCERY AND WITCHCRAFT

The Isle of Man enjoyed a reputation for sorcery and witchcraft from very early times. The Celtic poets made it the home of the nebulous Manannan and the scene of his magical activities; and pre-Christian navigators, creeping cautiously along the neighbouring coasts of Ireland and Scotland, saw dimly across the sea the necromancer's mantle capping the Island hills.

However uncertain Manannan may be considered, either as a Manx ruler or a Manx magician, there is at any rate some suggestion of the presence of wizards in Man at an early date; for a stone found on Ballaqueeny near Port St. Mary has an Ogham inscription in Irish of the fifth century: *Dovaidona maqui druata*—which has been translated, '[The stone] of Dovaidu son of the druid.'

And long centuries after the Island paganism had yielded to Irish missionaries, one hears an echo of the Druid powers in the claim of a Kirk Michael witch in 1690, when she boasted of a herb she had gathered in the fields of Bishopscourt, that if a man drank the drink of it he would forget himself, but if he drank of it twice he would forget himself for ever.

No details of sorcery are to be found in the Island records until the sixteenth century, though doubtless it was practised there through the Middle Ages, as in every other part of Europe. Martolene, a Governor of Man in 1338, is said to have written a book condemning the witchcraft prevalent there in his time; and, according to a fifteenth century chronicler, Manx witches were widely known for selling winds to sailors, in the shape of magical cords knotted in three or more places. A mariner requiring a moderate wind unloosened one knot; for a very strong wind, two. The three were undone to provide a tempest for the overwhelming of an enemy.

It was not until 1468, when Pope Innocent published his famous Bull against it, that drastic measures were taken to suppress the Black Art in Christian lands. The Isle of Man was inevitably affected by the witch hunt which then swept over Western Europe; but Man, like her neighbour, Ireland, appears to have escaped the excesses which followed elsewhere upon the prosecution of suspected witches.

It is probable that Manx witches had suffered death at an earlier period. The mountain, Slieau Whallian, has long been connected in popular tradition with stories of witches, though there is no record of an execution there. But its nearness to the Tynwald Hill and the nature of the witches' punishment said to have been inflicted there point to Viking times, when offenders were sometimes enclosed in spiked barrels, and so rolled to death down the precipitous slopes of a hill.

A parallel to the Tynwald and Slieau Whallian is to be found close to Duntulm Castle in Skye, an ancient seat of the successors, in the Hebrides, of the kings of Man and the Isles. There, two hillocks are pointed out—one known as the Hill of Justice, and the other, the Hill of Rolling, on which criminals were executed.

The Curragh Glass, 'the grey curragh', a bog also not far from Tynwald, was associated by tradition with witch trial by ordeal of water. If the suspect floated in it she was a witch; if she sank she was innocent. But no documentary evidence of a witch-killing there survives in proof.

Only three cases stand on record in Man in which the unhappy wretches arraigned for witchcraft were condemned to death. The first of these, Alice Ine Quay, was reprieved in 1569, after examination by a jury of matrons composed of 'six honest women'.

The others were a woman, Margrett Inequane, and her son. The precise nature of the charges brought against them is not recorded. After being found guilty in the ecclesiastical court by a jury of six drawn from the parishes affected by their alleged practices they were, according to law, handed over to the temporal power by the Bishop's chief executive officer, the General Sumner. In 1617 mother and son appeared in the Head Court before the Deemsters and a Jury of Twelve out of several sheadings, with the advice of Chapter Quest men. When they had deliberated on their verdict the foreman of the Jury for Life and Death was asked by the Deemster, according to the ancient custom,

Vod y fer-carree soie?—'May the Chancel-man sit?'

Cha vod—'He may not,' was the reply, for the Jury, like their fellows in the Ecclesiastical Court, had found the accused guilty, and the Bishop or Chancel-man, who occupied a place among the judges, left the Court to avoid being involved in the shedding of blood. Thereupon the dread sentence was pronounced: 'That she be brought by the Coroner of Glen Faba to the place of execution, there to be burned till life depart from her body.' A like fate befell Margrett's son, who, with his mother, died at the stake erected near the Market Cross at Castletown.

There is no doubt that the Manx judges and jurymen at that time were greatly influenced by contemporary events in Great Britain. The Scottish King James the Sixth, in his treatise on Demonology, published in 1597, had shown an extraordinary credulity regarding the reality of demons and witchcraft; and his convictions provided an excuse for the exercise of a sadistic vein in his character which enabled him to listen with complacency to the cries of suspected sorcerers put to the torture.

The year after his accession to the English throne in 1603 was marked by the passing, at his instigation, of an English statute against witchcraft which for more than a hundred years sent numerous victims, innocent and guilty, to the pillory, the scaffold and the stake. The Lordship of Man at that time was in dispute among members of the Stanley family, and was temporarily in the hands of the King whose influence was therefore directly felt in the Island.

But the burnings of 1617 mark the last time in Man when the extreme penalty was exacted for sorcery, and thenceforth the Manx records are not darkened by the horrors which attended the witch hunt in Great Britain and other countries during the seventeenth century.

For this one may thank the Manx Ecclesiastical Courts and the moderation of the average Island juryman, rather than his liberation from superstition. He had as profound a belief in the sinister possibilities of witchcraft as any Calvinist of his time, but he hated extremes and the legalised shedding of blood.

The cautious verdict returned by Kirk Arbory farmers in 1666, in a case in which any one of half a dozen counts would have sent a Scottish witch to the fire, is typical:

'We give for answer, that for as much as wee have not had any proofs that she is positively a witch, therefore wee doe cleere her, and say (being questioned) that she is not guilty to death, but notwithstanding, the proofs already by us taken into consideration by the spirituall officers, wee leave her to be punished at their discretion.'

She escaped with three Sunday penances, for which she stood barefoot and white-sheeted, carrying a white wand and with a paper on her breast proclaiming her offence. She went down on her knees before the congregations of Rushen, Arbory and Malew, in turn, confessed her sin and promised reformation.

The last witches to stand formal trial—Ealish Vrian of Ballaugh in 1712, and Jony of Kirk Braddan in 1717—were punished more severely. Bishop Wilson was trying to stamp out the practice of charming which had been stimulated by bad harvests and frequent deadly epidemics; and Ealish was confined in the crypt of St.

German's for thirty days, Jony for fourteen. In addition Jony did penance, Sunday after Sunday, in all the churches of the Island, and stood in sackcloth at the market crosses of the four towns.

John Curghey, the Spiritual judge, was quite aware of the drastic nature of Jony's punishment, and was careful to excuse it by stating that 'the offender, seeming yet to be utterly insensible of her wickedness, it is highly necessary to treat her with an uncommon Degree of Rigor in order to save her, if possible, from perishing eternally'.

IMITATIVE MAGIC

The earliest details of a witchcraft case were recorded in 1560, when *Juan Yernagh*—'John the Irishman'—who had a grudge against Stephen of Ballamoar in Ballaugh, one night set up a *muclagh* or pigsty on a pathway used by the owner of the farm. In it he hung a dead weasel. So to the insult was added the wishing on the farmer of the weasel's fate, by a magical transference through the dust on which the victim had trodden. Juan was found guilty of sorcery but appears to have escaped the extreme penalty.

Another instance of the same sort of imitative magic occurred in Ramsey in 1665, when the witch told her client to bury a goose egg, in the name of the person to be affected, in a dunghill, so that as the egg rotted away, the victim would also decay and die. It was for an alleged practice of this kind that the Duchess of Gloucester was accused in 1446. She was said to have made, with the aid of a notorious witch, a waxen image of Henry VI, so that as it melted away the King's health would decline. The story that she was imprisoned in Peel Castle has been denied.

Nowhere in the Civil or Ecclesiastical records is there evidence or indeed the vaguest tradition of witches' sabbats and other organised witchcraft in Man. In the seventeenth century a Kirk Arbory witch acted in collusion with another known as the *Ben Vane*—'the Fair Woman'; in Kirk Braddan mother and daughter shared their dark secrets; and in Ballaugh two sisters acted together. But these chance partnerships bear no resemblance to the witch companies which are alleged to have existed in Great Britain and on the Continent.

It is clear from the Court records that those believed to be expert practitioners of the Black Art in the Island were in poor circumstances and played upon the credulity of their neighbours to increase their scanty resources.

JANE CAESAR

One notable exception was Jane Caesar of Ballahick, whose husband was a member of the House of Keys in the seventeenth century. No doubt some aspects of her forceful personality set tongues wagging for there appears to have been a general belief in her occult powers, and she was said to have used them to keep her ailing husband alive for many years. Finally, in 1659, she was charged with diabolical practices—mainly on the evidence of a vindictive maid who said her mistress had steeped herbs to steal away the fertility of her neighbours' lands, and, for a sinister purpose, had taken parings from the hooves of a bullock before its sale.

A jury found her not guilty, but nevertheless the Governor who was apparently sceptical regarding her innocence ordered her to avow her freedom of any association with the Satanic powers, before the congregation of Kirk Malew. Sullen and resentful she at first refused, and it was only after the earnest pleadings of her husband, who, aware of her peril in case of non-compliance, repeatedly in a loud whisper begged her to say, 'I renounce the Divil,' that she made a reluctant submission; saying 'I defy the Divil and all his works,' and then cried, 'May those who brought me to this Scandal, never see their eldest children in the estate my youngest are in!'

Probably Manx people viewed occasional but enthusiastic amateurs like Jane Caesar with as great respect as the professionals, for these latter could be bought off, but a man's greatest fear was of a neighbour who, he had reason to believe, envied or hated, and whose malevolence could not be placated with gifts. And that last passionate outburst in Kirk Malew must have chilled the hearts of those who had testified against her.

THE TARRA

The charges against Manx witches follow the universal pattern. They include the power to take away the *tarra*, or increase, from a man's cattle or crops, and transfer it to another, to cast spells upon men and cattle, crops and churning, and to change, at will, into hares.

There is no tradition that Manx witches rode through the air on broomsticks, though they were sometimes credited with similar activities. At the last Manx witch trial in 1717 a witness reported that a traveller, benighted, sought shelter at Jony the witch's cottage, in Kirk Braddan. After he had gone to bed he saw, by the light of the fire at which Jony was sitting, a *saagh* or vessel moving upon the floor. The witch went into it, and both she and the *saagh* flew out of doors. At the latter end of the night she came home by the same convenient transport with a good store of fish.

At the same trial evidence was given of the witch's vindictiveness. 'It was a common saying', said Thomas Cubbon, 'that if anybody denied Jony anything he got no good of it.'

B

Ann Cretney said that Jony asked for milk but got none. At that time the herd of cattle was passing the door. One of the best cows immediately fell down and could not be made to rise. Eight men were engaged in lifting it, whilst the witch and her daughter, highly amused, watched the proceedings from a nearby hedge.

This indiscreet exhibition of a sense of humour did not favourably impress the court any more than the account given by a woman who suddenly saw Jony's figure loom up in the darkness, and, startled, called out to ask who it was. *She mish, yn ven-obbee vooar, ta ayn*—'It is I the great witch'—came the sardonic reply.

Harry Taggart, the miller of Ballaughton, too, described a visit of Jony to his mill when he was grinding. When she asked for flour he refused since it was wheat flour. She replied that the poor should be served of the best. When she had gone a little distance from the mill it stood and could not, by any endeavours, be made to go and grind, until they had changed the bewitched corn upon it. Then, he said, it fell to its grinding as formerly.

The magical transfer of productiveness was one of the commonest charges made against a *caillagh*, and Elizabeth the Kirk Arbory witch was said to have boasted that it was as easy to take away the substance of one man's corn and give it to another as it was to turn a cake of bread upon the griddle. Thomas Parr, Vicar of Kirk Malew for half a century, and Elizabeth's contemporary, had as great a belief in its possibility as any of his parishioners, and in 1650 wrote the following as a presentment from his parish:

'It is a common report that Margrett Ine Reah was seen in the shape and likeness of a haire and returned againe into a woeman.

'And att another time words were spoken by and touchinge the saide Margrett which are not tollerable, which wee desire that the Venerable Court would be pleased to take into examination, namely: the said Margrett sayd to John Bell (who was the man that saw her in the likeness of a haire),

' "Hould thou thy tongue and thou shall never want," and the same J. B. after that bought againe his lands, which he had formerly sould away to others when he was in poverty.'

This widespread belief that the *tarra* or fertility of a neighbour's crops and cattle could be stolen away by unholy charms and in-cantations caused constant anxiety to the Manx Church at a later period.

In the late eighteenth century form of service used in the annual perambulation of the parish boundaries great emphasis was laid upon the sin of covetousness and the witchcraft to which it led.

The outstanding date of such sorcery was May day when practitioners of the Black Art were said to walk before sunrise on the dew in their neighbours' fields, and, gathering some of it, magically transferred the increase to their own crops. In an old ballad the *phynnodderee*, the kindly Manx brownie or troll, is said to go to the meadows *Dy hroggal druight y vadran glass*—'to lift the dew in the grey morning'—to benefit his farmer friends.

Dust, too, was looked upon as an important agent in the magical transference of prosperity. In 1677 Henry Corrin's wife was accused of taking dust from the boundary hedges of neighbours at sowing time. She laid half of it up in her porch and had the other part sown with the first oats which would, as she thought, then have the added vigour and growth magically acquired from other people's fields.

The famous Irish witch, Dame Alice Kyteler, acting from the same motive, swept the dust of the Kilkenny streets towards her son's door, so that he might have the wealth of the town. And on the morning of New Year's day the Manx housewife swept the floor of the *thie-mooar* from the door towards the hearth, in order to keep prosperity within the house for the year.

WITCHES' QUARTER DAY

The beginning of each quarter of the Celtic year—February, May, August, and November—was an important date in the calendar of Manx witchcraft. It marked a renewal in the strength and activity of the sorcerer's operations: a renaissance of power which is hinted at in a belief once current in Scotland that on the first Monday of the quarter the smoke from a witch's chimney went against the wind.

There was therefore a corresponding need at such times for a renewal of protective charms on behalf of those who imagined themselves threatened; and in 1694 Thomas Gell of Rushen was punished by the Church Courts for safeguarding his property by making use of sorceries four times a year.

Some years earlier Elizabeth, the Kirk Arbory witch, was accused of frequenting her customers at the beginning of every quarter. One of them complained that the witch was accustomed to visit his farm at these times in quest of payment for protection, and that once when he had sent her away without the expected gift, he had suffered heavy losses in crops and cattle ever after.

Elizabeth appears to have visited her customers on these quarter-days as regularly as an insurance collector on his rounds, and with profit to herself. Her impoverished neighbours saw her returning from her periodic excursions into the countryside laden with her ill-gotten gains of meat, meal and fish; and, in the end, their fear of the witch was swallowed up by resentment and envy; and in 1666 they informed upon her.

The parish sumner arrested her on charges of having obtained contributions of food for sorcery and wicked practices, and by deluding poor ignorant people; and also because of many resorting to her house to get sorcery off her; and bad signs having been seen by credible persons.

One touch of humanity brightens the indictment and is, one would like to think, an example of the traditional Manx kindliness and tolerance. 'Whereupon', it says, 'she is committed into St. German's prison, and being remote from her friends, we therefore, Henry Maddrell of Ballamaddrell, and William Cubbon of Ballacubbon (to the end that she may have her enlargement out of prison) do become bound for the said Elizabeth.'

The evidence at her trial went to show that Elizabeth vented her spleen on those who annoyed her, by damaging or destroying their goods, and that she often appeared in the form of a hare.

Catherine Norris of Knock Rushen swore that for twelve years she could not rear a calf, but all died, nor make butter or cheese right; during all which time Elizabeth frequented the house of Knock Rushen using, Catherine believed, witchcraft and sorcery there, so that they were very low in estate every way. And the manservant who looked after the kiln for drying corn, could never go there, without meeting a hare about the kiln or lying near it in the gorse.

The hare was mentioned by several other witnesses. One said that he saw it by the Ballanorris sheepfolds, and then it disappeared into the pin-fold. To his surprise, when he looked over the hedge, there was the witch walking inside the pound. 'And', he said, 'being amazed at the sight, he went his way and left her there in that bodily shape that he ever did see her in.' Mrs. Norris, wife of Deemster Norris, who owned the sheep, testified that after the witch's visit to the folds the sheep became ill, and for a long time ceased to give milk.

Captain Stanley of Ballacagen told how with Tyldesley of the Friary, Calcott of Ballalough and others, he was riding to Peel through the Garee Moar, where Elizabeth was pulling ling, and Tyldesley spying her there said, 'Look, a hare!' Calcott replied, 'What! Do you call Elizabeth a hare?'

They rode on without further speech, the mare on which Calcott was mounted going very well. But on the return journey, when they reached the very place where he had named the witch, his mare fell sick and came to a stand. So he had to leave her there, and ride pillion on Stanley's horse. Shortly afterwards the mare died—in the view of the witness, clearly a victim of the vengeful witch.

THE EVIL EYE

The dislike which Manx people felt for a prying person who showed too lively an interest in his neighbour's affairs was partly due to the activities of the parish Church Wardens and the Chapter Quest who were sworn in annually to report breaches of the ecclesiastical law. But it probably sprang, too, from the deeply rooted belief in the Evil Eye. To look at your neighbour's crops too closely and in particular to count his flocks or herds was viewed with great suspicion.

In 1733, in a charge brought against a well-known Ballaugh character, Dan Cowle, the parish lockman, he was reported to have insinuated that the Rector had the Evil Eye, and that when he passed Cowle's team of oxen, one of them lay down, as Dan declared, 'before the Minister's face, a thing it had never done before or since.' Dan said he took dust from the Rector's footsteps and threw it over the ox, which immediately rose to its feet.

An interesting part of the statement is Dan's complaint that in passing him at the plough the Rector had not given him his blessing. Regarding this an eyewitness was made to say that 'it was not becoming to pass by a team, without bidding God Speed'. Gregor in his *Folk-Lore of North-east Scotland* says that ploughmen in that region showed a similar displeasure when the blessing was omitted. The usual Manx benediction was *Dy bishee Jee Ayr shiu*—'God the Father prosper you!' For his double crime of slandering the Rector and charming the ox, the lockman did penance in the churches of Ballaugh, Kirk Michael and Jurby.

In 1672 a Kirk Braddan farmer out after his lambs observed Thomas Thwaites, Vicar of Kirk Onchan, leaning on the field gate and watching with interest the rounding up of the flock. Later some of them died, and the owner, convinced that his loss arose from the Vicar's baleful eye, carried the carcasses to the Vicarage and piled them up in the porch.

It is not likely that the punishment visited upon the farmer—committal to the Bishop's prison and one hour sitting on the stool of correction on Douglas market day at the height of the market—altered his belief in the malevolence of the Vicar.

THE SIEVE AND SHEARS

One of the most ancient and enduring practices of sorcery was that of coscinomancy, or divination by the use of a sieve, for the discovery of thieves. Reference to it is found in Greek literature of the third century B.C., and it was used in Ireland and Scotland in the seventeenth century. Four Manx cases which attracted the censure of the Church belong to the eighteenth century, when the practice had largely fallen into disuse elsewhere, having been superseded by the 'Key and book'.

In ceremonial use the sieve was suspended from a thread, or balanced on the point of a pair of shears which was held upright by two fingers. The participants then prayed to the gods for assistance and repeated the names of persons suspected of the theft. The sieve swung round at mention of the culprit. Samuel Butler, the seventeenth century satirist, writes of 'The oracle of sieve and shears, That turn as certain as the spheres'.

Both instruments were believed to possess magical qualities. In the ancient world the sieve was the symbol of the rain-giving powers of the gods. Iron was credited with a potency against agents of evil, a belief which may date from the time when Bronze Age warriors had to yield to foes armed with weapons of iron.

The Manx case given in most detail happened in the parish of Kirk Braddan in 1733. The affair came to light owing to the protests of two men of the parish whose names had been submitted to the trial of the sieve, but who claimed to have been always of honest character. 'Yet', they wrote in their petition to the Vicars-General, 'James Kelley and his wife have very wickedly, by the diabolical practice of the Sieve and Shears, aspersed and slandered the petitioners as accomplices in a Theft and Robbery committed in the Parish some years ago.' The cautious charge made by the Vicar and parish officers was, 'Jane Kelley, wife to James, for turning a sive after the manner, as we think, to be charms or witchcraft.'

The witnesses testified that at a gathering in John Quilliam's house James Kelley proposed the turning of the sieve in order to discover a theft. He declared that the sieve was true, and that his mother had practised such divination. Jane and the housewife held the sieve—the former playing the principal part and naming suspects. She was not satisfied with the inertness of the sieve when the petitioners' names were spoken, and persisted in repeating them. It was this, very naturally, which aroused their indignation.

John Quilliam's wife pleaded entire ignorance of such wicked practices and said that she only held the sieve when James pressed and urged it. The two Kelleys were found guilty and sent to St. German's prison, later performing penance at the Parish Church.

THE CURSES

Among the most impressive weapons at the command of witches and occasional enthusiastic amateurs were the ritual curses. It was said of Ciaran of Clonmacnoise, one of the great Irish saints whose keeills and devotees were to be found in Man, that he was powerful in blessing and violent in cursing—two qualities greatly, if not equally, admired by the early Celtic church. And perhaps it was from it and the pagan cults preceding it that the Manx inherited a flair for picturesque cursing and vituperation which was stimulated by the practices of medieval society and survived the Reformation.

One must not, however, put all the blame for violent speech upon our Celtic ancestors. In 1758 John Cashen of Ramsey, imprisoned for the offence of uttering, as he admitted, 'rash and imprecatious expressions', pleaded that his language had been corrupted by his association with the British Navy into which he had been forced by the press-gang some years before.

Women apparently had a greater fund of striking phrases than men. 'The curse of God be his bed and boulster!' cried a Kirk German woman in 1782. It was assumed that the curse used on behalf of the poor and dependent was of peculiar efficacy. Two oft-used expressions were 'The curse of the widow', and 'The curse of the fatherless children'. There is also the case of forlorn Richard Quirk who in 1669 uttered *Y mollaght dooinney-treoghe*—'the curse of a widow-man.'

Among the imprecations of the greatest power were the euphemistic 'Curse of the King of Easter, of the King of Light, and of the King of the Sabbath'; and *Drogh ooir, drogh yerrey as beggan grayse* —'An ill hour, an ill end and little grace (of God).'

Of those coming down from pre-Christian times there were the *Shiaght mynney mollaght*—'the seven swearings of a curse;' and most potent and most terrifying of all, the *Skeab Lome*—'the bare broom,' or the besom of destruction.

The *Shiaght mynney mollaght* was, in early times, associated with a ritual in which the actor turned a round Swearing Stone seven times anti-clockwise in the cup-shaped hollow of a larger stone. This ceremonial was said to have sometimes taken place furtively at night on the summit of the Tynwald Hill, and at other times on its north side. The simple utterance of a curse was almost as greatly disliked by the Manx as one with ritual accompaniment. In 1677 a man working in John Moore's haggard at Pulrose said, 'I hear bad talk of my god-daughter. If it be true, my seven curses on her!' Moore immediately reported him to the Church authorities and he afterwards did penance at Kirk Braddan.

SKEAB LOME

The curse and ritual of the *Skeab Lome* does not appear to have an exact parallel in folklore elsewhere, though, of course, the association of the broom plant with witchcraft has been wide-spread. In some parts of Great Britain there is the old saying, 'If you sweep the house with the blossomed broom in May, you sweep the head of the house away.'

The Manx word *lome* (naked or bare) as it is used in the name *Skeab Lome* has the added significance of complete destruction. It has a similar implication in the now forgotten exclamation, *Losta lome!* literally, 'The naked fire!' or as Kelly's dictionary translates it, 'Hell fire!'—the fire of perdition: a cry used by the Manx in extreme and desperate urgency.

Skeab Lome was, therefore, a curse of annihilation, aimed first of all at the *chiollagh* or hearth, the gathering place and centre of the family, with its ever-burning turf fire, mystic symbol of life—in primitive times set in the middle of the one-roomed *thie mooar* or 'great house', and later at what was called 'the upper end of the house'.

In the full ritual of the *Skeab Lome* the person uttering the imprecation carried a besom with which she made the gestures of sweeping. Her hair was uncovered and fell loose upon her shoulders; her face was turned to the door of the enemy's house. And as she swept she cursed.

There were many variations and abridgments of the maledictory formula. The following, used in Rushen in 1744, is typical:

Dy jig Skeab Lome ort hene, er dty hiollagh, er dty hlaynt, er dty chooid as er dty chloan!—'May the Besom of Destruction come upon thee thyself, upon thy hearth, upon thy health, upon thy possessions and upon thy children!'

A Kirk Patrick curse of 1735 was *Skeab Lome, chiollagh gyn chloan, as follym faase gyn cass gyn rass, er y dooinney slesh y Cleigh!*
—'The besom of destruction upon the man belonging to the Cleigh, a fireside without offspring, and an empty desolation with neither root nor seed!'

In accordance with Celtic custom a person often knelt to pronounce a curse, for, like the removal of the coif and kerchief and the loosening of the hair, the act of kneeling was believed to magnify greatly the potency of the malediction. 'Rise off your knees! Curse nobody on your knees!' cried a horrified Kirk Maughold man, on seeing an aggrieved neighbour suddenly drop to the ground to curse a false accuser.

In 1713, at a time when professional lawyers had not yet appeared in the Manx courts, Henry Quay, arguing his case with an opponent before Deemster McYlrea, suddenly dropped upon his knees and bitterly cursed his opponent, 'using', it was said, 'such imprecations as are not fit to be repeated.' The scandalised judge passed him over to the Church to discipline him with the cold comfort of the Bishop's dungeon at Peel.

As time went on *Skeab Lome* lost much of its early significance. It was no longer reserved for great occasions of emotional hate, but was evoked casually by the trivial irritations of everyday life. *Skeab Lome!* was pronounced on the shingle the fisherman shook out of his net, on frogs and apple-stealers, on trespassing sheep and unproductive hens—to quote instances taken at random from the records. And when the Church Courts relaxed their discipline in face of the growing hostility of the community, the Curses which had been raised to an undeserved importance by Ecclesiastical censures, lost their terrifying qualities and largely fell out of use.

A woman of Rushen, however, is said to have used the broom ritual in the last half of the nineteenth century.

ANTIDOTES

There was a general belief that the most effective way of neutralising a witch's spells was to draw her blood above the breath—generally by scratching the forehead with a pin.

'She is a *caillagh ny pishag* (a witch of charms) and by pishags doth she live!' exclaimed Christian of Cranstal, Captain of Kirk Bride in 1695, speaking of a neighbour's wife; and called for a knife that he might draw her blood. It was in this way that the mistresses of Scarlett, Knock Rushen and the Friary sought for relief from the spells they believed Elizabeth the Kirk Arbory witch had cast upon their cattle, crops and churning. The housewives, who had not been able to make satisfactory butter and cheese for some time, fell in turn upon the witch at a convenient opportunity and scratched her face. Afterwards, as they complacently told the judges, they made butter and cheese well enough, and all things prospered with them.

At the trial of the Ballaugh witch, Ealish Vrian, John Corlett of Broughjiarg Beg told that Ealish and her sister came to his wedding feast, and that they were seen to take up dust near the threshold of the outer door, and put it under the chair where his bride sat. Thenceforth for years no heir was born to the house of Broughjiarg. Finally in desperation, Katreena his wife sought out the witches and scratched both above the breath, and her desire was soon gratified.

The legality of such barbarous assaults was recognised by the Manx Courts, as elsewhere. In 1617 the defendant in a blood-wipe was cleared with the consent of the Deemster because he did it in defence of his life and to avoid harm that might befall him by the witchcraft of the complainant.

Three other antidotes often used were dust, iron and fire. Dust was taken from the footsteps of the suspected sorcerer, or from crossroads and the church stile, where, sooner or later, all the people of the parish passed. When sprinkled over the bewitched victim it neutralised the evil influence. As this procedure can be carried out in secret it has survived to the present day.

An example of the common belief in the magical potency of iron is found in the tale of Jane Corrin who was combing wool at Ballacallin in Kirk Marown. She said that Jony of Kirk Braddan came in and received an alms from the mistress of the house. Jane, having heard ill things of the witch, then put the tongs into the fire in the name of Jony who was thereby kept against her will, and was only able to leave the house later in the evening, when the wool comber withdrew the tongs from the fire. Afterwards Jane Corrin had a long and severe illness which she attributed to the witch.

At a burial in Kirk Andreas in 1628 Philip Crebbin showed a similar belief in the restraining power of the metal. Apparently he feared that the spirit of the dead, of whose malignity he was apprehensive, would return to plague him. He therefore unobtrusively dropped a piece of iron into the partly filled grave; but was detected and did penance for his fault.

FIRE

Fire occupied the most important place among the safeguards against witches and agents of evil in general. On the eve of *Laa Boaldyn*, May Day, gorse bushes were set on fire everywhere to drive out the witches and fairies, so that, as an eyewitness wrote in 1837, the evening sky looked down upon the scene of a universal conflagration. The custom quickly declined in the last half of the nineteenth century, and had almost died out at its end.

The memory of the Druidical practice of giving protection to cattle by passing them between two fires persisted into the twentieth century and there are Manxmen still living who, years ago, secretly drove their animals through the smoke of a fire lit in some spot out of sight of their neighbours.

THE OURAL LOSHT

For protective and cleansing purposes fire was used in another way. In 1719 a farmer's wife in Rushen was accused of the diabolical practice of making *oural losht*, or a burnt sacrifice, in the church way, of a calf, to avert their ill luck in cattle. Incidentally, the informer in the case sought to justify the charge by pointing out the great success of the operation for, after it, he said, the farmer's cattle had escaped further loss and had multiplied.

Many other cases of burnings have been recorded up to the present century. There is nothing to suggest that the Manx *oural losht* was a sacrifice in the ordinary acceptance of the term, or an appeal to a supernatural being; though it is said, on somewhat shaky evidence, that cases of lambs burnt on May Day, *son oural*—for a sacrifice—occurred in the nineteenth century. The actors in the rite believed that the purifying virtue of fire would drive away or destroy the malignant spirit present in the dead or dying animal, and so prevent further misfortune.

In 1847, a man whose ducks were dying of a mysterious complaint, took the last dying bird and, building a great fire at cross roads within a mile of Douglas, surrounded the duck with a ring of burning ling. People who had gathered at the spot swore they saw the Evil Spirit rising from the flames as the duck expired.

The *Oural* was also intended to overcome the Evil Eye, or other malignant activity of the person responsible for the disease. This could be effected if dust from the enemy's footsteps were consumed in the fire. This done the evil-doer would not only lose his power but would be magically attracted to the place, and be the first to arrive.

For the scene of his fire, therefore, the farmer invariably chose a highway in frequent use, and along which travelled the people suspected by him. In 1713 the wife of the Captain of Kirk Arbory burnt a calf in the high road at the Ballabeg. The fire lasted more than a day, its fumes causing great annoyance to passers-by and the people of the neighbourhood, and the lady was presented.

The court, however, treated her tenderly and adjourned the case indefinitely, for she was socially important, and moreover, it would have been difficult to bring home a charge of witchcraft, since incantations were apparently not used in such circumstances.

In a later case which occurred a hundred years ago a dead cow was burned on a fire of turf, coal and gorse, on the Starvey Road two miles from Peel. When an old man well-informed in the practice arrived he found that the thrifty farmer had skinned the animal and sent the hide to the tanner's. He declared that this destroyed the value of the proceedings, which were stayed. The hide was brought back by the reluctant owner and then the whole animal burnt, to everyone's satisfaction.

At this point the spectators saw, through the drifting reek and smoke, a figure approaching. It was a reveller returning with unsteady steps from a *mellia* or reapers' feast. Instantly they cried out that he was the worker of witchcraft. Sobered by fear he took to his heels and so escaped the rough treatment which he might have received from the excited and uncritical crowd.

CHARMS

Like their Druid predecessors the witches claimed a knowledge of charms and curative herbs to overcome sickness, and their sinister reputation did not prevent constant demands for their services by a community which seldom saw a doctor. In 1713 when Gilbert Cain who had a sick child was asked by the Spiritual Judge why he had sought help from Ealish Vrian he replied rather pathetically that if it was in her power to hurt his child, it must surely also be in her power to do her good. Ealish sold charms to rid the fields of weeds, and restore fertility; and on one occasion when refused a present by a farmer, reminded him that at his request she had cleared his fields of the *basthag bwee* (yellow marigold). She sold love potions which, according to the evidence, were not always successful.

The heads of one family called Teare of Ballawhane in Kirk Andreas restricted their activities to White Witchcraft; and for at least five generations clients came to them from all parts of the Island in search of charms for sickness, wounds, success in fishing and other contingencies. They were also believed to be able to foretell the future; and in 1741 a witness in the Church Courts told how he had met a sad and anxious Kirk Braddan man making his way on foot twenty weary miles over the mountains to Ballawhane, to find out if his sick wife was going to recover.

In vain did Bishop Wilson and his clergy preach against charms and point out that King Saul received divine punishment for consulting a charmer. The Church's counsel went for the most part unheeded, and even in the last half of the nineteenth century, highly respected and respectable members of Church and Chapel, when need arose, sent to the witchdoctor of Kirk Andreas for herbal charms to counteract evil influences and prosper the churning.

Many protective charms were used at the time of the four great festivals of the Celtic year. On *Oie Voaldyn*, May Day eve, leaves of the trammon or elder tree and primroses were strewn on the thresholds, and crosses made from a twig of the *cuirn* or mountain ash were placed above the doors, fastened on animals and worn on the person.

The *bollan bane*, St. John's wort, or mugwort, was used as a charm at the Midsummer feast. It was worn in olden times by those who attended the annual meeting of the Tynwald at St. John's, and this use of it was revived over twenty years ago.

Among unusual charms was one which a Kirk Santan farmer disclosed in 1690 when he innocently asked the Vicar 'to give him libertie to tie some of his sister-in-law's haire to the steeple of the church above the bell, to cure her of the falling evill, this to be done three Sundays before sunrise, it being a charm given him by a wise woman of Ballasalla'.

Although snakes were banished from Man under the same happy dispensation as that bestowed on Ireland, lizards remained and were made use of as a charm. A *jialgan leaghyr* or mancreeper lizard was steeped in water and the liquid sprinkled over the cattle to promote fertility.

THE FAIRIES

There are many accounts of fairies in Manx folklore, but remarkably few references to them in sworn evidence. Where they are mentioned it is clear that, as in Scotland, they were regarded as malevolent beings with none of the pretty accessories given them by imaginative writers in modern times. Charges of commerce with fairies as with witches, were looked upon as of the greatest gravity, and were bitterly resented by the accused.

Two of the most ancient of Manx charms were directed against them. The first arose from the belief that the flint arrowheads found on pre-historic sites were of fairy origin. A projecting part of the brooighs of Ballaugh is known as the *Gob ny Shee*—'the promontory of the fairies'—for the field on the top was a Stone-age settlement and is thickly sown with flint chips and with occasional arrowheads.

Fairies were supposed to use ill-disposed mortals to fire the arrows. The charm against elf-shots runs: 'If it came out of the earth or the air or from under the tide of the sea let it return again.'

Judging from the charms which have survived in writing most of them were prayers depending for potency upon the names of God and the Saints. The most attractive is the well-known protective charm against fairies and all other evil influences of the night, with its invocation of St. Columba:

> *Shee Yee as shee ghooinney,*
> *Shee Yee er Columb Killey,*
> *Er dagh uinnag, er dagh ghorrys,*
> *Er dagh howl goaill stiagh yn Re-hollys,*
> *Er kiare corneillyn y thie,*
> *Er y voayl ta mee my lhie,*
> *As shee Yee orrym-pene.*

Peace of God and peace of man,
Peace of God on Columb Killey,
On each window, on each door,
On each hole admitting moonlight,
On the four corners of the house,
On the place of my rest,
And the peace of God on myself!

II

EARLY MANX DOCTORS

When A. W. Moore sat down in 1901 to record the names of notable Manx figures in medicine and surgery he was only able to find three whom he considered suitable for inclusion in his volume of *Manx Worthies*, and all were of the nineteenth century.

One, Samuel Nelson, was son of John Nelson, Rector of Kirk Bride, and brother of the ill-fated poet Esther Nelson. He was long remembered for the nobility of his character and his disinterested services to the poor.

The other two—Charles Bland Radcliffe and his brother, John Netten Radcliffe—were connected with Ballaradcliffe in Kirk Andreas, and won places in the Dictionary of National Biography. The younger man, Charles, was a distinguished epidemiologist. He discovered the source of the cholera outbreak in London in 1866 and was an authority on the then infant science of public hygiene.

The only practitioner's name of the eighteenth century which has survived the oblivion of time is that of a Frenchman, Dominique de la Mothe. He was surgeon on one of the semi-piratical privateers of the period. His vessel captured several British ships, but was eventually taken by the prisoners on board and brought into Douglas. De la Mothe was released on parole and contrived to conceal himself when his comrades were being drafted to England. His good fortune continued. He cured the Governor's wife of an indisposition, was released, and married a Castletown girl. The late Deemster Lamothe was his descendant, and many other Manx people can claim consanguinity with the surgeon from Gascony.

The picturesque circumstances of his settlement here made some writers assert that there were no trained doctors in Man until his arrival.

But the 'House', as the whole establishment of Governor, officials, garrison and Castle was termed, was provided with a surgeon at least as early as the sixteenth century, and a Doctor Moryson was practising in Castletown round about 1585. His descendant, Daniel Moryson, who died in 1704, was the most prominent member of his

31

profession for more than a generation. His charges for daily visits to the Nunnery, where Major Robert Calcot lay ill in 1682, were two and sixpence a day.

With this one may compare the fixed salary of William Fowler, Surgeon to the House in 1580, when he received four nobles a year, equivalent to sixpence a week. Of course the vastly greater buying power of money at that time must be considered. Otherwise one might come to wrong conclusions with regard to the hygiene of the Houses, on finding that the total cost of soap for Castle Rushen and its occupants in 1601 was one shilling. As for food, prices varied from year to year, but at that time sheep supplied to the House were sixpence each and hens three a penny—no doubt a cheaper rate than that accepted in the open market.

In common with the other officials the Surgeon to the House enjoyed various perquisites—lodging, bread, beer, turf for firing, candles, etc.—received fees for special services and enjoyed the fruits of his private practice.

Moore's *History* gives the name of Doctor John Lace (*d.* 1654) as a proof that medical men were to be found in Man in the seventeenth century. But although Lace was held in some repute and credited with the possession of extraordinary powers bordering on witchcraft, the doyen of the profession in the mid-seventeenth century was Thomas Shaw. Like nearly all the doctors of the period he lived at Castletown and his appeals at law for payment of accounts show that the modern reluctance to give the doctor his due is not a new aspect of human nature.

In 1673 he was concerned in the case of a boatman wounded in a fracas at Peeltown. John Whiteside, a trader from Belfast, had employed Donald Christian and his boat's crew to load herring. When the time of payment came the Irishman offered half a crown, but the boatman demanded four shillings, and, when it was refused, threatened to have Whiteside's vessel arrested for debt.

This aroused the anger of the trader, who was also irritated by Christian's speaking in Manx. Suddenly drawing his rapier he lunged at the sailor and, missing a lethal spot, ran him through the arm.

The affair was reported to the Governor, who appointed Dr. Shaw, his assistant Thomas Radcliffe and James Sprewll, apothecary, to examine the wound. Their written report is a pleasing example of a pious non-committal expression of opinion which left their professional reputations unblemished, whatever happened.

'Humbly saying', they began, 'that the wound is not in itself mortall, but, with diligence and care, can be made, by God's blessing, recovered. But, as to that question, we reserve the judgment of others that may have better skill, next unto God himself, who hath not only the negative vote in all things [that] comes to pass, but doth absolutly determine them by His omniscency.'

The wounded man recovered, whereupon the Court ordered Whiteside to pay thirty shillings to the surgeon and his assistants, and twenty shillings compensation to Christian. A soldier was set to guard the offender until he settled his account.

On a previous occasion in 1662 Shaw had been asked to make a report on alleged wounds in a mysterious case involving Robert Vinch, on whose land Finch Road, Douglas, was built one hundred and fifty years later. The Governor, having been informed that Vinch had been grievously wounded by John Quayle, Junior, of Douglas, had impetuously ordered Quayle's commitment to the Castle, and then sent the surgeon to view Robert's body. Shaw took with him two soldiers from the Bulwark (i.e. Douglas Fort)—William Flexney and Sylvester Moore—as witnesses and in case Vinch objected to being viewed. To their great surprise they could find no wound or mark on his body; and the chagrined Governor in a statement of the case must have been speaking from the heart when he wrote, 'It is the duty of all good Christian people to certify to the truth to the utmost of their knowledge.'

The Doctor did not always display the diplomatic humility implicit in the report of the Peeltown wounding, and in 1657, John Pigott brought an action against him for 'his slanderouse reproachfull and opprobrious expressions . . . towards the plaintiff's wife relating to the late cure', which Shaw had undertaken but failed to perform; and claimed the sum of ten pounds, damages.

Like everyone else of his period, from the Governor and Deemsters downwards, Shaw did not limit his activities to his own calling, and sold snuff and tobacco. His charge for blood-letting—a favourite and sometimes deadly remedy—was eighteen pence.

When a patient was not satisfied with the help provided by Manx doctors, and was well enough off to afford the expense, he sailed to Dublin. In 1692, Susanna, the ailing daughter of David Murrey, a prosperous Castletown merchant, was sent to the Irish capital and paid heavily for the services of a doctor from Poland whom she found there, but without avail.

On the whole the countryside saw very little of doctors. Malew had no physician in 1665, though so close to the Manx capital, and spokesmen for Arbory in that year declared, 'Concerning the practice of physic or chirurgery or midwives we know nothing, for it was never usuall among us. . . .'

c

Ballaugh, however, had a doctor in 1687, his wife being brought before the Ecclesiastical courts for failing to go to Church. A Doctor Abraham Silk appeared in Jurby in the first decade of the eighteenth century. He answered to the description applied by Vicar-General Robert Parr to an Island visitant of a previous generation: 'A wandering fellow and went up and down the countries and had no resting place.'

Silk acquired fame for his inebriety rather than for cures. His habit of falling over unfortunate patients he was called in to see, and his frequent inability to keep on his horse's back without assistance, soon brought him under the censures of the Church. A wordy combat with a dissatisfied patient whom he encountered on the highroad in Lezayre, when both men cursed one another with extraordinary vigour and fluency, once more attracted the attention of the authorities, and after his trial he disappeared from the Island.

Silk was the contemporary of two other doctors—Laurie and Calcott. Laurie, a Scotsman, caused a great sensation in Castletown in 1714 by hinting at the possession of necromantic powers. He said he would sacrifice a black cock, and then make the moon stand still. At the beginning of the eighteenth century very few of the clergy or their people could accept such a threat with indifference, and Laurie was hurried off to the Bishop's dungeon at Peel, where he was not likely to get a bird suitable for his purposes.

Robert Calcott also came into conflict with the Church, being charged with tippling—a widespread vice in a century of cheap liquor—and neglect of Sabbath observance. His excuse for non-attendance at Church might have come from a hardworked Health Service practitioner of the present day. He put the blame upon his patients, 'who', he said, 'urgently press upon him for administering of Phisick and drawing blood.'

Calcott belonged to a family whose founder is said to have married the dispossessed Prioress when the Nunnery of Douglas was dissolved, and settled there in the sixteenth century. The traditional Illiam Dhone ballad includes the Calcotts among his enemies, and correctly predicts the disappearance of the family. Robert himself died in 1713.

The story of one case in which Doctor Moryson was concerned is attractive in its revelation of the pathetic efforts of a dying man to save his friend from suspicion of foul play.

One evening in 1678 Philip Brew of Kirk Santan was making his way homeward when he was overtaken by William Bredson, who, in greeting him with an affectionate slap on the shoulder, caused him to stumble on the uneven path and lose his footing. In the fall his leg was broken. When the surgeon enquired into the causes of the accident the injured man declared that it had happened when he was alone. Moryson apparently doubted the truth of this story, but Philip persisted that he himself was solely responsible for his mishap. Even when his case was desperate and the Sacrament had been administered he loyally stuck to his original statement. But at last with the near approach of death the enormity of his sin in lying at such a time, and, as the Manx of his time firmly believed, thus forfeiting the grace of God and the hope of salvation, weighed heavily upon him. He sent for the Vicar, John Cosnahan, and told him the truth, and the reason for his denials.

'He had no hurt in his heart towards me,' pleaded the dying man, and William Bredson standing by his friend agreed, with tears in his eyes. Later the Coroner's jury found for accidental death.

Doctor Patrick Christian, a Ramsey physician who was born in 1691 and reached the age of eighty-nine, perhaps by avoiding his own remedies, has left at least one prescription behind him. Written in Latin, it falls into two parts. The first mentions roots of sarsaparilla, ginger and raspberry; green willow, St. John's wort (in Manx, *luss y chiolg*) and juniper berries. In the second, among other things, are powders made of red coral, crab shell, and millepedes—small wormlike animals with many legs.

His patient died and the Doctor's failure drew upon him the reproaches, merited or not, of the relatives.

'The famous and ingenious Doctor, one Patrick Christian,' wrote the patient's father, 'an imperfect and pretended doctor of physick, who thinks neither a sin or shame to enter his claime for six pounds against your petitioner for service done to his son, which your petitioner had very great reason to wish that he had let alone, and to have given him as much more for doing the same. . . .'

Doctor Christian's prescription of coral goes a long way back. Red coral, pulverised by fire and mixed with water, was one of the chief magical draughts of the ancient Druids, and red coral amulets are still used in Italy as a protection against the Evil Eye.

To the Manx country people of the seventeenth and eighteenth centuries, periodically scourged by fevers and epidemics, there seemed little difference in result between the medicinal herbs of Patrick with his coral and millipedes, and the medicinal herbs and incantations of the charmers.

Possibly, thought the Manx, the white witches with their claim to supernatural powers might be the more effective, and Bishop Wilson, in 1712 and later, fulminated against the sin and use of charms with little success.

III

THE LORD OF THE ISLE

THE LORD'S PREROGATIVE

The meagre medieval records of Man afford no evidence of the existence of serfdom in the Island when the new Lord obtained possession in 1406, or afterwards; though thousands of people in Great Britain were of servile status even in Elizabethan times. The Cistercians, like the other Monastic Orders of the Middle Ages, were owners of serfs, but here again there is no indication that Rushen Abbey had bondmen at the beginning of the fifteenth century.

Many of the customary laws, however, appear to have sprung from the usage of the medieval Manor, with its tradition of servitude. How far the native Kings of the Norse dynasty went in introducing the practices of feudalism is not clear, but it is probable that they and the rulers who succeeded them imposed upon the institutions they found in Man many of the forms and customs of the English feudal lordship.

At the root of Manorial practice was the 'Profit' of the Lord, and this was held up as one of the main objectives in every department of the Island Government. Fortunately for the Manx, a favourable financial return generally depended upon the provision of a stable, cheap and reasonably just and efficient administration, for which the Stanleys—the Lords of whom we know most—were able to supply competent officials from their great estates in England.

The Lords of the Isle were, it has been said, feudatory princes with sovereign power, but the story of their rule affords little evidence of the kingly virtue which is based upon sacrifice by the ruler for the good of his people.

The 'Lord's Profit' was so often the subject of debate that the phrase came as glibly to the lips of the ordinary citizen as to the officials who were so insistently urged by ordinance and the terms of their appointment to guard and augment it. In 1721, Waldron, a revenue officer stationed at Douglas and author of a famous account of the Island, owned a fine cockerel in which he took great pride. It was stolen, and his anger was unbounded. 'If I catch the thief', he exploded, 'I will see that the Lord gets some profit!'

36

'Justice is a great profit!' ran the medieval adage, and from this source the Lords of Man received substantial amounts in fines and forfeits. The insistence on financial benefit in the administration of justice sometimes had its advantages. Coroners, for instance, who presented people accused of misdemeanours and did not get a verdict of guilty with a fine, were not paid anything for their pains, which no doubt deterred them from proceeding on insufficient grounds. In the sixteenth century the extreme penalty, too, was sometimes avoided by money payment. Thus in 1539 when a felon was taken to the *Knock Dhoo*, 'the Black Hill', near Ballasalla, for execution, he bought a pardon by the payment of sixty shillings, in addition to his already forfeited goods.

In the sixteenth century this absence of rigidity in the administration of the law made it possible for Robert Fletcher of Kirby (then called Ballafletcher) to seek the Controller's intervention with the Governor for the temporary release of the Kirby shepherd, who was in Castle Rushen, indicted for the theft of a young goat. Fletcher expressed astonishment at his servant's conduct.

> 'Truly,' he wrote, 'I never knew such demeaner, which I have had him five yeares, but god knowes all. Lettin you know that all my ship [i.e. sheep] that I had of wedow More [Pulrose] with most of my other shipe yr gone frome me and I have nott one that knowes them. I desyre you to speak to Mr. Deputy that I may have him out of Castle to the Head Court day, that he may gether my shipe to gether and I will be in thre bonds that he shall a peare if he have ys lyff.
>
> From K. bradon 25 Aprill 1584.'

Where a criminal was penniless and therefore unable to provide the fees of the officials responsible for his execution the officers were encouraged to relieve the Island of his unprofitable presence by banishment. The judges themselves often showed compassion for people driven to crime by poverty, and were obviously anxious to save them from capital punishment.

In 1669 J. R. was indicted by a jury for stealing a silver dish from Balladoole. But the Court considering the circumstances 'and the poverty and ignorance of the party, and also that *the Lord hath no advantage* by her tryall,' passed by her arraignment and ordered her to be whipped.

ABJURATION

When an offender accepted exile as an alternative to the imposition of the death penalty he appeared before the Governor and officers, and the following oath of abjuration was administered to him:

> 'You swear upon this Holy Evangelists that you shall by the next conveniency depart this Isle and never to return to the same hereafter, unless you shall be casually compelled by extremity of weather from off sea, without the especiall warrant of the Rt. Hon. the Lord of the Isle first obtained. . . . So help you God.'

Cases of renunciation of country are to be found in the Records until the end of the eighteenth century, and occasional grants of pardon to home-sick exiles.

In 1786 two Castletown men broke into a warehouse and stole £25. They were sentenced to death but recommended to mercy, and their punishment reduced to transportation for seven years. Owing to the failure of Whitehall to make the necessary financial adjustments at the Revestment in 1765, there was no money in the public funds to pay for their journey to the Thames hulks, and they had to be kept in Castle Rushen.

Driven to desperation through lack of food, and exposure to the weather in the ruinous Castle, they broke out, apparently to the great delight of the Governor and all concerned, and escaped to Liverpool. They were detected and brought back to prison. Once more the hungry prisoners escaped to Liverpool, and once more were returned by the over-zealous police. In the end the embarrassed Manx authorities who had not yet solved the financial problem, were glad to get rid of the felons by allowing them to abjure the Island.

In 1797, two sheep stealers were granted the same relief on condition that they joined the Navy, this being the last occasion when such clemency was exercised. Sixteen years later an abjured felon, probably one of the sheep-stealers, was arrested on returning to Man and so breaking his oath of renunciation.

The Church courts provided one source from which the Lord obtained an income. Offenders committed to the Bishop's prison obtained release by finding bonds of £3 *ad usum Domini*, and the money was forfeited to the Lord in case of the offender's default. In 1703 a Convocation at Bishopscourt abolished the commutation of penances for money payment with the approval of the Earl of Derby, but later one of the complaints made by the Lord's officers against Bishop Wilson and the ecclesiastical judges was that they were too merciful, and often reduced or remitted fines and forfeits which, as in the case of the commutations, would have gone into the Lord's treasury.

Whatever indulgence the Stanley rulers were disposed to show to native customs, they clung naturally enough to the ancient prerogatives, perquisites and monopolies of a manorial proprietor; and were not above displaying an arbitrary temper at times, as in 1577 when Earl Henry pardoned a felon and ordered him to wear an iron collar 'revetted round about his neck for two years and two dayes and bound to all services dureing his life'; or when, following the same feudal tradition, Earl Edward married the widow of Deemster Thomas Norris to a soldier of the Peel, under a threat of loss of the Deemster's estate.

Though in later centuries the successors of the Tudor autocrats conformed more to the established law they still, on occasion, took a profit out of marriage. In Kirk Michael in 1729, articles of marriage were drawn up between the two families involved. The girl, however, changed her mind and eloped with another man. Thereupon the frustrated bridegroom brought an action for breach of contract against the elopers and their parents. He was awarded £30 damages, half of which was claimed by the Lord.

DEODAND

Of the numerous feudal dues in rents, forfeits and services with which the Lord's tenants were harassed, one of the strangest was that of Deodand (i.e. given to God). A deodand was a personal chattel—animal or goods—which had been the cause of the death of a human being, and was in consequence given to God as an expiatory offering, to be devoted to alms or other pious uses.

In practice the deodand was forfeited to the Lord for his own purposes. In 1674, John Sayle of the Craige, Kirk Andreas, was killed by his bull and the animal was taken by the Lord's officers. In 1697 John Shimmin of Billown in Kirk Malew fell from his horse and was dragged a hundred yards in the lane of Gary Kelly, his foot caught fast in a home-made stirrup made from a halter. The jury declared that since the rider's death had been caused by the horse and halter they were deodand to the Lord.

Among the other forfeits which fell into his hands were the goods of a stranger guilty of manslaughter, of excommunicated persons, and of an alien dying in the island, who had not sworn fealty to the Lord. When Lieutenant Haythorne, an English officer of the garrison, died, not naturalised, in 1669, a deed of gift to his needy young son was accepted as a will by the compassionate Spiritual judge. But the Temporal Court condemned this act as a diminution of the Lord's prerogative.

Animals which had strayed for more than a year without a lawful claim being made became the Lord's property, even when the original owner was known.

Of felon's property the Lord took for himself all horses and cattle above two years old, and sheep above one year and swine of any age. Nevertheless the rights of a felon's guiltless wife (or husband) and children in the property were recognised. 'If any forfeit his goodes to the Lord by Felony his wife shall not forfeit her part of goods, because the woman is but subject and obedient to the man.'

THE LORD'S WARREN

The maintenance of the Lord's rights in the Commons (known as the Lord's Forest), the warrens, rivers and seashore, was a perennial source of trouble to his officials, and to the lessees of his rights. In spite of harsh penalties for poachers, the resentful Manx countrymen never ceased their inroads on the deer in the hills, the salmon and trout in the rivers and the game in the warrens.

The Northside warren was the most extensive preserve in the lowlands, though there was another near Peel at the Congary, 'the Rabbit Sheiling,' and a third in Rushen. The right to trap and kill rabbits in the Northside warren was periodically let to tenants able and willing to buy the lease. The game preserve extended along the coast from the Ballaugh *Cass ny Hawin*, (Burn-foot), northward round the Point of Ayre to Ramsey and the mouth of the Sulby. Within its boundaries it was forbidden to pull the bent, so highly prized for thatching, since it provided cover for game. The warren comprised 'the shore, sea-banks and skirts and borders of the shore.' In this vague official definition of their grant the lease-holders found a good excuse for encroaching on land which its owners considered to be outside the Warren, and they were not slow to express disapproval.

In 1750 the lessee, Major Christian of Milntown, complained of obstruction when he went to Jurby with his assistants to catch coneys with purse and hay-nets, not far from the Lhen Mooar. He was met by the landowner armed with a scythe who came upon the hunters in a most furious manner, and cried threateningly, 'What the devil brought you here? Are you come to steal our goods? I will cut all before me with this iron!'

He was accompanied by his wife, swinging a long rake, and by two cur-dogs. They pressed closely on Christian's party, disarranging their nets and not ceasing with fiery threats until they had driven the trappers away.

The farmer and his wife were sent to Castle Rushen from whence he made an unavailing appeal, stigmatising Christian and his helpers as trespassers and robbers—for was not he himself owner of the land to the full sea-mark? But the Courts decided against him, it being held that rights of warrenage were an ancient reservation and the prerogative of the Lord.

Salmon and trout were taken by unauthorised fishermen from the Dhoo and Glass, and Radcliffe of Knockaloe reported similar losses of fish from his leased waters of the Neb. In 1763 Conister or St. Mary's Rock was let for oyster cultivation, but the beds were plundered by Douglas people. Five years later two newcomers leased the salmon and trout fishery, and found themselves faced with every sort of resistance by the poachers who used fish-spears or listers, nets, creels and boats in their attack on the fish.

There were frequent prosecutions in the last half of the eighteenth century in an attempt to discourage unlicensed hunters and fishermen. In 1772, for example, a poacher of salmon at Namode on the river Glass was sentenced to stand on a platform three feet high erected on Douglas market-place, with a paper on his breast to indicate his offence; and the Town Captain was enjoined to see that the Coroner carried out the punishment.

The assertion of the Lord's claim to a right of hunting all over the Island met with great opposition in 1755. In that year the farmers of Lonan, Onchan, Braddan, Santan and Marown complained that the Governor had granted a licence to hunt with beagles to a set of people, mostly strangers but who included, 'to their reproach,' some few natives.

Fences were broken, cattle and sheep damaged and lost; whilst the ring-leaders of the hunters—Bacon, Mountgomery and Ross—menaced objectors with loaded whips and threatened to pistol the farmers. An opposition party headed by the Heywoods of the Nunnery assembled in Douglas, armed with clubs, bludgeons and guns, 'like highwaymen,' and raided Bacon's kennels, wounding, and in one case killing, several dogs. They threatened death to the owners' servants.

When the case was settled in 1762, and the Lord's right of hunting established, the defendants were all fined twenty shillings and sentenced to three weeks in Castle Rushen. But the hunters who no doubt had obtained great enjoyment from their skirmishes with the opposition, magnanimously pleaded with the Court to remit the imprisonment.

HEAD OF THE CHURCH

The Lord of Man very quickly imitated his suzerain, Henry the Eighth, in claiming to be Head of the Manx Church. In 1541 three commissioners appointed by Edward, Earl of Derby, declared that the Lord was 'Metropolitan and Chief of Holy Church', and that the

Bishop was to act only at the pleasure of the Lord. At Tynwald in 1581, Bishop Meyrick dramatically emphasised his subordinate position by holding the Earl's stirrup when he mounted his horse; though this may have been homage for the Bishop's Barony.

In 1675, when Edward Crowe, Vicar of Lezayre, refused to officiate because of his inadequate stipend, Bishop Bridgman sequestered the Lezayre tithes so that the Vicar's just grievance might be rectified. But Lord William annulled the sequestration by virtue of his prerogative as Head of the Church. The last emphatic claim to Manx ecclesiastical supremacy came from the Stanley heiress, the dowager Duchess of Atholl, who wrote to the Home Office in 1784, 'Whilst I live none else but myself has any right to appoint a bishop of Mann!' and she proceeded to choose Claudius Crigan, one of the least admirable of the occupants of the See.

THE LORD'S SOLDIERS, 1406–1765

The administrative officials whom the first Stanley Lord of Man appointed to his new possession in 1406, were accompanied by a small body of soldiers. One gathers from their names—Halsall, Litherland, Norres, etc.—that they were, in the main, recruited from the Stanley estates in Lancashire.

Bound together by the fact that they were an inconsiderable force in a strange country which at first turned an unfriendly face to them, they were encouraged to develop *esprit de corps*, and their attachment to the ruling family was strengthened by their contacts with the Lord and his deputy. They garrisoned the Lord's Castle residences— officially known as the 'Houses'—and were household troops.

It was laid down in 1422 that for their equipment each was to provide bow and arrows, a sufficient doublet or habergeon, a sword and buckler, and spurs and saddle. By another thrifty regulation no recruit was accepted unless he agreed that the armour and weapons he brought with him should, at his death, remain in the armoury 'for the better maintenance and defence of the Isle and Houses'. In the fifteenth and sixteenth centuries a white jacket having the badge of the Three Legs in red cloth on front and back was a distinctive part of his dress.

The garrison troops shared in the unpopularity of the early Stanley administration until the purge of its dishonest and tyrannical officials in 1428. But the imported soldiers soon formed connections by marriage, acquired land and, in the end, became more Manx than the Manx.

Vacancies in their ranks were generally filled by natives, though there appears to have been no bar to recruits from other countries.

Thus 'William Flexney, a soldier, came out of Ireland' in 1650, and his descendants intermarried with prominent Manx families. The position of soldier of the House, with its opportunities of perquisites and fees obtained from the performance of police and prison duties, was a desirable one and, according to the practice touching many public offices of the time, was saleable. In 1631, for example, the tenements of Scarlett and Thalloo Quaye were sold by Richard to Thomas Norris for a soldier's place and fifty shillings.

Ordinarily the household troops lived in their own dwellings outside the Houses, taking their regular turn of duty in the fortress; and most of them obtained formal permission from the Governor to supplement their wages by trade and farming. They were encouraged to keep lodgings, and in 1553 it was ordered that they should be given preference in the granting of licences to those wishing to provide accommodation for travellers.

In 1653, William Preston of Castletown is described as 'soldier and glover', whilst Thomas Crellin, master gunner of Castle Peel (*d.* 1644), owned and farmed Ballaquane and was, as his will reveals, a man of substance. He possessed a fishing boat and six feather beds, among other evidences of his social standing. Turner Ingoldsby, a soldier of Douglas Fort in the eighteenth century, pursued the trade of barber.

The Lord's soldiers were the last resort in cases of disobedience to the Civil Courts. Failure to obey the Moars and Coroners was punished by fine, but resistance to a soldier was treason and entailed the loss of body and goods. And when he rode into the countryside to escort an absentee to trial or to support a parish Moar in the extraction of rents from reluctant tenants his prestige was such that he seldom had to seek further help from his garrison.

There was, however, occasionally some Manxman ready, in a spirit of impishness and obstinacy, to wage unequal contest with the authorities. In 1593 Thomas Moore of Kirk Onchan voiced the grievances of the farmers over the payment of customary rents of corn, victuals and turf. These were commuted according to an ancient money scale which had not been adjusted to ever rising prices. Thomas refused to give his cattle and sheep at the old accustomed rate, and was fined.

When the lockman bearing the Deemster's token or warrant, came to collect a pawn (i.e. goods, generally more than sufficient to cover the debt or fine), Moore refused to give it, saying that 'he would not deliver a pawn for never a Demster in th' Isle before he saw a copy of a Reconinge'. It was admitted in Court that the defendant had not been presented with an account of his liabilities, and the fine was mitigated and forgiven.

Later, when warned by a soldier to satisfy the collector or else come to Court, he refused unless the soldier would carry him on his back. 'Therefore', says the record, 'he hath forfeited body and goods to the Lord.' He escaped forfeiture by timely submission, but was in similar trouble in 1599. He promised reformation but broke his word—as the long-suffering Court, obviously disinclined to use the full rigour of the law, plaintively pointed out, when he was again brought before it in 1601.

JURY OF THE HOUSE

Violations of the ancient rules and traditions of the Houses were tried before a jury of soldiers and the Judge of the House—the Controller, an important Household officer who controlled or supervised the receipt of rents and other revenues.

The soldiers were held strictly to their oath of loyalty to the Lord of the Isle. In 1691 John Stevenson, a soldier of the House, was drinking with others at Jony Pickard's in Castletown; and in the course of conversation his brother-in-law, William Banke of Whitehaven, exclaimed, 'My Lord Darby is a fool!'

The company professed horror at this commission of *lèse-majesté*, and Stevenson hastened to express his resentment. 'If you were not my brother,' he said, 'I would break your head for that!'

And Jony observed with sinister implication, 'You do better take notice of what your brother Banke hath said!'

Stevenson ignored the warning and did not report the offending speech. His failure to take action became known to the authorities, and a jury of the House found him guilty of perjury; for a person was held to be perjured when he failed to keep the oath he had taken to obey and perform the ancient rules of the House. John Stevenson had committed such a sin of omission—a very grave one where the reputation of the Lord was concerned—and he was forthwith discharged from his place as soldier.

The first indication of the strength of the Lord's troops occurs in the Exchequer Book of 1593, when the Castles were each garrisoned by thirty-six men. From time to time threatened danger from without caused temporary increases in the establishment. Thus in 1540, Earl Edward obtained the Privy Council's permission to recruit one hundred men in England for the defence of Man against attacks from the North. That the danger was real is shown in a dispatch five years later from Henry the Eighth's Deputy in Ireland, who reported that McConnell, Lord of the Isles, was raiding with 4,000 men in 180 galleys, and had reached Carrickfergus.

The Civil War in the next century also brought large additions to the Insular military strength. In 1765 when the government of the Isle was surrendered to the Crown the garrison of Castle Rushen had declined to 22, of Peel to 13. The figures for Douglas, Ramsey and Derby Forts were 7, 4 and 4, respectively—a total of 50.

On the disbandment of the Lord's Soldiers, a gaoler and 19 constables were appointed to carry out their civil duties, and three companies of an English Foot regiment, with a troop of Dragoons, went into quarters at Castle Rushen.

THE LORD'S LICENCE

Until the third decade of the nineteenth century it was illegal for a Manxman to leave the country without having obtained a licence known as the 'Governor's Pass'. In 1810 this cost ninepence, of which threepence went to the Pass-master, and sixpence was the perquisite of the Governor who paid for the printing.

The first mention of such a permit is in 1422, when the Deemsters and Keys gave for law that 'noe man of what condition soever he be go out of the Land without special Lycense of the Lord or his Lieutenant with Vessell, upon pain of forfeiting the Vessell and all the goods therein'.

This was designed to prevent the departure of debtors and felons, and the loss of export duties, and of goods and currency needed at home.

One mysterious case in which the law was contravened arose in 1602, when Deemster John Curghie of Ballakillingan left the Island without the necessary permit. Later witnesses testified that the Deemster with Standish of the Ellanbane appeared one day on the Kirk Andreas shore and asked Gilbert Christian and John Crenilt of that parish to transport them to Whithorne in Galloway. When the boat owners demurred in the absence of a licence, Curghie and his companion—who apparently were on urgent business, though its nature was never disclosed—pushed the boat into the water. The Andreas men, unwilling to see their vessel disappear in the hands of others, jumped in with them, and they voyaged together to Scotland.

On their return they were arrested and the Deemster confined in Castle Rushen. There was no precedent for this position, and the officers, Deemsters and Keys having met to deem what the Law was in such circumstances, declared that according to the Statute the boat that carried the Deemster, and what goods he had on board were forfeited to the Lord.

In 1676 two Ramsey fishing boats were seized for going away to England without licence. The boatmen, John Christian Michal, and

John Cannan, said that they had been sent by a merchant for hops, as there was none in the Island. Their story was confirmed by the Customer. Their plea of ignorance of the regulations was accepted, and their boats returned to them, but they were fined five shillings each. The Deputy-Governor, Richard Stevenson, excusing his lenience said that John Cannan was 'a young man, and a beginner in the world'.

Officials, whose lack of vigilance allowed people or goods to leave the country unlicensed were liable for any loss to the Lord or to private persons.

In 1596, Henry Curwin, who had been illegally appointed Archdeacon by Earl William in 1595, was dismissed from the post after Tynwald had declared the law, and was committed to the custody of the Constable of Castle Rushen until he refunded the income he had received; but he made his escape from prison and reached England, leaving his creditors unpaid. The Constable was found liable for his debts, and in his turn fled from the Island. Boat owners were still getting into trouble in the nineteenth century for carrying away people without a licence, but the punishment had become a money fine, generally £1.

EMIGRATION

The Lord's licence represented an attempt upon a problem which still remained unsolved three centuries later—the emigration of useful members of the community, particularly those who worked for hire. Repeated enactments and prohibitions were unable to stop the outward flow of enterprising young people escaping from a sometimes distasteful and always ill-requited servitude.

In 1561, the wages of the highest class of man-servant, the ploughman, were limited by law to 13s. 4d. a year with diet, the driver of the ox team 10s., the horseman 8s.; and maidservants had to be content with the Deemsters' interpretation of the phrase, 'as she deserves'.

The employers struggled with little success to keep wages at the ancient rate. There was a fine for farmers who increased the set hire, but servants were scarce and the law was broken. There were, too, the inevitable comparisons with conditions in former times; and when Kenyon was Governor in 1690, great complaint was made that the labouring men about Castletown were very unreasonable and extortive and would not work under 6d. a day. An order was then issued, no doubt with the connivance of the Keys who were all employers of labour, that the labourers were to have 2d. a day, with meat, and 4d. a day without. Those who refused were threatened with close confinement in prison.

Skilled workers received more. In 1679 Tynwald fixed the pay of mowers of hay at 4d. a day with sufficient meat and drink, a day's work being fixed at a *daymath*—an area less than an acre.

YARDING

Hired workers were subject to an oppressive system of conscription called 'yarding', by which the Lord and officers of government— Deemsters, Coroners and Moars—were entitled to call upon persons of their choice to serve them, willy-nilly, for a year, sometimes when the servant was already working for a master. The Keys and Clergy, however, could not be deprived of their workers in this way.

One great grievance was that workers yarded for the Lord received only half the normal rate, but this injustice was rectified at the end of the seventeenth century. The custom created much resentment among the victims. In 1735 the Sumner of Ballaugh came to Cowley of the Kiardagh, and laying his rod of office ('the yard') upon the shoulder of the smith's manservant, claimed him for another.

Cowley broke out in violent anger: *Dy der y Jouyl lesh ersooyl fo thalloo, personyn as saggartyn, sunderyn, guilleyn glass as toshee yoarrey!*—'May the Devil take away under ground Vicars-General and clergy, sumners, lockmen and coroners!' But the threat of St. German's dungeon quickly cooled his wrath, and he was glad to escape with the performance of penance for his 'horrid imprecations'.

The harshness of yarding was somewhat mitigated by custom. A yarded servant was freed from forced service for four years after his term. An infirm cottager or crofter could ask for one of his children to be exempt from yarding. A Kirk Braddan application of 1699 runs: '. . . Robert Kelly of the said parish hath this day entered his daughter Alice Kelly as his choice child to aid and assist him in his old and helpless condition whereby she may be freed from yarding and jury of servants—provided that the jury of servants in that parish approve.'

Custom required that a servant's porridge should be of such consistency that the potstick would stand upright in it immediately after cooking. The barley cakes given to him should be as thick as the length of a barley corn.

For refusal to obey the 'yard' and for other serious misdemeanours servants were liable to whipping or to imprisonment until they became amenable, their meagre fare in confinement consisting of one barley cake a day and water.

One curious case affecting relationship between master and servant occurred in 1664, when a ploughman, annoyed by the erratic movement of his ox team, assaulted his driver and drew blood. Normally the offender would have been fined, but in this case the charge was dismissed, since it was the master who drew blood on his servant. A. W. Moore, commenting on a similar instance and result in 1651, said that it appeared to be an infamous decision of the Deemsters. But their ruling was evidently in accord with the customary law, for a judge in 1564 dealing with a similar complaint pointed out that, since it was the master who drew blood on his servant, by ancient custom the case could not proceed (*ideo non procedit per antiquam consuetudinem*).

The servant was required to give timely notice if he wished to leave his place at the end of his term. If his employer was absent through accident or design he went to where the master sat at meat or by the fire and, in the presence of a witness, cut a nick in the chair. If the house door was fastened against him he nicked the threshold.

In 1763 the wages of yarded servants which had not been materially altered for two hundred years were raised to 40s. per year for men and 20s. for women. Seven years later yarding was abolished, and the Statutes relating to the wages and labour of servants were repealed.

CASTLE RUSHEN, 1795

The Lord's house is seen behind the gateway

IV

EARLY MANX SETTLERS IN AMERICA

BARBADOS

One day in October, 1646, a Bristol ship, the *Fortune*, appeared in Douglas Bay, and, piloted by local fishermen, came in on the flood tide to a berth in the harbour. When the Customer (i.e. the customs officer) and the Town Captain had made their examination the ship-master, William Brooke, hurried off to Castletown. There he obtained permission from Governor Greenhalgh to issue a public notice offering, on terms, a sea-passage to men, youths and boys—except such as were under military command—wishing to go to Barbados and St. Christopher in the West Indies.

At that time the Island was in the midst of preparations for its defence against Parliamentary attacks, and in addition to the demands for recruits to the Earl's armed forces there was a perennial shortage of agricultural labourers.

On what grounds Brooke was allowed to carry off a number of able-bodied males is not known. But there was much destitution among the poorer classes. Both the land and sea harvests had failed, and the continuance of wet summers and poor fishing during the following years was to result in famine. The Governor may also have been influenced in his decision by the fact that Barbados was under Cavalier rule; but in any case it is doubtful if Brooke could have obtained any Manx recruits had they known what lay before them.

On the face of it his conditions must have appeared fair enough, in view of agricultural wages and the purchasing power of money in the seventeenth century. Emigrants were promised free food and ship accommodation till their arrival in the West Indies. In return they had to sign a contract engaging themselves to serve for a period in the plantations. This was four years for men, five or six years for youths and boys. Their employers were to provide them with meat and drink and lodgings; and at the end of their service they were each to receive ten pounds sterling or its value in commodities grown in the islands—sugar, indigo, cotton or tobacco. After the expiry of his indenture a servant was made free of the country and could set up in business for himself.

Barbados, approximately two-thirds the size of the Isle of Man, had fallen into English hands nineteen years before the arrival of the *Fortune* in Douglas Bay. St. Christopher (Kitts) had been occupied in 1624. Their rich tropical fertility quickly attracted settlers and was exploited by the rapacious Cavalier planters whose inhumane treatment of their workers caused a scarcity of white labour.

In 1647 when the hopeful and unsuspecting Manxmen were brought to the islands the daily routine for indentured servants was as follows: From 6 a.m. to 11 a.m., when the tropical heat brought work to a standstill, they were in the fields or attending to the sugar mills and boiling rooms. The food they then received consisted of *loblolly* which was crushed Indian corn meal worked into a paste with water and served cold on trays.

From 1 p.m. to 6 p.m. they were in their huts and received another meal of *loblolly* or mashed potatoes. They were given no bread, and water was their only drink. Their beds were boards unprovided with coverings.

The owners, as a rule, were only concerned in getting back their original outlay on the bond-servant and making the largest possible profit out of him during his term of service. Their overseers were often sadistic bullies who gave severe beatings to sick, slow or complaining workers. If a labourer became so ill as to be of no further value he was turned off the plantation, to die by the wayside, where his body was left to rot.

Writing about Barbadian life before the Restoration a recent history declares: 'The conditions under which white labour was procured and utilised in Barbados were persistently severe, occasionally dishonourable, and generally a disgrace to the English name.'[1]

The thirty-six men and boys who, filled with what high hopes, sailed out of Douglas one autumn day in 1646, appear to have come from every part of Man. Their names include Teare, Callie (Caley), Moore, More, Quayle (2), Christian (3), Skelly, Hutchin, Cottar (Cottier), Carran, Kennis(h), Galle (Gale), Falle (Fayle), Clague, Nores (2), Lace, Crooe (Crowe), and Woods. One, William Standish, was probably a connection of the celebrated Miles Standish who had landed in New England twenty-six years before.

Nobody will ever know how many of the indentured Manxmen outlived the Atlantic passage and the cruelties of the plantations. But at least one on the official list—Robert Quayle—is found twenty years later in his native land. Either because his return out of great tribulation was regarded as unusual, or because of the constant recital of his incredible experiences, he gained the nickname 'Bar-

[1] V. Harlow, *History of Barbados.*

badoes'. As 'Robert Quayle Barbadoes' he figures in a number of civil lawsuits, one of which in 1672 shows that he had some connection with Ballahaine in Rushen.

In 1650 Barbados contained Manxmen whose names are absent from Captain Brooke's list. In a letter addressed 'To his loving friend Will Cown', Phillip Kermine (Kermeen) of Kirk Lonan wrote in that year by the hand of John Rattliffe,

'My love remembered unto you and to your wife and children hoping in God you are all in good health as I am at these presents writing thanks bee to God. These are to certifie you that I am in the Barbades in the West Indes and doe not knowe when I shall bee soe happy as to see my owne contry againe. . . .'

He therefore asks his friend Will Cown to distribute some of his property among his children. There is pathos in his anxiety for them, and in his unsatisfied longing for his native soil: 'I doe remember my love to Phillip Moore in Douglas hee is the last man that I spoke to in the Isle of Man. I desire you of all love to see these goods payd unto my children. . . .'

'By me John Rattliffe in the parish of St. Andrews,' wrote the scribe, 'pray remember me to my friends.'

The Governor appointed a Commission to find out the nature of Phillip's assets, and the children received half of the amount desired by their father. He had apparently been a crofter or a small farmer. There is nothing to show what his status in Barbados was, or that he ever returned to his 'owne contry'.

In spite of the low speed of the leaky broad-beamed trading vessels of the seventeenth century and the dangers of sea travel, trade with newly settled places sprang up with surprising quickness. Less than twenty years after the English occupation of Barbados, 'Barbados canvases,' made from its hemp, were being used in the Isle of Man.

Stories of the miserable conditions of employment in the West Indies spread with a like speed, and the resulting disinclination of white men to seek work there forced the planters to treat their white employees with more humanity. But the shortage continued, and unscrupulous ship-masters found it a profitable venture to coast along the shores of the Irish Sea, taking by surprise and kidnapping for transport across the Atlantic.

It was in such a way that the notable Captain Skillicorn, when a boy, playing his flute on the rocks below Ballarragh, was carried off by a Bristol ship apparently engaged in this detestable traffic. He avenged himself on his captors by composing uncomplimentary rhymes in Manx which he sang to the unconscious objects of his abuse. One verse with which he has been credited voices his longing for home, and its end has a suspicion of the spirit which enabled him to survive and triumph:

> *Ogh as ogh, my graih Ballarragh!*
> *Vallarragh my chree, cha vaikym oo arragh.*
> *Ta mee my hassoo as my ghreeym rish y voalley,*
> *Cummal seose kiaull gys cloan ny moddee.*

> Alas, alas, my sweet Ballarragh!
> Ballarragh of my heart, I shall see thee no more.
> Here I stand with my back to the wall,
> Keeping up music to the children of dogs.

Not all the Manxmen in Barbados in the first half-century of its colonisation came there as indentured servants. Charles Stevenson, brother of Captain Richard Stevenson of Balladoole, was resident in the West Indian island with his kinsman John Whetstone, and died there in 1686. In his will he left £35 to relatives in Man, the rest of his property, including a silver watch, going to William Lucas, another Barbadian Manxman.

Disregard of tropical hygiene, the prevalence of lethal fevers, hurricanes and periodic threats of enemy attack, made life very uncertain in Barbados. Robert Corlett, a prosperous trader, brother of Thomas Corlett of Ballakeoig, Ballaugh, and stepson of the first Deemster Dan McYlrea, in his last letter home in 1707 spoke of 'being now daily in expectation of the Island being invaded by the French', and says he is going 'to marry a virtuous lady, Mrs. Frances Mann'. In a few weeks he was dead.

A later immigrant, Robert Looney, son of John Looney of Kirk Onchan and his wife Anne Cannon, died in 1732, after more than thirty years in the colony. He was a master blacksmith, having served his time to the craft in Wicklow, and had prospered in the West Indies; for, among other legacies, he left the then considerable sum of £200 to relatives in his native parish and Ireland, and his Negro slave to a Barbadian friend.

Until the surrender of the Lordship of Man to the British Crown in 1765, there was constant direct communication between Man and Barbados, and the Manx flag was often seen in West Indian ports. But after the Revestment all foreign commerce was forbidden to Manx vessels. In memorials of 1769 and 1771 the Keys complained bitterly that under Crown rule the Insular merchants were deprived of even supplying a ship with fresh provision, and not allowed to ship salt to cure herrings, nor to export salt-fish into Great Britain or the Empire.

Repeated deputations to London failed to obtain for the merchants the restoration of their trade with Europe and America; and the right to trade freely with foreign countries was not conceded until 1853.

NEW JERSEY

About one Manx emigrant of the seventeenth century sufficient facts have survived the passage of the years to reveal the quality of the people who, continuously from time immemorial, have left the Island to find a living in other lands.

He was John Kaighin and reached North America before 1682. It is not known whether his emigration was an escape from persecution because of his Quaker beliefs, or whether he joined that sect after his arrival in the American Colonies. Two letters which, faded and in several places indecipherable, survive in the hands of descendants, throw light on his ancestry and his own fervent religious faith. His father, John Kaighin, who owned the quarterland farm of Ballacregga with Cooil Darragh in Kirk Michael, married Jane Cannell of the Lhergy Vreck in 1656, and also had possession of that estate more than thirty years later, but surrendered it to his brother-in-law.

He was Parish Clerk, and it was probably he who on one occasion in 1670, when his stipend was in arrear, made a strong protest to the Ecclesiastical Court:

> 'Pray remember that I will not any longer officiate the service of the Churche of Kirk Michaell without a reasonable consideration for my paines which I desire the worshipfull court to take into consideration and give out an order to that intent or else I shall surcease.
>
> Yr humble servant
>
> John Kaighin'

He was one of the Keys from 1689 to his death in 1701, and by default of his Quaker heir, was succeeded in Ballacregga by a younger son, Charles, who became Captain of the Parish.

John, the emigrant, settled in New Jersey near Philadelphia and prospered greatly. He was engaged in the linen trade and other activities, and in 1696 bought 455 acres of land by the Delaware River, later called Kaighn's Point[1] and now part of the City of Camden. He was a zealous member of the Society of Friends, was one of the Judges of Gloucester (later Camden) County in 1699–1702, and a member of the Assembly of the Province of New Jersey in 1710. He died in 1724.

[1] 'Kaighn' is the American form of the surname. The story of John and his American descendants was communicated by one of them—David K. Bennett, N.J.

Though he was married three times, only his second union with a widow, Sarah Griscom, produced survivors to perpetuate his stock: John and Joseph. John Junior's son, Samuel, in spite of his Quaker beliefs, served as a Captain in the Revolutionary war with the New Jersey troops.

Joseph's grandson, John (1730–1770), a bachelor, was a Doctor of Medicine, and is notable as having in 1758 received the earliest known medical diploma to practise medicine in the Colonies. It now hangs in the rooms of the College of Physicians and Surgeons in Philadelphia.

The doctor's two brothers, Joseph (1734–1797) and James (1752–1811) created a great stir in their time by their generous act of humanity in freeing their slaves, and were founders of the two branches of the family, with numerous descendants—a family which has played an important part in the development of Camden. As its chronicler, Charles S. Boyer, has pointed out, it is a typical cross-section of American society—composed largely of lawyers, doctors, educators, farmers, business men, tradesmen and mechanics.

The first of the letters already mentioned was written by the mother, Jane Kaighin, in August 1702, the year following her husband's death, and is addressed

'To Mr. John Kaighin, Linener.
In West New Jersey nigh on
Delaware River side opposit
To Philadelphia Citty. In
America.

'Deare and loving son,' she begins, 'After my deare and tender love to you yor wife and all yors remembered hoping to god that you are in good health. . . .

'Deare son, I must now Aquaint you with that dolefull and sorrowfull newes of yor fathers death who dyed in November last to my great sorrow and greife, his love and care was soe much over me. . . . I cannot put him out of my sight. Within few . . . of his death I took the fever which continued with me more than a quarter of a yeare which caused me to be very feeble but have now come pretty well to my selfe yet cannot expect to be done with my infirmityes by reason of age.

'Yor sister Ellen who was not borne when you left the Isle is married to Jon Leece's son [Balla leece] in the parish of Kk. Garman since yor father dyed. I being left with my son Charls and his wife in Balnacrega had noe great comfort or contentment as might draw away from me my melloncolly and troublesom burden of greife and was forced to remove and leave my own house to come to my daughter Jonys house, in Kk. Andreas where I now lieve with much content and Comfort. My son-in-law Daniel Lace is very . . .

and carefull over me in so much that he has been the means of
raising me . . . so that I continue with dayly prayer joyned in that
he and his wife may lieve to see my gray heayrs in the grave, mine and
my children deare love to you all. I desire to here from you as
soone . . . can.

Yor loveing mother,
Jane Kaighen'

John's answer has no date or signature, and appears to be a
preliminary draft of the letter which he presumably sent. It is largely
made up of references to his religious beliefs, with reiteration of the
spiritual gain in this life which comes 'to those that retire their minds
to God alone in stillness and silence of all flesh far from the noises
hurry tumult and vanity of this world'.

'Dear tender mother,' he begins, 'after my kind love and duty to
thyself and respects to all my brothers and sisters families and relatives and wishing all health and prosperity in this world and that
which is to come . . . I have been informed of my dear fathers
decease and thy own great exercises, which make deep impressions
in my mind, and am concerned that we are so far apart that we
cannot be so helpfull one to another under these weights and
pressures. . . .'

and he goes on to praise the virtue of submission to the Divine will.

He himself has had his share of sorrow and hardship; among them
the loss of

'my two good loveing wives in a few years time, and being left
alone with young babes is a deep and he(a)rt piercing exercise. It
is now going on six years since it pleased the Lord to call for my
wife out of this life and left me 3 children, two boys and one girl.
The youngest [Joseph] is still at nurse and so I still remain hiring
servants to keep my house. My concerns [i.e. business] is considerable and the danger in these troublesome times great.'

But he gets spiritual gain from the chastisements 'which the Lord
inflicts sometimes for humbling proud man', and consolation and
peace descend upon him. 'I keep my mind retired to the Lord, not
thinking my own thoughts, nor speaking my own words, but feeling
the rays of his Divine presence to enlighten my soul.'

His second wife Sarah Griscom had been the widow of a car-
penter who came to Philadelphia during the William Penn régime
and acquired large tracts of land. Her son Joseph's half-brother,
Tobias Griscom, had a grand-daughter who became a national figure.
This was Betsy Griscom (later Ross), popularly known as the 'Quaker
Rebel', because of her active sympathies with the American Revolution.

She was a flag-maker and it is claimed that she made the first
Stars and Stripes. This has been vehemently denied; but a house of

the Colonial period in Philadelphia, known as 'Betsy Ross's House', is now maintained as a public monument by believers in the tradition. There, they say, she carried on her business. In 1952, the bicentenary of her birth, the United States Government gave support to the story of the Quaker Rebel's achievement by issuing a commemorative 3 cents postage stamp. It bears a picture of Betsy in 1777 displaying the new flag to an appreciative committee of three, headed by George Washington.

The names of Jane Kaighin's daughter Jony and Daniel Lace, for whose affection the mother was so grateful, are found on one of the most interesting sepulchral stones in the churchyard of Kirk Andreas. It apparently was an ancient decorated cross, smoothed by a seventeenth century vandal to receive inscriptions which record three generations of the family of Ballavoddan. The first,

'1686 O Captn Lace too soone extinct by death
Wth thy dear wife art buried here beneath,'

relates to the John Lace who led his parish militia in the rising of 1651, and was expelled from the Keys, but later taken back into official favour.

Daniel, his son, was also one of the Twenty-four and Parish Clerk. The second inscription records his death in 1736, and of his wife Jony's in 1716, at the early age of forty-nine. But Jane Kaighin's prayer that she should not out-live her daughter and the kindly Daniel was answered, for she died in 1708.

V

CORONER AND MOAR

In ancient times Manx Coroners were called Moars, and the earliest accounts of Tynwald speak of the Moar, not the Coroner, of Glenfaba. The Manx Gaelic equivalents *meoir* and *toshiagh joarrey* had their parallel in the Highlands—the *toshach dera* and *maeor*.

Discussing feudal changes in the province of Mar[1] Dr. Douglas Simpson says that these two officers were Celtic survivals as late as the fifteenth century. The *toshach dera* was usually expressed as 'coroner' in early writs; while the *maeor* was apparently a royal representative within the province and a kind of pre-feudal sheriff. After the establishment of sheriffdoms in the thirteenth century the *maeor* sank in importance to a minor official at the sheriff's court.

Perhaps the Scottish occupation of Man during the same period was responsible for similar changes in the status of the *Moar* who yielded place to the Coroner as chief executive officer in the Sheading. This is the more possible owing to the inclusion of Man for a time in a Scottish sheriffdom—that of Inverness.[2]

THE PARISH MOAR

The old title survived in the parish Moar who was a collector of customary rents and a subordinate officer of the courts, serving his year of office in turn with other landowners of his parish. When the Coroner had made one of his periodical raids upon unlicensed drink sellers and users of illegal measures, the Moar publicly announced the names of the culprits and collected their fines.

The measures in question were the *ferlot*, used for grain, etc., and holding sixteen gallons; the tailors' and weavers' yard; the quart wooden can; and the miller's *kishan*, equal to eight quarts. No measure could be legally used in trade unless it had been compared with the Castle standard and officially sealed.

As a court officer the Moar was responsible for the commandeering of horses, when needed for members of the Court travelling on

---

[1] *The Province of Mar*, 1944.
[2] Dickinson: 'The Sheriff Court Book of Fife, 1515–22.'

the circuit of the Sheadings. But during the stormy political and religious disputes of the seventeenth century his chief court duty was to present cases of blood-wipe, which brought him a fee of 6d.

The blood-shedding was sometimes of a ritual nature. At a gathering in Kirk Onchan in 1722 William Kashin's wife accused another woman of witchcraft and stealing by magic the productiveness of Kashin's cattle; and Kashin laid his hand on her face, after which there was a scratch on her brow, as if made by a pin.

Then Kashin's wife exclaimed, 'If there be blood upon thee, show it to the Moar! Thou has milch cows but mine are dry!'

'I will pay sixpence for it,' said Kashin from beyond the door. 'There is blood upon thee and it was I bled thee. Go with it to the Moar.'

Some indication of the Moar's once greater importance is to be found in the practice which gave Deemster and Moar a choice of yarded servants before the Coroner, and an equal share in the division of certain perquisites. The office was abolished when the Lord's Rent ceased to be collected in 1908.

The presence of the Coroners at Tynwald, armed with sword or battle-axe and ready to deal with disorder in the assembly, was a spectacular demonstration of one of their chief duties—to maintain the peace in their Sheadings, and particularly to secure felons and bring them to justice. For this and other purposes they summoned juries and witnesses, and held inquests of death and of enquiry into petty trespass. They served summonses and other processes.

They levied fines and executions and, in case of necessity, were supported by military force. They had the right of search in houses and elsewhere when there was suspicion of felony, or a threat to the Lord's profit. One of their more extraordinary tasks was to destroy diseased horses by casting them over a sea-cliff. This barbarous method of destruction was last used in 1752, when a Marown man was found guilty of keeping a 'scabbed' horse, and the Coroner carried out the ancient law.

SANCTUARY

Until Prowess, or private vengeance, was made illegal by a Tynwald Court held at Keeill Abban in 1429, a manslayer fleeing from the relatives of the victim often took refuge in Church or on other holy ground. But he was not as secure as in many Christian countries.

'If', said the Deemsters and the Twenty-four declaring the ancient law in 1422, 'any man have done any point of Treason and taketh Sanctuary for dread of punishment, the Sanctuary shall not avail him by the Law of Man.'

Similarly, within three days of a manslayer's entry into the holy place the Coroner was empowered to break sanctuary and take him out if he did not acknowledge his guilt. The prisoner was then presented with three choices—a stay of not more than three days in sanctuary—which he must then abandon and take his chance—standing trial, or banishment.

If he chose the last, the Coroner was to place him in the middle of the highway leading to the harbour of his departure. If he strayed from the way he was liable to arrest by the Coroner, and lodgment for trial; and whether he kept the road or not he stood in the greatest peril from the avengers of blood.

The law therefore laid it down that if he was taken by his enemies on the excuse that he had left the road, they had to bring two witnesses in proof that they had not slain or captured him on the appointed way.

CORONERS' FEES

A Coroner paid Office Silver to the Lord out of his fees and perquisites, which were sometimes considerable. Of a felon's debt-free goods he received all horses, mares, oxen and kine two years old and under, and all sheep a year old and under; in the case of a suicide, the deceased person's outermost garment, his share of the household goods, all beasts under three years old, and any broken rucks of corn, hay, etc., in the haggard.

A manslayer forfeited his weapons. In 1590 when a visiting Englishman was guilty of manslaughter the jury found that at the time of his arrest he had no goods and chattels, but only 11s. 4d., which, they said, was due to the Lord; and a rapier and dagger which the Coroner took of right for his fee.

Like the Moar the Coroner was granted one quarterland free of Lord's rent, and exacted an annual fee of 4d. from each quarterland in his Sheading, and lesser sums from the small holdings. He was exempt from Watch and Ward.

THE LOCKMAN

The Coroner had an assistant in each parish, the Lockman, who appears to have got his title from Scotland, where formerly the Lockman was the public executioner. The name is said to have come from the 'lock' or small quantity of meal which he received as a fee from each bag of marketed meal. Train tells how he had seen the hangman at Ayr collecting his dues with an iron ladle.

The word 'lock' was certainly used in the Island with the same meaning. In 1713, for example, the young wife of a Kirk Andreas farmer was charged with patronising a witch and rejected the accusation. She said she took the sorceress for one desirous of receiving the alms of good farmers, and gave her a lock of meal.

On the other hand Man inherited Norse traditions and the name Lockman may be derived from Old Norse *lokus-veinn*, 'janitor, jailer'. His Manx name, *Guilley-glass*, is based on the assumption that 'lock' refers to prison bars. In Man the Lockman assisted the Coroner in carrying out the ultimate punishment decreed by law, and probably this sinister association with the gallows-tree is hinted at in the cryptic old saying,

> *Tra ta'n gheay 'sy villey, yiow shiu yn Guilley-glass:*
> 'When the wind is in the tree, you will get the Lockman.'

He also administered lesser punishments, as in 1693, when Adam M. was sentenced to be whipped at Kirk Michael Church by the Lockman on the next holy day.

No specimen of the Coroner's Rod or Yard has survived. It is given the Latin name *virga* in early documents and was no doubt a descendant of the long stick which one sees held threateningly by overseers in medieval pictures. The modern staff of office is $15\frac{1}{2}$ inches long and 1 inch in diameter.

An incident in 1725 shows that it was then sufficiently slender to be broken without great difficulty. One Curghie was involved in a pinfold dispute and William Curlett, the Coroner of Michael intervened, as was his duty, to command the peace. Holding out his Rod to quell the disturbance he cried, 'Peace, in my Lord Derby's name!' Curghie, however, audaciously seized the symbol of authority, broke it, and struck the Coroner with the pieces.

The evidence of William Kelly of Kirk Michael who was present is a good example of cautious understatement. 'They spoke', he said, 'in English that I did not understand, but I am certain the said Curghie was provoking.' The culprit was fined £3, the statutory penalty for disobedience to the Rod.

During the Stanley period the Coroner was chosen more often than not from the leading landowners. Up to the middle of the eighteenth century, and before a legal training was an essential preparation for a judicial appointment, the Coronership was a stepping stone to the Deemster's bench. John McCorkell of Lewaigue, Coroner of Garff in 1497, and John McCristen of Milntown, Coroner of Ayre in 1498, were Deemsters some years later. Dan Mylrea of the Dollough passed by the same way to the Deemstership at the end of the seventeenth century.

The office was frequently held by members of the Keys. In 1610 all six Coroners belonged to that body—Dollin Caine, the East

Nappin; William Tyldesley, the Friary; Phil Garrett, Ballabrooie, Lezayre; William Bridson; John Moore; and Richard Cowle.

When, as often happened in the seventeenth and eighteenth centuries, the Coroner was also Captain of the Parish and Warden of the Watch, he wielded great influence within his Sheading. At that time the position was sufficiently desirable to tempt a Kirk Marown man to approach the Governor with the offer of a bribe—a pearl taken from a fresh water mussel in the Dhoo—in return for the Coronership of Middle. The indignant official promptly denounced the offender, and after trial in 1695 he was fined and sentenced to one hour in the pillory with his ears nailed to it.

The Statute Book gives early evidence that the powers attached to the Coronership were open to abuse when exercised by unscrupulous men. In the fifteenth century Tynwald made an attack on those who had brought their office into disrepute by dishonest, malicious and tyrannical acts, 'to the hinderance and destruction of the comonalty —wherefore be it ordained that the Coroners stand in office but one yeare.' At the same time their right to make arrest without warrant was limited to cases of treason, felony and breach of the peace.

William Callow of Claghbane, writing *circa* 1730, says that some of the practices condemned by Tynwald were still encountered. 'It is in their power', he said 'to plague such people as they are displeased with by returning them frequently upon juries, or picking a jury, upon occasion, to serve a friend of the officers [i.e. members of the Administration], of which we had too frequent instances. By this means, besides hand-suits, etc., it's in their power to ruin their neighbours.'

In the early nineteenth century both the Duke of Atholl and the party opposed to him were for once in agreement that the Coronership required regulation. A bill was drafted to deprive Coroners of the power to pack juries, and after long delay such a measure was passed in 1832.

One of the complaints of the time was that a party got judgment in the summary courts and was enabled to sell the goods of the debtor with great rapidity, and that there was no law enabling a debtor to pay by instalments. It was said that the number of executions for the recovery of debts was almost incredible, and that the Coroners received considerable fees for summoning parties and witnesses.

But these emoluments together with their fixed pay of £6 per annum—£3 in 1777—had long ceased to attract suitable candidates for so burdensome an office. In 1827 a member of Council reported, 'Two or three at the most are at all equal to their duties;' and in 1829, 'The Douglas Coroner keeps a low public-house and is to my knowledge a very unfit person to be a Coroner. . . . The Coroner of Garff follows the same occupation and is equally unfit.'

One at least of the incompetents had a turn for literary expression, as shown in the petition of a discredited Southside ex-Coroner who had lost his position owing to misconduct or, as he held, through unreasonable prejudice. Writing in 1830 he complained that two prominent advocates, George Dumbell and Thomas Gawne, had said that he should be 'hung', for his duplicity.

'And what could it avail them,' he asked, 'to call me a beggar man and say that I was receiving help from the contending parties, while it appears that I am in a poor situation and therefore would not refuse the kindness of any man? My poor wife goes about for charity, but the false report of my enemies has turned the hearts of my dear friends against me. So I live a life of grief and pain, and my heart dies within me.'

The Coroners' powers were further curtailed in 1852, when they ceased to hold inquests of the dead, and in 1855 an increased scale of remuneration proved attractive to men equal to the responsibilities of the office.

VI

CAPTAIN OF THE PARISH

The title, Captain of the Parish, is the only purely Manx honour, apart from salaried appointments, which can be bestowed upon an Islander, and is first recorded in 1626, when Tynwald ordered the Captains to bring in complete muster rolls of their parishes with an account of the arms and accoutrements possessed by the countrymen.

It is a territorial distinction attached to each of the seventeen ancient parishes and, by tradition and practice, is limited to a native or resident of the parish in question. The official responsibilities of the position have now dwindled to attendance annually at Tynwald in July, and at a Selection Board; and the occasional calling of public meetings.

MILITARY DUTIES

In former times, as his commission still indicates, the Captain's most important duties were military. He supervised the Watch and Ward which was maintained night and day, and he commanded, trained and disciplined a militia company consisting of all the able-bodied males in his parish between the ages of sixteen and sixty. He had commissioned subordinates—a Lieutenant and, later, an Ensign —but these disappeared when the parish musters had ceased to be regularly held towards the end of the eighteenth century. No one knows when the name, Captain of the Parish, was first used—probably not earlier than the second half of the sixteenth century, when Henry the fourth Earl of Derby (1572–1593) paid several visits to his Island Lordship and tightened up its civil and military administration.

In the time of the native Kings of the Norse dynasty, the unit of military organisation was the Sheading, under the command of its *Moar* who was later known as Coroner. But the formation of the parishes in the twelfth century created new administrative units which reduced the power and duties of this official. The change was gradual, and the earliest surviving lists of Watch and Ward personnel, 1496–1507, show that the coast guard was still, if nominally, a Sheading organisation. The parishes, however, had each its own

Watch hill and Warden at that time, and it is probable that he carried out the duties later assigned to the Captain.

WATCH AND WARD

The duties of Watch and Ward were regarded as of vital importance, and the oath taken by an alien seeking Manx nationality specially mentioned this obligation. In 1672 a Scot named Andrew McBryde came into the Deemster's Court and craved he might be naturalised and made 'a free denizen of the Isle'. He offered a sum of money as fee which the Court thought too small, and he then increased it to five shillings. After further argument the Deemster accepted that amount, excusing his leniency and defeat in the bargaining by saying that McBryde had been coming to the Isle for many years and 'had used good dealinge'.

He took the oath on his knees, swearing allegiance to the Lord of the Isle and his heirs, with a reservation in favour of the Suzerain Lord, the King of England. 'You shall be obedient', the oath ran, 'to the Governor or his Deputy of the said Isle and the Government thereof, and perform all Watches and Wards whereunto you shall be required for the safetie and defence of the Isle to your best abillitie and power.'

The Manx custom of Watch and Ward was of Norse origin and introduced by the Viking settlers. It was an extremely oppressive duty, and by law no one was exempt save the officers of the parish Company, the Keys, the Coroners and Lock-men, the Moars, the Customs Officers, and the principal smith and miller of the parish. Four men were on Watch at a time—the Day Watch from sun-rise till sun-set, when they were relieved by the Night Watch.

Thus fifty-six men of each parish were called on in rota every week; and in the smaller parishes during times of sickness, or when many men were away in the boats fishing or trading, a man's turn came round very quickly.

The Day Watch was posted on an eminence very often crowned by an ancient burial mound, giving a wide view over the sea, and chosen for its visibility to the other posts. Some of the northern Watch Hills can be seen from seven or eight parishes. Several of these old look-out points are commemorated—as in Jurby, Malew and Rushen—by the name *Cronk ny Arrey Laa*, the Hill of the Day Watch. The night watches were generally established on the shore near the best landing place of the parish. When necessary the Watch coming on duty carried ling for fire in the shelter, and for the beacon.

The men of the Watch were supposed to bring their own weapons, and no doubt this was true of early times when every man carried

TYNWALD DAY, 1795

Streams of people are moving towards the Green and the canopied Hill

arms. But in the seventeenth and eighteenth centuries the government from time to time supplemented the scanty and varied equipment of the countryman—swords, dirks, pikes, calivers, javelins and muskets—with small quantities of weapons and ammunition, and periodically made levies to pay for their repair.

THE MUSTERING CROSS

The Parish Muster Roll supervised by the Captain and Minister, indicated the order in which men served on the Watch, and they were reminded of it by the Watch Cross which was passed around among those due to serve. It was made of wood but no specimen or detailed description has survived, though Kelly's Dictionary says it was a wooden sword in the form of a cross. It is not known how the Watch differed, if at all, from the Mustering Cross. The Captain had a number of Crosses ready for use in emergency, as shown in the Rising of 1651 when the Malew and Lonan commanders each sent out several crosses to raise his Parish.

The importance attached to Watch and Ward is reflected in the respect which was paid to the Cross, and the punishments given for its misuse. In 1611, for example, William Cubbon, Warden of the Day Watch at Cronk Arystine in Arbory, complained that two men had failed to attend the Watch owing to the fault of Moore of the Mylnes who had kept the Cross for two days, and did not pass it on. The Governor granted his token to the Warden to take two sheep from the offender.

Failure to appear in the appointed course at the Watch Hill drew a fine of a sheep for the first night, a cow for the second; and for the third, loss of goods and life at the discretion of the Lord. Absence at a Parish Muster was treated with equal severity. In 1595 the Captain of Man and his Council ordered that

'Upon warning given everyone do come to the place appointed by the Captain and there to bring his best weapon upon pain of forfeiting life, body and goods. Everyone that absenteth himself from the muster for the first time to be a year imprisoned and to forfeit all his goods to the Lord; and the second time to be at the Lord's disposition for his life, unless he be hindered by sickness.'

Passed from house to house the Cross was useful in the orderly summoning of the coast guards, and for parish musters, as in 1730, for example, when the Captains were ordered to raise the country for the apprehension of escaped prisoners. But its efficacy, as has been seen, could be gravely impaired by the failure of one person to hand it on. Sudden dangers from the sea, to which the Island was liable until the nineteenth century, called for a quicker means of rallying

E

the garrisons and assembling the militia. Both drum and bell are named in the fifteenth century regulations governing the castles of Peel and Rushen, and in times of crisis the drum provided the usual summons to arms in the parishes.

It was not always obeyed with the speed which the circumstances demanded, as in 1601 when several ships thought to be pirates appeared off Castletown. An alarm was given by beating the drum and hoisting the flag on the Castle; and the authorities complained of the lack of response from those within sight and sound of the signals. Upon deliberation by Governor, Deemsters and the Twenty-four, it was deemed that those who failed to obey such a summons deserved immediate death.

The drummer of a militia company had a special responsibility in the sounding of the Alarm. It might be mentioned that, in all the records of the Island Militia, a drummer was its only member to be rewarded for his services. In 1663, twelve years after the siege and capture of the Loyal Fort in Kirk Andreas it was remembered that

> 'Thomas Kinreade was the drummer in the said Fort and be-
> haved himself well and was true and trusty to the last. These are
> therefore for the better encouragement of all such persons, and he
> being also a public officer of Kirk Christ Lezayre therefore I think
> fit to free the said Kinreade from all duty and services whatever
> except when he shall be called on by his Captain or any other
> superior officer.
>
> H. M. Nowell, Governor.'

SEA RAIDERS

The part of the Island most vulnerable to attack was the north, with its numerous creeks and sandy beaches. There is a tradition of persistent raids in the first half of the sixteenth century, when a free-booter from Galloway named Cutlar McCulloch used to make sudden descents upon the shores of Jurby and Kirk Andreas, take what plunder he could and make off before the parishes could be raised. But the most notable incursion, of which there are details, took place at a time when the Island was full of preparations for defence and when it might be supposed that any hostile vessel approaching the coast would be at once detected and repelled.

In September, 1643, Scottish pirates landed near Port Cranstal and plundered Christian, Ballacallow, and others. Their booty included eight cattle, one of which they killed on the shore; fifty sheep; thirty geese, and two fishing boats with their nets. They carried off all the food, domestic utensils and clothing they could lay their hands on: a hundred salt cod, four dozen cheeses, jerkins, breeches, stockings, bedclothes, pewter and piggins. They even stole Christian's psalter—a pilfery which must have brought conviction to the victims with regard to the raiders' nationality.

The despoiling of Ballacallow was not the only example of lawlessness on the Manx coasts. During the period of the Civil War (1642–1651) the Irish Sea was infested by piratical craft owing an easy allegiance to one side or the other, and ready to rob indiscriminately. In 1648 William Hill complained to the Captain of Peel that he had been pillaged and robbed at sea by Captain Kissag and his crew in a frigate belonging to Wexford. He still had fifty-five shillings hidden in his stockings when the vessel came to rest in the lee of the Castle. But this also was taken from him by one of the crew who drew a dagger across his throat, and moved a slow match about his head and tortured him.

In the following year Captain Brooks put into Douglas and anchored under the guns of the Bulwark, secure in his welcome as an avowed Royalist. On board he had prisoners—passengers from a bark taken by him on her way from Ireland to Wales. Foolishly he allowed his captives to stretch their legs ashore, and they immediately made complaint to the Captain of the Town. They had all been robbed, women as well as men, one of whom had been stripped of his clothes and shoes. Brooks was ordered to return the stolen property, and then impudently asked for the surrender of the prisoners. He was refused, and sailed off in search of fresh plunder.

The failure of the Governor's Council to deal with the thievish Royalist as he deserved may have been due to the fact that the circumstances of the Civil War had lowered the normal standards of behaviour. The island had become a place of refuge for adherents of the King's party, and some of them were as unscrupulous as the seacaptain. The fire-eating Cavaliers who swaggered and quarrelled at the Earl's Court in Castletown added to the disorders of the time, when a blow was the almost inevitable climax of a warm argument; and when brawling in the garrisons had become so frequent and dangerous that in 1645 Earl James decreed the punishment of cutting off the right hand for anyone striking and drawing blood within the Castles.

SIR ARTHUR ASTON

It is possible that this savage and inhuman punishment was suggested to Lord Derby by the most remarkable of the Royalist leaders who took refuge in Man during the concluding years of the war. This was Sir Arthur Aston, a soldier of fortune, connected with a good Cheshire family. He had had a long and varied military career, was in Russia on a mission from 1613 to 1618; fought under

Sigismund of Poland against the Turks; for Lithuania against Gustavus Adolphus, and then for Gustavus against the Austrian Count Tilly; always ready to sell his sword to the highest bidder. As Clarendon said of him, he was 'a man of rough nature and so given up to an immoderate love of money that he cared not by what unrighteous ways he exacted it'.

On his return to England in 1640 he was given high rank in the army operating against the Scots and was knighted for his services. After some hesitation he joined the Royalists on the outbreak of the Civil War and enhanced his outstanding reputation as an army commander. But he was cruel and ruthless; on one occasion having a soldier's hand sawn off to satisfy a grudge against the victim; and he appears to have been detested and feared by everyone who had dealings with him.

As governor of Reading with a garrison of 4,000 men he successfully resisted a long siege by a Parliamentary army; and when Charles's Court was at Oxford, Henrietta Maria obtained his appointment to the Governorship of that city, on the plea that he was a Catholic like herself and would look after her security. In 1644 he lost a leg as the result of a fall, a mishap which debarred him from further service in the field.

Four years later he was in Man, and, according to Blundell, was responsible for the erection of a military work on the seaward slope of Peel Hill commanding the crossing to St. Patrick's Isle; but no recognisable remains are now visible. In 1645 the Earl had made Governor John Greenhalghe Lieutenant-General of the Insular armed forces, and Aston declared that a 'martiall' man was needed for the post. Some of his acquaintances in Peel told him that he ought to be in charge of the defences. 'It is an ill dog', he replied bitterly, 'that is not worth the whistling.'

Fortunately for the Manx the Earl did not whistle, and the disappointed knight vented his spleen on the Governor. Greenhalghe was obviously anxious to treat Aston tenderly and, in an attempt to settle their differences, made a journey to Peel where Aston was then living. He summoned the truculent soldier to appear before him, but Sir Arthur refused to present himself; and thereupon the Governor confined him to his chamber with a guard of six musketeers, at Aston's expense. This assault on the most vulnerable point of his defences—his pocket—quickly produced an apology and a plea for pardon.

His stay in Man, which appears to have escaped the notice of his biographers, ended shortly afterwards; and he crossed to Ireland where the Royalist leader, Ormond, gave him the command at

Drogheda. The town which had strong fortifications manned by 2,800 men, was invested by the Parliamentary forces under Cromwell; and on September 10th, 1649, after a repulse, the English troops penetrated the defences and, on Cromwell's order, put the garrison to the sword, many civilians also being included in the slaughter. Aston, easily distinguishable with his wooden leg, shared the fate of his officers and men and was savagely hacked to death. Thirty survivors of the massacre, with hundreds of Irish, were later shipped to the plantations in Barbados.

THE GREAT STANLEY

The story of the Isle of Man during the Civil War is dominated by the personality of James, seventh Earl of Derby, who succeeded to the title and the Lordship of Man in 1642, and spent a large part of the nine years of conflict in the Island. The *Stanlagh Mooar*, 'The Great Stanley,' as the Manx called him, was a man of outstanding character and ability, with a quick and cultivated mind, a gift of literary expression, a shrewd understanding of human nature, and a courage which matched his unfaltering loyalty to two unworthy princes of the house of Stuart.

He had a sincere desire for the welfare of the Manx people, introduced some reforms, and had schemes for the founding of a college and the development of trade. But his attitude to the problems of his Lordship was clouded by the prejudices of his class and times—an autocratic objection to opposition, and an assumption common to the Lords of Man that the Island was merely a property or instrument in his hands for the prosecution of his designs and the profit of his family.

He pursued his course with finesse. Instructing his son in the art of managing men he wrote, 'If in anything you are obliged to be harsh, of that let another bear share; and when you deny or afflict let another mouth pronounce it.' The levies, assessments and other exactions with which he burdened the Manx people during the war were all passed in correct form by Governor, Council and Keys in Tynwald; the Earl keeping in the background and discreetly using persuasion, promises and covert threats to gain his end.

GOVERNOR GREENHALGHE

In consequence his mouthpiece the Governor, John Greenhalghe, became the scapegoat to whom were attributed many of the hardships of the time; though it is true that the Earl defended his representative from criticism, and deplored the unappreciative attitude of his subjects. Replying to one complaint, he wrote, 'They had cause to bless me who took such care of these poor people. There never came amongst them better poor man's friend, or that took more paines to do all men justice.'

From one thing Greenhalghe could not shield his master—the odium attached to his scheme of robbing the landowners of their customary tenure, and converting their farms into leasehold; and this attack on their ancient rights caused a deep resentment which finally found expression in the Rising of 1651.

As early as 1643 only prompt action by the Earl averted an outbreak, Edward Christian, commander of the Island armed forces, being charged with conspiracy against the peace, and sentenced to perpetual imprisonment in Peel, at the Lord's pleasure. In the following year the Parish Captains were ordered to repair with their companies to training camps, and the Bride and Andreas men were assembled at Knock y Doonee.

There, it was reported to the authorities, John Lace the Elder had uttered seditious words. Summoned to Castletown, he confessed that there was talk of a refusal to keep camp unless they had pay from the Lord, who, he said, had broken their tenure; and he heard the same was being said in other parishes. Many found fault with Greenhalghe who, expecting trouble, had attended Tynwald 'with so many soldiers, and their muskets charged with powder and bullet'. It was rumoured, Lace said, that there would be another Governor.

Before the Tynwald of 1644, the Earl had taken steps to strengthen the Captains' loyalty by summoning them to Castletown where they took a fresh oath of obedience to the Lord of the Isle. In the Exchequer Book of that year there is a list of those present. One, John Sayle of the Craige, Andreas, failed to attend. For some unknown reason Lezayre was at this time given a second Captain, an innovation which was maintained until the end of the next century. The list is as follows:

William Gawne, Ballagawne; Richard Stevenson, Balladoole; William Hudleston, Ballachott; John Moore, Knock y Loghan, Santan; John Moore, Marown; Robert Moore, Pooil Roish, Braddan; Edward Christian, Bemahague, Onchan; Philip Moore, Lonan; John Christian, Maughold; Sam Radcliffe, Gourdon; Thomas Tubman, Ballakilmoirrey; John Cannell, Michael; Thomas Thompson, Ballakinnag; John Teare, Ballateare; David Christian, Cranstal; John Christian, Milntown, and John Curghie, Ballakillingan, for the North and South Divisions of Lezayre.

From this time military preparations went forward with ever-increasing strain on the population. A troop of cavalry raised at the end of 1643, four men from each parish, was increased to two troops in 1644, the cost of maintenance being laid on the parishes and clergy. Four years later the numbers were increased to 288 troopers. In addition householders had to give free quartering to the troops, and periodical requisitions were made on the country for the upkeep of the garrisons manning the castles and forts. The presence of a body of English troops prevented any further attempt to upset the Government, and Earl James also sought to curb dangerous freedom of speech by causing an enactment of 1601 to be formally brought to his notice. This law declared that

> 'whosoever shall sclander condeme or accuse any of the 24 or any cheefe officer within the Isle sworne to maintayne lawes and justice touching either their othes or the state or government or any other scandelous speeches . . . and be not able to prove it shall be fyned for every tyme soe offending in ten pounds and their eares to be cutt off for punishment. . . .'

The Exchequer Book copy bears the endorsement:

> 'Castle Rushen 21 of July 1647: I do well aprove of this to be a Lawe for any Scandalous Speeches against any cheif Officer Spirituall or Temporall, or any of the 24 Keyes and will this, my consent, to be proclaimed at the next Tindwall.
>
> L. Derby.'

The Earl spent the last seven years of his life in Man. In 1649 he was formally required by Parliament to surrender the Island. To this he replied in a bombastic vein that if they troubled him with any more messages he would burn the paper and hang the bearer; and he issued an invitation to all adherents of the young Charles to repair to the Island. Parliament's answer was to give the Lordship of Man to Lord Fairfax.

In August, 1651, the Earl left Castletown for the last time, with 300 Manx soldiers, to take command of the insurrectionary Royalist forces in Lancashire and Cheshire. A letter survives which he wrote to the Manx Vicars-General some months before. What he asks for is not evident, but it reveals a pleasing sensibility and a concern for his Manx subjects whom he had so deeply involved in his political fortunes.

'I hope,' he wrote, 'that I have deserved so well from you that you will easily comply with my desires in such a necessitous time as this is, though perhaps that which I am forced to expect from you for the ease of the poor people may be somewhat beyond your present abilities. . . .' It may be that he was referring to the dearth of the necessaries of life in the preceding three years, brought about by bad harvests and his own exactions. An entry in the Records speaks of the

> 'sad condition poor people were in for want of bread and other food, many having dyed through hunger, and most part of the poorest sort scarce able to stand for want of sustenance. . . . It is ordered that every farmer and housekeeper within this Isle shall

twice every week spare from themselves and their famillys the usual proportion of victualls for one meale distributed amongst the poorest sort that come to their houses; this to continue till new corn come in.'

The Earl crossed over to Lancashire under no illusion as to the precarious nature of his venture. 'Fame', he had once quoted in his diary, 'which ploughs up the air and sows in the wind, has often been dangerous to the living; and what the dead get by it let the dead tell. I and some others who'are almost dead have in the meantime some guess.'

On August 26th his troops were engaged at Wigan Lane by a superior Parliamentary force and cut to pieces; though, according to contemporary reports the Manxmen 'fought stoutly and with much couradge'. The survivors were scattered through the countryside, and some managed to make their way back to the Island. In 1671 Mrs. Lowcay, wife of the Chaplain of Castletown, made a successful appeal for the life of a condemned felon on the grounds that it was his first offence, and that he had 'ventured his life at Wiggan in a good cause with our late Noble Lord James of never dying memory.'

Following this defeat the Earl joined the King at Worcester, was captured in the retreat from that place, and after trial at Chester was executed at Bolton on October 15th. He had left the Countess in charge of the Isle of Man with complete powers to act for him. Whatever admiration Charlotte de la Tremoille had aroused in the minds of the Manx by her heroic defence of Latham there is no evidence that her personality had won their liking or affection; and the departure of the Earl and his expeditionary force, left the way open for his discontented subjects to act for the redress of their grievances.

THE CAPTAINS' REVOLT

The initiative was taken by William Christian—*Illiam Dhone*, 'Brown-haired William'—commander of the armed forces—who called a meeting of the Parish Captains and companies of the Southside. Crosses were sent out in the parishes and 800 armed men assembled at Ronaldsway, where they took an oath 'to withstand the Lady Derby in her designs until she had yielded or condescended to their aggrievances'.

These were generally accepted to be the change of land tenure, free quartering of troops, and the Countess's action in opening secret negotiations with the commander of the Parliamentary fleet on its way to reduce the Island. There was a belief that they were being sacrificed; that, to use the current phrase at the time, the country was being sold for twopence or threepence apiece.

Dollin Clarke, Lieutenant of Jurby, gave another reason for the rising. He said that on October 20th the Jurby men were under arms by orders of Lady Derby because of a fleet coming against the Island; whereupon he said, 'they resolved that there was no better way for the preservation and safety of the country than to rise against my Lady.' The horrors of Drogheda were still fresh in their minds and they had no desire to provoke a similar slaughter in Man.

All the Northside companies obeyed the summons of the war crosses, and marched on the forts at Ramsey and Andreas. These, with a troop at Bishopscourt, surrendered without bloodshed. John Sayle, the Craige, Captain of Andreas, was not in favour of the rebellion and the Company was led by his Lieutenant, John Lace the Younger of Ballavoddan. Three other Captains also held aloof: Richard Stevenson, Balladoole, Arbory, and Robert Calcot the Nunnery, Braddan, whose Companies took no part in the Rising; and William Hudleston, Ballachott, Malew.

On the completion of their task the Northside militia marched to Cronk Lheannag, north of Sandhouse and less than two miles from Peel, where Captain Samsbury Radcliffe of Gordon had assembled the Patrick and German men for an attack on the Castle. It was captured on October 24th, the first time in its history. But the militia, who had been aided by members of the garrison, were not sufficiently experienced in the art of war to take advantage of their success and were driven out by a counter-rally. One captain whose name is unknown was mortally wounded—perhaps Thomas Tubman of Ballakilmoirrey who died about that time.

Only one case of damage to property during the Rising is recorded —the burning of the kiln of Captain John Sayle who was in the Fort at Andreas during its investment and refused to come out— an eloquent testimonial to the decent behaviour of the countrymen.

On October 25th the Parliamentary fleet of 44 sail appeared off the coast, and William Christian and his associates made haste to assure the English commander, Col. Duckenfield, that a landing would not be opposed. On the following morning the Islanders' representatives went aboard the flagship to surrender the Island, only asking that the Manx should be allowed to retain their ancient laws and liberties. The occupying forces disembarked on October 28th, and dividing into two, marched on the fortresses at Castletown and Peel which soon surrendered. Quarter was given to the garrisons, and Lady Derby, with her entourage, was allowed to leave for England.

THE END OF ILLIAM DHONE

In February, 1652, Lord Fairfax was formally proclaimed Lord of the Isle; but on the restoration of the British monarchy eight years

later the Stanleys were reinstated; and the Great Earl's son Charles
came to Man burning with a desire to avenge the affront to his mother
and family implicit in the Rebellion of 1651. The arch-offender,
William Christian, had been living in England, and, misled by the
King's grant of a general amnesty for all who had been concerned in
the Civil War, incautiously returned to the Island. He was arrested
in September, 1662, for 'illegal actions and rebellions' in 1651; and
was indicted for treason by a packed jury of six.

When the Court of General Gaol Delivery sat in November,
Christian refused to come into the Court to abide the law. This was a
grave error of judgment for, according to customary law, a refusal to
plead was considered a tacit confession of guilt. The Deemster and
Keys were consulted, and answered that in such a case the accused
was at the mercy of the Lord for his life and goods.

To make this decision unanimous the Earl had ordered the dis-
missal of seven Keys who had been active in the Rising—Edward
Christian, William's nephew and assistant Deemster; and six Parish
Captains and Lieutenants: Sam Radcliffe, William Gawne, John
Caine, John Lace, Dollin Clarke and Ewan Curghie. Their places
were filled by the Earl's nominees: Thomas Woods, Knocksharry;
William Caine, Ballagawne, Michael; William Christian, Balla-
yonaige; John Moore, Balnehow, Santan; John Taubman, the
Bowling Green; Thomas Huddleston, Jun., Ballachott; and William
Corlett, the Cleanagh.

On December 31st, the Deemsters pronounced sentence of death
by shooting, and two days later Christian met his end at Hango Hill.
He was mourned by the Manx as a patriot who had lost his life on
their behalf. Twelve members of the Council—including the three
Parish Captains Stevenson, Calcot and Hudleston, who had not
joined in the Rising—had sat in the Court which found *Illiam Dhone*
guilty; and the disasters which later fell upon the families of Calcot,
Norris, Tyldesley and others, were popularly attributed to the share
their representatives had had in the leader's condemnation. An old
ballad says,

> *Gow gys yn Vannister ny Cailleeyn-ghoo;*
> *As eie son clein Cholcad derrey vrisheys dty ghoo;*
> *Ta'n ennym shen caillit v'euish, Vanninee ghooie;*
> *As dty vaase, Illiam Dhone, te brishey nyn gree!*

> Go to the Nunnery of the black-robed nuns,
> And call for Clan Calcott until thy voice breaks;
> That name is lost from you, ye native Manxmen;
> And thy death, Illiam Dhone, 'tis that breaks our heart!

Gow gys ny Cregganyn, ny gys yn Vallalogh,
Cha vow fer jeh'n ennym shen jir rhyt, 'Cheet stiagh!'
Ec joarreeyn ta nyn dhieyn, nyn dhalloo as nhee;
As dty vaase, Illiam Dhone, te brishey nyn gree!

Go unto the Creggans or to the Ballalough,
There is no man of that name will say to thee, 'Come in!'
Strangers have their houses, their land, and their all;
And thy death, Illiam Dhone, 'tis that breaks our heart!

AFTER THE RESTORATION

For more than a century after the Rising the Parish Captains continued in their duties of mustering and training their companies, and providing for the maintenance of the Watch, for it was not until the conclusion of the Napoleonic Wars, in 1815, that the Manx coast was free from the danger of sea raiders. No doubt there was some relaxation of vigilance during the brief periods of peace in the seventeenth and eighteenth centuries. But the emergence of new political crises—the outbreak of war with a Continental power, an Irish or a Scottish rising, the danger of imported plague—periodically caused a tightening up of the militia organisation, the renewal of Parish musters and assessments to pay for arms.

In 1689 for example, the Governor announced that 'by reason of the present troubles and disturbances the Isle may be exposed to the incursion of pirotts, pickerroons and such like as may come in hostile manner to robb plunder and annoy', and camps were to be set up at Hanmer Hould (Ballaugh), Shellag Point, Bankes Howe, Santan, Cass ny Hawin and the Calf. The Captains were ordered to divide their Companies into four, each part taking a week's duty in rotation.

As in the past the Bishop and clergy were ordered to provide arms —the Bishop, eight muskets; the Archdeacon, four; the Rectors, two each; and the Vicars, one each. These exacting demands on the parishes could not long continue, and in 1695 there is an official complaint that, although danger still threatens from the sea, arms are neglected, and the Town Companies in particular are unfit for service.

One curious intrusion of politics into the economy of the Parish Companies occurred in 1699, at a time when the Manx people were engaged in the final phases of their long struggle against the attack first made by the Great Earl and maintained by his son and grandson upon the ancient land tenure. The Keys had gone to London in 1698 to state their case, and Paul Gellin and John Oates, Captains of Braddan and Onchan respectively, urged a collection on the Braddan Company to pay towards the cost of the Keys' journey.

The Braddan men refused, but some of them agreed that an assessment for the repair of the Parish arms should be diverted to the Keys' fund. They stipulated, however, that Gellin should repay the money if it was ever demanded by the Authorities. A dissentient from the scheme reported the irregularity, to the great discomfiture of the two Captains.

FALSE ALARM

In 1720 fear of plague brought by ships from the Mediterranean engaged the public attention. King's Orders in Council excluded all Manx and Channel Islands ships from English ports, and the rumour spread in England that the Island was plague-stricken. Governor Horne vehemently protested to London that there was no truth in this; but that, as a consequence, all papers and letters were refused at Whitehaven, the Manx packet boat having been fired upon when it attempted to communicate with the shore. His dispatches had had to be sent by way of Ireland. He went on to describe in detail the extreme precautions which he had taken for the safe interrogation of strange vessels approaching the coast, and the strictness with which Watch and Ward was maintained to prevent unauthorised landings.

The embargo greatly inconvenienced the Island, and Earl James II was asked to intervene with the English Government. His reply was in keeping with the ungenerous attitude to the Manx which historians have attributed to him. He said that he was doing what he could; but, he pointed out sarcastically, since the Twenty-four found it necessary to obey Orders in Council in the Christian of Ronaldsway dispute, and the Bishop had insisted on an Act of Henry VIII—two cases in which his own wishes were thus thwarted—he did not see why they should not accept the present Order in Council with the same alacrity.

In spite of Horne's emphatic orders for a close and constant Watch on the coast, John Oates of Bibaloe was reported to have failed to provide for this duty. He admitted that as Captain he was responsible for the Watch, but excused his dereliction by pointing out that Onchan was only a small parish, so that each man's turn came about every ten days, and he did not wish to be hard upon the people or give them trouble. Besides, he said, Port Onchan was only a small creek, and there was no danger of a boat landing there.

His pleas were not successful. The Governor was extremely angry to find that the coast guard was not so complete and excluding as he had imagined; and Oates's good nature lost him his Captaincy. He was also imprisoned in Castle Rushen for ten days, but a fine of £10 was remitted two years later.

Occasional lapses by the rank and file of the Watch met with the ancient penalties. The Captain of Arbory in 1721 and of Malew in 1737 reported men who had failed to stand watch or send substitutes. They were first offenders and each paid a wether to the Warden. On St. Mark's Eve, 1721, the Kirk Michael Watch deserted their post before dawn and the arrival of the day relief. They denied leaving before day-break, but said they were starved with the cold and called at a cottage for a pint of ale. They were adjudged to have forfeited body and goods to the Lord, and the meagre inventories of their possessions still survive.

In 1719 and again in 1739 assessments for the purchase of arms were made to supply deficiencies in the Companies. As in former times they were never completely successful, and in 1748 it was ordered that each landowner and house-keeper should buy his own weapons under the supervision of his Captain.

The declaration of war with France in 1743 and the Young Pretender's preparations for a descent on the British Isles brought fears of invasion, and in 1745 when enemy attempts to land were daily expected the Companies were frequently exercised and the Watches doubled. Judging from the amount of ammunition available it is however doubtful whether a landing in force could have been long resisted. For the whole Island the Lord's Administration provided only five barrels of gunpowder: four for the garrisons and one to be divided in an emergency among the parishes.

THE REVESTMENT

After 1765, when the Lordship of Man was vested in the British Crown, the customs of Watch and Ward and the Parish Muster fell into disuse, save for short periods during the French wars. The new Royal Governors showed little disposition to put the Militia laws into force, Lieutenant-Governor Dawson declaring in 1777 that they were rigorous and oppressive; and that the Keys were disinclined to bear the expense of arming. He asked instead for a permanent garrison of English troops, to protect an Island left defenceless. No repairs, he said, had been done in the Castles and Forts since 1646, and they were in a ruinous state, with unmounted guns.

In 1781 he informed Whitehall that the Island was exposed to the depredations of privateers, not very different from pirates. An English ship of that class had forcibly taken four Castletown men on board. Fortunately, two of the ship's officers were ashore at the time, and were lodged in the Castle until the captives were returned. Smugglers, too, frequently landed their goods, protected by armed men, and distributed them through the country without fear of molestation. And every summer the Isle was visited by many hundreds of lawless Irish fishermen who disturbed the peace and committed all sorts of disorder with impunity.

The Governor's desire for a stable military establishment was not gratified, but at various times between 1780 and 1815 Fencibles and Volunteers were recruited and shared guard duties with detachments of English regulars stationed for short periods in the Island. Some of the Parish officers were given volunteer commissions, but otherwise the Militia as such played a very minor part.

In 1779 the Parish Captains were ordered to choose places of retreat in the hills to which the cattle were to be driven out of reach of invaders. In 1798 the Irish Rebellion caused much anxiety and the Captains were ordered to set up strict Watch and Ward over the Isle, and to warn their people 'to turn out in case of alarm, agreeably to the antient Manx laws, to defend their country'. The Militia were mustered for the last time and 4,181 able-bodied men answered the call.

On the renewal of the French War in 1803 the Governor asked the Captains for a return of able-bodied men willing to shoulder a pike in the event of invasion. A total of 2,319 offered—an excellent response, when the number already serving in the Navy, Fencibles and Volunteers is remembered. In the following year 400 pikemen were enrolled (there were only 435 pikes available) and served with the Captains as auxiliaries to the Volunteers.

THE FOUR HORSEMEN

From time immemorial each Manx parish provided four horsemen who, with the Parish Captain, rode armed to Castletown to form an escort for the Lord of the Isle or his Deputy when he went with his retinue in annual procession to the Tynwald on Midsummer Day. Watchers on the hills signalled the progress of the glittering cavalcade as it passed northwards with colours flying, with jingle of harness and ring of steel, to the sacred Hill where the Deemsters and Keys, the Bishop and the People, awaited it. One catches a glimpse of the picturesque quality of this ceremonial ride in the description of the first Atholl Lord's coming in 1736, when he was escorted to St. Johns by three squadrons of the Horsemen—bay, black and grey—well mounted and armed, carrying standards and marching to the music of horn and drum.

The Horsemen were generally substantial landowners who acted as liaison officers between Watch, Captain and Governor. Danold Quark, a Horseman of Onchan, giving evidence in 1775, told how, forty-four years before, he had supervised the Watch at Port Onchan, going on duty every fourth night in turn with the other Horsemen.

He took his horse along with him, ready, he said, to obey the Captain's order with an express to the Governor or others. His duty, he recalled with pride, was to attend the Governor at Tynwald. In addition the Horsemen were expected to see that the arms and equipment of the Watch were in serviceable condition. They provided their own horses and accoutrements, including helmets, and received some trifling parochial exemptions in return.

Owing to their obligatory attendance at Tynwald with their Captains, they survived the disappearance of the Watch and Ward at the end of the Napoleonic Wars, until the time when the Governors no longer went on horseback to St. John's.

One of the last documentary references to them is found in a return from Kirk Bride. In the hungry thirties and forties of last century there was a shortage of food and much suffering among the poor; and in 1836 the Captain, William Christian, Ballayonaige, was asked to find out the quantity of potatoes available for sale in the parish. He reported that he had 'sent the Four Horsemen to each quarter of our parish—Cranstal, Ballavaranagh, the South and the West Ends', to collect information.

THE CAPTAIN'S CIVIL DUTIES

In addition to his purely military duties the Captain had the obligation to suppress riots and other disorders and maintain the peace. Quarrels ending in blows often arose in the ale houses, which were the only places of public resort for social purposes, and were used by people of every class.

In 1681 several men, including Ewan Curghie of Ballakillingan and John Kneale of Regaby, were met in a house in Ramsey, and one of them, a Captain and agent for Lord Derby in his cattle dealing, had drunk too much and became abusive and threatening. Then in came Ewan Christian of Cranstal, Captain of Bride. He gave the agent a clap on the shoulder and 'required the Lord's peace', pointing out that he could put him into prison if he disobeyed. The drunken man drew his sword and placed himself in a posture of defence, but, stepping on to a slippery place, he fell; and Cranstal, seizing the sword by the blade, forced it against the table edge and broke it. The agent was then confined in prison until he found sureties for his good behaviour and attendance at the next Court.

There were no civil police until after 1765, and the Captain sometimes had to call upon his men to furnish guards for offenders. In 1667 a Jurby farmer made a murderous assault on Conly of Ballaconly, and the Parish Captain set a guard of neighbours upon the aggressor until he could be conveyed to Castle Rushen.

SULBY CLADDAGH

The periodical fairs, which were usually held near the Parish Cross and were an essential feature of rural life, had increased in size with the growth of trade at the end of the seventeenth century, and often caused damage to the churchyard fences. When Trinity Fair was held at Lezayre in 1728 buyers, sellers, and cattle not only levelled the hedge but overflowed into the churchyard and damaged the church windows. A strong protest was made by the churchwardens, and in 1735 Tynwald ordered the removal of the fair to Sulby Claddagh, the Captains being instructed at the same time to supervise their local fairs, see that order was kept and apportion the fair ground to the general advantage.

The Claddagh had once been the corn-land of Ballamannagh. But in August, 1673, after abnormally heavy rains, the flooded Sulby river swept over the flats, carrying away the soil and destroying their fertility. The Governor, Henry Nowell, ordered the Captains of Bride, Andreas and Lezayre, to muster their Companies and to bring spades, creels and sled-cars 'to the greatest breach at the broken point towards Ballacarghey's [i.e. the Carrick] side'; and there they built a defending wall of stone and sod. The owners of Ballamannagh obtained a reduction of their customary rents by a quarter and the wasted land became common.

There are numerous cases in the Records of the Parish Companies being called in to help in similar public work. In 1692, for example, the Captains of Rushen and Arbory were ordered to bring their men with spades and creels to clear away stones—ballast—jettisoned from boats in Derby Haven; and in the same year the Malew and Arbory Companies repaired the common highway from Castletown to Peel, by way of Arbory, which had become 'very unpassable in the wintry season'.

But there was a growing reluctance among the countrymen to do unpaid work for the general good, outside their own parishes; and the eighteenth century saw the abandonment of the muster, in favour of an assessment levied impartially on the community concerned. There were, however, instances of a muster for work within a parish as late as 1750, when John Wattleworth, Captain of Kirk Andreas ordered his Company to repair the *Raad Killagh*—'Church Road'—which ran through the fields from the south side of the Church to the Knock Beg.

THE COINAGE

The Parish Captains provided convenient agents by which administrative orders could be made known to the countryside, and then enforced. One subject which was a constant source of concern to the Insular Government until 1840, was the coinage. The Island suffered from a perennial shortage of this medium, in spite of an old law forbidding the taking of money out of the land; and various expedients were used to balance the deficiency. A number of foreign coins were in circulation and some of them had officially fixed exchange values. In 1645 Spanish pieces of eight were worth four shillings and fourpence, provided their weight was equal to four shillings and ninepence sterling; in 1647 the Venetian silver ducatoon was tender for five shillings; and in 1703 a levadoon was worth nineteen shillings and sixpence.

A 'Manx mark' is mentioned in the Book of Pleas of 1587; but apart from this cryptic phrase and that it was worth 4 shillings nothing is known of it. The first exclusively Manx coins of which we have knowledge were made in 1668 by John Murrey, a merchant of Douglas. They were penny tokens which were made legal tender by Act of Tynwald.

A large part of the Insular trade was conducted with Ireland, and tokens such as 'Butcher's or Pot Halfpence', were introduced from that country. It was not until 1709 that the Lord authorised an issue of Manx copper pence and halfpence, exchangeable at the rate of fourteen Manx to twelve British; and in the eighteenth century Manx merchants and their book keepers spent much time working out their accounts in terms of the Manx, British and Irish values.

The next Manx issue—£900 in pence and halfpence—appeared in 1733. It was made, according to tradition, from guns once mounted at Castle Rushen; and the London Mint criticised it as being bad in weight and metal. The only Manx money coined in the Atholl period came into circulation in 1758. The penny was considered by the Mint to have only half the value of an English one, but was an improvement on that of 1733, and the quality of the copper little inferior to the English penny. After the Revestment there were four more issues— in 1786, 1798, 1813, and 1839. In 1840 the Manx coinage was called in, to the accompaniment of public demonstrations and riots, the holders being aggrieved at the rate of exchange.

At different times during the seventeenth and much of the eighteenth century, Man was flooded with counterfeit rapps from Ireland and base coins from Birmingham; and people were forced to use them, owing to the gradual disappearance of the legal Manx currency in a black market. Strangers coming to the Island changed their shillings for fourteen pence Manx, and then passed the Manx coins upon their unsuspecting countrymen in England, thus obtaining a modest but dishonest profit of two pence on the shilling.

F

In the times of the Stanley and Atholl Lords the Captains were expected to keep watch on the currency position in their parishes and report anyone detected passing or making spurious coins. In 1723 the blacksmith of Ballasalla, who also sold ale, gave two brass coins or rapps in change to a customer. At that moment the Captain of Kirk Malew walked into the smithy house, and seeing the coins in the drinker's hand, examined them and pronounced them counterfeit. He searched the smith and found another rapp in his pocket. Suspecting the smith and his son of manufacturing the coins he sent them to Castle Rushen. When they came up for trial they were found innocent of the charge; and ten years later the son was employed by the Lord to make the copper coinage of 1733.

In that year an Act of Tynwald made the coining or uttering of counterfeit money a capital offence; and the Captains were ordered to give notice at the parish churches in June of each year that all persons who had any of the new currency in their custody were to bring them to the Captains to be examined for false pieces and counted, a return of the amount being made to Castletown.

ALEHOUSES

Another important duty performed by the Captains was recommending the grant of licences for the brewing and selling of ale. Ale was a necessity in a society in which tea, coffee and cocoa had either not yet appeared or were expensive luxuries, and brewing was a normal task in the houses of many of the clergy and prosperous farmers, though most of the brewhouses were in the towns.

In the country the selling of ale was rarely the only means of livelihood of a licence holder, who might be a miller, the wife of a Key, a schoolmaster, cottager or a clergyman's daughter. The alehouses were not, as in modern times, specially built for the purpose of selling drink. They were the average type of house or cottage found everywhere in the Island, and the drinking took place in the *thie mooar*—the kitchen.

Immoderate indulgence in liquor increased towards the end of the seventeenth century, and unduly large quantities of barley were diverted to the making of malt, even when the harvests had been poor and there was a dearth of grain. On the other hand two cases in 1702 show the importance attached even to the weak home-brewed ale as a necessity of life. Several persons had been punished for unlicensed brewing, but begged for the remission of their fines, arguing that they had brewed from sheer necessity. One man had used a *kishan* (eight quarts) of malt to obtain 'the benefit of the small beer to relieve his sick family'; and Margery Watterson brewed a ferlot (thirty-nine quarts) because 'her father and mother were both in their death of sickness, and she could not get them in the parish a pennyworth of small beer'.

The Captains received orders from time to time, and especially in bad seasons, emphasising the need to restrict the amount of corn to be turned into malt. The increase in drinking was linked up with the existence of what in 1728 was called 'a vast number' of alehouses. In that year the Captains and Clergy drew up lists of drinking houses in their parishes and were instructed to limit the number of licences. Their efforts were not noticeably successful, and more than a century had passed before there was a radical reform.

The considerable influence and power which the Captain exercised in his Parish in the seventeenth and eighteenth centuries was greatly reduced by the administrative changes which followed the Revestment—the appointment of Constables and High Bailiffs and, in more recent times, the development of local government. But his licensing duties in the past are recalled by his present-day attendance at a Selection Board which meets annually to elect members of the District Licensing Court, and for which he may be chosen. Similarly his obligation to attend the Governor at Tynwald still remains, though he no longer carries arms or wears the martial dress of his predecessors when, long ago, in picturesque cavalcade, they rode with music to St. John's.

VII

CAPTAIN OF THE TOWN

The Captain of the Town, like the Parish Captain, had a military origin, but, unlike him, received pay for his services—at Castletown and Peel as Assistant Constable of the fortress, and at Douglas and Ramsey as Captain of the fort and garrison. The title Captain of Douglas (or Ramsey) came into use after 1650, when the officers in control of the local forts also commanded and trained the newly formed town militia companies; though in a document more than a hundred years earlier 'Captain' is used with reference to Ramsey.

In 1533 a Scot, with a safe conduct to come to Man to fish, complained that whilst he was talking to 'the Captain at Rammyssey haven', his vessel was boarded in the night by four Manxmen who cut the cable and sailed off to Peel in Furness. In this case the 'Captain' was probably the Lord's customs officer, known as the Searcher.

The Captain's authority extended over the urban community protected by his garrison and, as time went on, his civil duties became increasingly onerous and touched on every aspect of town life—the maintenance of law and order, paving and sanitation, markets, the supervision of people entering or leaving the port, etc. In Castletown the Governor himself often intervened in the affairs of the place, and initiated local reforms; and the Captain's duties were in the main restricted to his military office.

In 1696, for example, the irascible Governor Sankey, stimulated no doubt by personal experience, issued an order directing that

> 'as by the general want of chimneys . . . more especially . . . in the market towns, the smoke coming out of the doors is a very great inconvenience both to the inhabitants and passers by, and the better to prevent fire householders are to provide not only a sufficient chimney but also a convenient range for more effectual carrying up the smoke.'

The smoke was generally from fires of turf and ling, but sea-coal was being more used and, where there was no chimney, its smoke became an intolerable nuisance.

LODGINGS AND BREWING

The importance of providing accommodation for traders and other visitors was realised in early times, and four hundred years ago people in Castletown were encouraged to keep beds for strangers, by an order of the Governor, Henry Stanley, who stipulated that no one was to brew ale for sale unless he was an approved householder able to take people in when required. In 1595 those desirous of letting beds had to sign a document which said

'We whose names be subscribed shall not only be ready at all tymes, when we are legally appointed to harbour or lodge, but also shall not keep any discordant or bad person or any other men's servants drinking in our houses at an unlawful time of the night.'

The twenty-three signatures are headed by that of Sir Danold Corkill, Chaplain of St. Mary's; and it is interesting to note that less than a third are native surnames.

The obligation to provide beds for strangers as a condition of obtaining a licence to brew ale, long remained. In 1648 Governor Greenhalgh rode to Peel on business, and stopped to drink at the house of the strong-minded Barbary Wattleworth, alias Caesar. She audaciously charged him more than the legal price, 'enhancing the rate of her drincke by 3d. a quart', on the ground of its excellent quality.

When the Governor warned her that her over-charge would have serious consequences, 'she withall stood peremptorily upon it, saying that noe man should sett a rate upon *her* drincke.' Her defiance of the law and the Lord's deputy was punished, as might have been expected, with a fine of forty shillings and the loss of her licence for brewing and lodgings.

THE TOWN MARKET

One of the Captains' most engrossing tasks was the control of the local market which was generally held twice a week. He appointed a Market Jury of four who were sworn by the Coroner to act justly. They presented traders and customers who took an unfair advantage by doing business before the market bell gave the signal. They investigated cases of defective goods and false weights and measures.

In 1691, for example, the Castletown jury examined corn for sale from a Malew farm and declared that it was not well dried or cleaned, and was unfit for grinding. In 1694 they found that the shoes of a leather seller of the town were unlawfully tanned and seized the defective goods—seven pairs—fixing their price, 'to the utmost of our wisdom,' at 1s. 6d. the pair, about half the normal rate. Apparently the leather had not been examined and passed by the sealmaster. Each of the four towns had such an official who exacted a fee of 1d. from the tanner for the guarantee of good quality given by his stamp.

Market juries were still appointed in the last half of the nineteenth century.

In the days before the Industrial revolution, the provisioning of towns often provided difficult problems for the authorities. The townspeople depended for their supplies of food almost entirely upon the contiguous country districts. If the harvest had been bad the towns were the first to suffer from the consequent shortages. To secure a townward flow of country produce the Manx government limited the freedom of the farmers to sell where they wished and directed them to take their goods to a named town. Thus the parishes of Rushen, Arbory, Malew, Santan, Marown and Patrick were forbidden to sell their commodities at any other market than that at Castletown.

It was not easy to divert effectively the stream of trade from its natural course; and in 1703 the inhabitants of Castletown, the proud capital, complained bitterly of the failure of the farmers to obey the regulations. They said

'Most of the inhabitants and families of the seven Parishes that are by law obliged to supply the markett do constantly sell their corn and other provisions at other markets which not only deprives your Honours complainants of all manner of necessaries but also forces them to repair to Farmers houses where they in vain importune for such goods as they have very much want for.

'Besides that this Metropolis, the place of your Honour's and the officers' residence scarcely appears to be a markett town, which exposes us to the contempt and ridicule of all strangers.'

RAMSEY

The Captain of Ramsey commanded the Fort Royal built by the Great Earl in 1648. No plan or drawing of the structure is known to exist, but it was probably round, like the Fort at Douglas, and Derby Fort which he erected in 1645. At the beginning of the eighteenth century the Ramsey Fort was rebuilt on a rectangular plan. When it had fallen into ruins in 1760, its site, bought by a merchant, was said to have a frontage of fifty-three feet; and on or near it stands a building which formerly served as a lighthouse and, at an earlier period, also as a prison.

The erection of the fortification was due to the great impression produced by the unresisted raid on Kirk Bride in 1643, when Ballacallow was looted; and a fort was begun at Port Cranstal, but abandoned in favour of one at Ramsey.

It was garrisoned by three rank and file, and in times of emergency Watch and Ward was kept there by militia levies. There were no police, and the Captain depended upon the garrison soldiers for assistance in quelling disturbances and in making arrests. Prisoners were kept in the Fort to await an escort to Castle Rushen. More than once juries were locked up in the Fort until they agreed upon their verdict. On one occasion in 1727 the twelve members of the Great Enquest of Ayre were shut up in the Fort for four days and nights, stubbornly refusing to agree over a licence to enclose a piece of claddagh in Glen Auldyn, in spite of the great discomfort they were undergoing through lack of fire, food and bedding.

Among other duties the Captain had to see that the streets were in repair, and cleaned once a week by the householders, to aid revenue officers in the suppression of smuggling, and to prevent boats sailing from the harbour without the Governor's pass. But for more than a hundred years that which most pressed upon his attention was the problem of preserving Ramsey town from destruction.

RAMSEY FENCE

Perched precariously upon a *mooiragh* or sea-bank of sand and gravel, Old Ramsey was never safe from the ravages of the sea. In 1630 the inhabitants complained sadly to the Governor,

'That we the inhabitants of the said town being yonger brethren and hath no meanse to leive upon but only our giftes and best indevours to leive upon our portion, where God and our parents hath ordained for us, have bestowed the most partt of our goods in buildings of houses and other nessesaries for the intertainment of strangers and the Comonwealth of the Cuntry; we your pore supliants doe submissively complaine and crave we may have better comfortt to leive in the said towne than ever we'll have had hear-to-fore; for divers times we are over-flowed by the sea . . . the most partt of all our houses was all full of watter, beinge a most fearfull and wofull sight unto us. . . .'

Their request that the Captains of Maughold, Lezayre and Bride should be ordered to bring their companies to build a protective embankment of loose stones was granted and this, known as Ramsey Fence, for a long time saved the town from the worst consequences of the Spring tides which, in times past, had swept away gardens and houses. To strengthen the sea wall every boat coming to the fishing in Ramsey Bay was ordered to bring annually two boat landings of stones from the rocks; and periodically the Captain appointed four overseers to collect assessments for the repair of breaches made by the sea.

John Llewelyn, remembered in the hill slope, Pairk Llewelyn, where he introduced grouse into the Island in 1745, John Frissell of Lhergy Frissell, John Kerruish and others advocated groins to break the violence of the sea and save the town from being entirely destroyed; but it was not till after 1745, in which year several houses were swept away, that the town was made reasonably secure from the attacks of the sea.

The Captain was sometimes ordered to perform duties repugnant to his best feelings. In 1670 Captain Ainscough, a Lancashire man, was reprimanded for tolerating Ramsey Quakers, and even allowing a Quaker's wife to keep a school in the town. The Manx members of this sect shared the uncompromising views of the early followers of Fox, refused to pay tithes, take oaths or come to Church, and as Isaac Barrow the Sword-Bishop—for he was Governor as well as Bishop—pointed out in an appeal to them, displayed a self-righteousness out of keeping with the Christian virtue of humility.

The Bishop, who had initiated a campaign to suppress the sect, found fault with the Captain for allowing Quakers to live in their own houses, instead of arresting them and bringing them before the Courts for excommunication and banishment. 'I wonder', he wrote, 'how he did suffer the same. I once more admonish and require Captain Ainscough of Ramsey that he forthwith put the order in full execution against the Quakers as he shall answer at his peril.'

A RAMSEY MERCHANT

Ramsey shared Castletown's interest in providing lodgings for merchants and other strangers, and most of the householders of the little town had beds to let. One of the most prominent Ramsey traders, John Black, has left details of his establishment in the year 1664. He was a Scot who settled in Ramsey and in 1654 by an expenditure of thirteen shillings and fourpence became a naturalised Manxman, this giving him important advantages over an alien merchant. His house and shop stood on or near the site of the present Lough House at the Old Cross, and on the adjacent land, known in later times as Black's Lough, he kept three cows, a horse and three pigs. He also owned a herring boat.

His house was two storied, containing six rooms including the shop. Every room, except the *thie mooar* (living room) and shop, contained beds, ten in all. The equipment of the *thie mooar* resembled that of the average Manx farm kitchen of the seventeenth century. There were the fire-side fittings: the *slouree* (a chain from which to hang cooking pots), pothooks, spits, griddle, gridiron, flesh hook and cooking pans of brass, copper and iron; and there was a little grate.

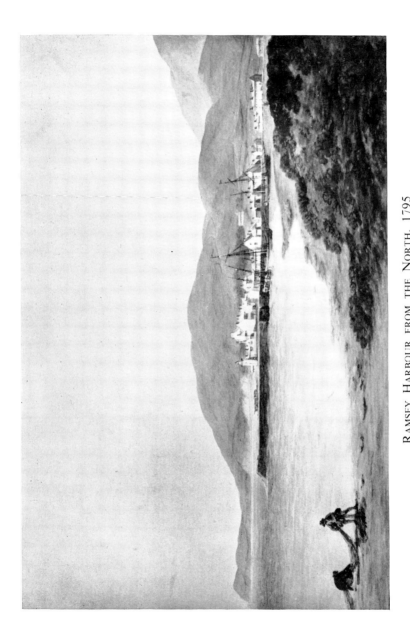

Ramsey Harbour from the North, 1795

Showing mounted guns in front of the Fort site

The cupboard held twelve noggins, two piggins and eighteen trenchers in treen (wood). There were twenty-four earthenware dishes and plates and six flagons; forty-eight pounds of pewter ware; horn and pewter spoons. The furniture included two tables, the tops being movable, two forms, six chairs and six stools. One iron and two brass candlesticks were used for illumination. There were two spinning-wheels and wool and flax cards; and a staff churn, with wooden pails, milk cans and sieves. A kieve or brewing tub on its stand indicated another important activity of the Black household.

The shop was stocked with a wide variety of goods—among them clothing, horse furniture, books and writing material, spices, spectacles, chemicals, treen ware, tools, children's belts, looking glasses, dyes, and 'apothecary stuffe'. The clothing materials included Scotch cloth, holland, bandstrings, taffety ribbon; hatbands for the tall wide-brimmed hats then worn; hooks and eyes for fastening doublet and breeches; and buttons for cloaks. There were psalters, grammars, inkhorns and hornbooks; and among the apothecary medicines were coral and stagshorn.

RAMSEY CAPTAINS

The Captains of Ramsey were nearly all Christians, drawn from the related families of Ballure, Ballastowell and the Flat—who, in turn, like the Christians of Ballakilley and Cranstal, belonged to the great Milntown clan.

One of the last Captains and probably the most notable was Matthias Christian of the Flatt and Pooldhooie—the Flatt being the name given to the land stretching from the Lake (now the Market place) to the Lezayre Road; and bounded on the North by the harbour.

In his time and for a century afterwards Manx townspeople and country labourers greatly resented the export of Manx grain by the landowners, when, as often happened, there was a famine shortage in the Island. In 1767 an English tenant of Ballavoddan in Kirk Andreas loaded a vessel in Ramsey Harbour with corn. The market jury, acting on an old regulation that no grain was to be exported until it had been exposed for sale in the market, went on board with John Callow of Ballaglass and ten other Ramsey men and unloaded the cargo.

Their spirited action was unfavourably received by the newly appointed Crown Governor, and they were sent to Castle Rushen; but three years later he issued instructions to the Captains to enforce the rule upon which the jury had acted.

DOUGLAS

The Captains of Douglas commanded the round Fort built in the seventeenth century on an outcrop called the Pollock Rocks and remembered in the present day by Fort Street, part of a way running towards the Fort. It was garrisoned by five rank and file. Like the Ramsey counterpart it was used as a temporary prison, and as a Watch post manned by militia levies from Onchan and Marown. Its dilapidated remains were removed in 1816.

During the rule of the Captains, that is, from 1660 to 1777, the Manx towns, and Douglas in particular, were visited by ships from the Americas and the West Indies, and from all the coasts of Europe. There was, in Douglas, a resultant cosmopolitan section of the population largely composed of immigrants from Scotland, Ireland, France and other Continental countries, attracted to Man by the 'Running Trade'. From the nature of their interests it was not to be expected that these strangers, many of them only temporary residents, would add to the decorum of Douglas or have a healthy moral influence on the native Manx with whom they came into contact. And the Captain and his men were often called upon to quell disturbances generally caused by the excessive drinking which was one of the evil consequences of the contraband traffic.

In 1720, for example, a young trader, Joseph Bacon, with three companions, who had been carousing, came to the Fort and threatened the deputy commander, David Christian. They drew their swords and pistols and ordered him to go down on his knees and beg their pardon. Eventually the drunken men were hustled into the Fort, where they were held until they found sureties to keep the peace and come up for trial.

CHURCH AND STATE

In the first three decades of the eighteenth century the age-long struggle for power between the Manx Church and State came to a head. The Manx countryside accepted without much demur the Ecclesiastical discipline which Bishop Wilson strove to maintain, and their opinion was largely reflected by the Keys when, in 1722, they wrote to the Bishop

> '. . . as to the charge of exercising a spiritual tyranny we do solemnly testify (as we are in Justice bound) that there is no cause to us known for so strange an imputation being verily persuaded that you have been so far from assuming to yourselves any undue authority that the Church was never better governed than in your time nor Justice more impartially administered in the Ecclesiastical Courts of this Isle.'

There was, however, a section of opinion in the official, commercial and well-to-do classes of the towns, and of Douglas in particular, which not only revolted against the disciplinary claims of the Church but went out of its way to show its contempt for its laws and pastors. In this the rebels were supported by a series of Governors and high officials imported from England whose arbitrary conduct, shady and illegal actions and personal boorishness cast a shadow over the last decades of the Stanley domination of Man.

CAPTAINS OF DOUGLAS

Outstanding among the clique of undisciplined young men—Manx and alien—who rejected the sober religious traditions of the Island and pursued a vicious course of life, unrestrained by considerations of decency, was Thomas Heywood of the Nunnery. Governor Horton made him Captain of Douglas in 1725, so that, it was said, he would as a soldier in the Lord's service be outside the jurisdiction of the Spiritual Court, before which he had been summoned to appear on a charge of immoral conduct. Shortly afterwards he was accused of smashing the windows of Douglas Chapel—later St. Matthew's—in a drunken frolic. He refused to swear that he had not done it; but before the Court could take the usual course in such circumstances and pronounce him guilty, an immigrant trader declared that he himself had caused the damage when drunk. Public opinion hesitated to accept this confession; but it was charitably held by some that perhaps the Captain's attitude was due to his occupancy of the Nunnery, ancient Abbey land, with a right of trial in an Abbey Court.

Heywood's refusal to submit to ecclesiastical censures brought upon him a sentence of excommunication, which he ignored. He impudently swaggered into Kirk Braddan at service time accompanied by armed soldiers from the Fort, and the Vicar was too indifferent, or too afraid, to exclude him. When he appeared with the other Captains at the Tynwald Chapel, Bishop Wilson abandoned the service rather than tolerate the presence of an excommunicant. Earl William was of a different mind. In 1730 he re-asserted the claim of the Lord to be Head of the Manx Church, and declared the excommunication void.

The tragic deaths of boon companions seem, however, to have made a profound impression on Heywood, and in 1732 he submitted to the discipline of the Church. The Bishop, who had suffered many affronts from the prodigal, was convinced of the sincerity of his change of heart, and at Kirk Braddan publicly received him back into the Church. Later he became Chairman of the Keys.

Among other Captains of Douglas were Robert Quayle, son of the Deemster of that name who owned the Ballabeg, now 'Farm Hill'; and Robert Calcott who took great pride in the Town Company, marching at its head with what he called a leading staff: a javelin with a Brazil-wood shaft; and Paul Bridson, whose military career had been jeopardised by his inexperience when a junior officer at the Fort.

He was sent by the Captain to the South-side to arrest a deserter. With a file of soldiers he took the wanted man into custody and made for Douglas. Night fell with violent wind and rain as they came to Santan, and there they took refuge in a cottage. The ensign moved up to the glowing turf fire to dry and warm himself, and the escort momentarily took their eyes off the prisoner.

He seized his chance. There was the sound of a door opening and closing, and he had vanished into the storm and blackness of the night. When the shamefaced Ensign reported his mishap, the Captains of the Parishes north of Douglas were ordered to muster their Companies for the pursuit. The Captain of Kirk Braddan did not send the Cross to the northern part of the Parish, for the fugitive came from Baldwin, and it was realistically accepted that he would be helped rather than captured by his kinsmen and neighbours. Eventually he escaped to Scotland and the Ensign was punished for his lack of caution.

JACOBITES

The Jacobite Risings of 1715 and 1745 created a considerable stir in Man and the authorities were nervous and uneasy. In 1715 Governor Horne made a proclamation that all persons reflecting on Government and drinking the Old Pretender's health should be reported to the Captains or other officials within two days. He declared that 'A few seeds of disaffection have taken root even among many of the natives of this Isle'; and the Temporal Power was supported by Bishop Wilson who exhorted the people

> 'to be quiet and to mind their own business; to be subject to those whom God hath set over us, not only for wrath, but also for conscience sake. Remember that whosoever resisteth the Power, resisteth the ordinance of God.'

Demonstrations of sympathy for the Stuarts were mainly confined to the towns with their colonies of Scottish traders, and did not take any more active form than a toast to 'the King over the water'. Nevertheless at such times of stress and tension, people had to be as guarded in conversation as the citizens of modern totalitarian states. On June 23rd, 1740, a few months after the declaration of war between England and Spain, a Castletown man was enquiring for a horse to carry him next day to Midsummer Fair, and asked one Christopher McDonald if he was going. He said he was and added, 'We shall blow you all up off the Hill as soon as you go upon it.' He then declared that he was a Spaniard. He was at once cast into prison on suspicion of plotting against the safety of the Isle; and was not released until he had brought witnesses to prove that he was drunk at the time, and had found sureties for his good behaviour.

In 1746 Captain Bridson was having his morning drink in a Douglas inn kitchen, when John Duffield entered and in his cups foolishly boasted that he had been in Carlisle the previous year when Prince Charles and his Highlanders were there. The Captain immediately arrested him on suspicion as a rebel, and sent him with an escort to the Castle. The unfortunate man petitioned for release, saying that he had been confined for thirteen days, lying on the cold ground in his clothes; and that his wife and six children in Douglas only kept alive through the kindness of Thomas Heywood, then Captain of Kirk Braddan, who had given a barrel of meal on credit. Duffield was released until the time of his trial.

After the Revestment of 1765 when the Lord of the Isle sold his regalities to the Crown, and detachments of English troops were, from time to time, in garrison, the Militia Companies were no longer mustered; but the Town Captains continued as civil officers for another twelve years. In 1769 an Order was issued to remind them of their duties, and emphasis was laid on the assistance they were to give to Officers of Customs with search warrants; on the supervision of the newly appointed constables; and on the guardianship of public buildings.

In 1777 the office of Captain of the Town was abolished, the civil duties attached to it being performed by stipendiary magistrates called High Bailiffs until 1860, after which popularly elected bodies began to take over the control of street repair, sanitation, and other matters of local concern.

VIII

MILNTOWN

Among all the private residences in the Isle of Man with historical associations, probably Milntown makes the most alluring appeal to the imagination. It is sad to think that the ancient estate, of which it is a part, with its rich fields and enchanting prospects, has not, apparently, been protected from the hazards of ribbon development and other forms of modern progress.

For Milntown was not only the scene of the most famous battle of Manx history, when in 1079 Godred Crovan, whom historians identify with the traditional King Orry, defeated the Manx at Skyhill and established a dynasty of native Kings which endured for two centuries. It was also the cradle of the Christians of Milntown, the most powerful Island family known to the Manx for six hundred years—a family whose long and varied history is interwoven with that of Man. For generation after generation members of the Christian main line and its branches filled at one time or another every public office from the Governorship downwards.

Two outstanding personalities among them were Edward Christian of Maughold and William Christian of Milntown and Ronaldsway, both of whom died prematurely in the political strife of the seventeenth century because they championed the rights of Manxmen and resisted the will of the Lord of the Isle.

Edward Christian, the most democratic Manxman of his time, was at first the favoured servant of the Earl. But later the *Stanlagh Mooar* would gladly have seen him hanged, and complained bitterly that whilst Manx landowners were ready enough to send sheepstealers to the scaffold, they showed no anxiety to do so in the case of those who opposed the Earl's authority. Christian died in the Lord's prison in Peel Castle in 1661, after many years of confinement there, and his gravestone is to be seen in Maughold churchyard.

William Christian—*Illiam Dhone*, Brown-haired William—the most dramatic figure in Manx history, was shot to death at Hango Hill in 1663.

Here in this house he spent his boyhood and must often have seen his father, Deemster Ewan Christian, holding his court in fine weather, before the front door, and in later times joined him on the judges' bench. His tragic but courageous end made him more than ever the symbol of the age-long resistance of the Manx to the arbitrary actions of the Stanley Lords and their officials.

In the fifteenth, sixteenth and seventeenth centuries Milntown was regularly used as the meeting place of the Sheading Courts. When the Captain or Lieutenant of Man, as the Governor was called during the first two hundred years of the Stanley Lordship, went on circuit with the Deemsters, Receiver, Comptroller and Water Bailiff, he began with Glenfaba. From there the cavalcade of judges and clerks, accompanied by the records carried in leather trunks slung in horse-creels, rode over the rough uneven bridle-paths to Kirk Michael where the sessions were, as elsewhere, often held in the Church.

The Sheading of Ayre was next visited, and then the Southern Division. Two days were generally spent in each place, and the Captain received an allowance of one shilling and sixpence a day with food, the other high officers one shilling. The value of the judges' allowances is more easily understood when the bill for victuals for one day's Court at Milntown in 1608 is examined.

The chief items were 38 penny loaves; $1\frac{1}{4}$ barrels of beer, 11s. 4d.; 3 sheep at 3s. 4d. each; 1 lamb, 1s. 2d.; 2 hens, 6d.; 1 capon, 6d.; 8 chickens, 1s. 2d.; eggs, 1s.; butter, 7 lbs., 2s. 3d.; a pudding consisting of flour, 10d., $\frac{1}{2}$ lb. 'currens', 4d., $\frac{1}{2}$ lb. raisins, 4d., $\frac{1}{4}$ lb. sugar, 6d.; cheese, 1s.; oatmeal groats, 2d.; pepper 1s.; vinegar, 1 pint, 3d.

In addition 2 lbs. of candles at 6d. a lb., and 12 loads of turf at 1d. a load, were burned.

In 1496, the Coroner of Ayre, John McCristen (later Deemster), returned the expenses of his Court at Milntown, as eight shillings and sixpence.

If the space in front of the house conjures up a picture of Deemsters on the seat of judgment, and of excited plaintiffs and defendants pleading their own causes in expressive Manx Gaelic—for professional advocates did not appear until the eighteenth century—the mill-stream on the other side of the mansion is redolent of a still more antique past.

From the Crossag path, when the evening is falling, one sees the mill-stream as it flows down between the trees, making a picture of exquisite melancholy beauty, and in that magic wood anything may happen. It is no wonder that in past times, when the countryside was full of stories of fairies and other supernatural beings, people were afraid to pass the trees in the dark, and late wanderers confessed to flight from strange monsters lurking near the mill.

The name 'Milntown' is at least five hundred years old, having been used as early as 1448 when William McCristen was Comptroller of Man. In all likelihood a mill of the horizontal-wheel type was set up here in the early days of Viking colonisation. The newcomers gave Glen Auldyn its name—*Alptardalr*, the Glen of the Wild Swans— and the mill-stream may have been running for a thousand years.

During the long period of the Stanley rule mills offered an opportunity of modest profit, and landowners, influential and prosperous enough to obtain mill grants and pay for them, competed for the Lord's leases. The owners of Milntown were always in control of water mills in other parts of Lezayre, in Maughold, and for a time, in Jurby.

One has a glimpse of the simplicity of early seventeenth century society in an account given by a Kirk Andreas man in 1669, describing how, many years before, he had seen Deemster Ewan Christian, with his own team of oxen drawing a sledge loaded with a new millstone, on his way from Ramsey to the mill at the Lhen Mooar.

The date at which the Christians settled at Milntown is not known, but a statement made by Deemster John Christian in 1665 implies that his family was established there before the middle of the fourteenth century. Resisting a claim for customs of fish made by the Lord's officers he declared that Milntown had had a fishing boat for more than three hundred years and had never paid the customs.

According to tradition the massive walls which form the core of Milntown House were part of a building raised by Deemster John Christian (fifth of the line) who died in 1535. He was also responsible for a tower which stood above what is now the scullery on the north side of the house. It became unsafe and was pulled down by another Deemster John Christian in 1830.

Some alterations or additions were evidently made during the time of Ewan Christian (1579–1656), Deemster from 1605 to 1655, for Mrs. Rita Browne,[1] the last surviving Christian in the direct line, possesses a piece of wood cut out of the beam above the front door when a porch was added in 1830, which bears the inscription, 'E.C. 1611.'

Ewan's tenure of office marks the peak of the Christian influence. The Milntowns had blood and marriage connections in every part of the Island and Earl James who disliked them heartily was compelled by reasons of expediency to make use of them. Nevertheless he sometimes showed the claws below the velvet and let Ewan know that he was only the servant of a feudal lord.

In a letter criticising the Deemster's suspicious slowness in dealing with a land dispute near Castletown the Earl, then Lord Strange, wrote brusquely:

[1] The writer is much indebted to Mrs. Browne for information relating to Milntown.

'Christian,

'I have receaved yor letter of the 28th of Aprill wherin you certifie mee how the case standes betwen Calcott and the poore people; but since he still claymes and pretenteth right unto the same and that it concerneth many and myself also, with that it is fit there be some cours used to bringe the same unto an end, according to the lawes of the lande (which I am bounde to see done and so will)

'Therefore I would have you give them warning that they bringe what proofes they can before the 24 for this shall be the last heering of it

'And for you to absent yourself I know no reason, for if I have chosen you Deemster you must do your office there, for if you be not fit to do his buisness you must not doe another neither

'And so Farwell for this Time
              Yor Mr
                       Strange
lathome 23rd of May 1632'

The Great Earl administered sugar with the pill in accordance with his avowed technique, adding a post-script in which he said:

'Your son [his heir John, assistant Deemster, and later Deemster] hath followed your business well and caryes himself soberly, give him charge to doe soe still, and I will take the time for some employment for him.'

Ewan bought the estate of Ewanrigg in Cumberland some time before 1644. He acquired Ronaldsway in 1626 and gave it to his son Illiam Dhone. The Deemster in his old age similarly made Milntown over to his heir Deemster John Christian, and spent the remaining years of his life in turn on his Cumberland property, at Ballahutchin in Kirk Marown and at Ronaldsway. Long after his death a room at that house was known as the 'Old Demster's Chamber'.

Milntown witnessed a curious incident in 1673. John had nominated his younger son Ewan, a merchant of Newcastle, as executor, and on the Deemster's death the disposition of the property produced conflicting claims from various members of the family. The Bishop, as supreme judge in the Church Court dealing with wills and testaments, was called in to settle the dispute quickly, since a large amount of perishable goods was in question.

He decreed that a candle should be lit in the hall of the house at twelve of the clock on a day in January, 1674; and that then the goods should be put to auction and sold 'within the space of the burning of the candle'. The next of kin were to have the pre-emption where equal sums were bidden.

G

In the eighteenth century the head of the house lived at Ewanrigg; and from 1742 until 1830, Milntown was let, one of the last of the tenants being Deemster Thomas Gawne, who used it as his headquarters when he commanded the Northern troop of the Manx Yeomanry Cavalry during the Napoleonic Wars.

One of the most remarkable members of the family was John Christian Curwen of Ewanrigg (1756–1828) who added Curwen to his name after a second marriage with his heiress cousin Isabella Curwen of Workington Hall. He had a long and distinguished career in the House of Commons and was noted for his advocacy of social and political reform and of improved methods in agriculture. He was also one of the Keys, and in 1808 received a testimonial from the Manx anti-Atholl party for his 'strenuous and successful efforts in Parliament in defence of their country's rights and independence and for the benefits the rising agriculture has received from his protection and example'.

Milntown House owes its modern form to Curwen's eldest son, John Christian (1776–1852), by his first wife Margaret Taubman. John received legal training and was a member of the English Bar. He was made Deemster in 1823, it being a condition of his appointment that he should bring his family to Man. This provision arose from long experience of English lawyers in the office of Attorney-General, who had other sources of income, disliked the sea-crossing and grossly neglected their duties in the Insular Courts.

Deemster Christian took up residence at Fort Anne and embarked upon a great and expensive scheme of alteration of his ancestral home, with a lavishness symbolised by a story current at the time that all the mortar was mixed with beer.

A new battlement façade was erected—probably in imitation of the old part of Ewanrigg Hall, and a servants' wing added to the main building. Many of the interior fittings were removed, but the beautiful inlaid woodwork in the library escaped the fate of wainscoting and fine stucco ceilings destroyed in other parts of the house. The bog-oak used in the library is said to have come from the Close Lake, once a Christian possession. Above this room is the chief bedroom, reported to be haunted by the ghost of a man. The mahogany doors to the living-rooms, said to have come from a wrecked Spanish ship, though, like the library oak, traditionally ascribed to Deemster Ewan Christian, probably belong to the eighteenth century.

The main work of reconstruction was completed in the early eighteen-thirties and was accompanied by substantial changes in the grounds. The present drive took the place of an old entrance opposite the road to the White Bridge and the Bayr Dhowin. The course of the Auldyn river was changed to make room for the existing road between the mill and the newly erected farm buildings.

The Deemster was a great tree-lover and was the first Christian to plant Skyhill. He was also responsible for the avenue of trees in the Lezayre Road towards Ramsey. Like his father he sometimes had ideas in advance of his times, as in his provision of a sunken lead bath and shower in the apple-house near the mill-stream.

If the ancient interior of Milntown House suffered at the hands of the improver a worse fate was to befall the family papers. After the Deemster's death in 1852 a member of the household, with unbelievable irresponsibility, spent a whole day in emptying the muniment chests and making a bonfire of the family records—deeds, wills, certificates of appointments, letters, diaries and other papers—and so wiped out the precious accumulation of many generations. Only three documents escaped the destruction.

The Deemster's son, William Bell Christian (1815–1886), was the last proprietor of Milntown to occupy a prominent position in Manx public affairs. He entered the Church and was Vicar of Lezayre for a time, but gave up clerical work and was elected to the Keys, where he acted as Deputy-Speaker. For the last three years of his life he was Receiver-General.

His son, a civil engineer of great ability, was the twenty-first head of the family since the fourteenth century and the last male of his line. He died at Milntown in 1918, so bringing the long story of the Milntown Christians to an end.

IX

THE KILLING OF WILLIAM
MAC A FAILLE, LEZAYRE, 1639

The broken body of William Mac a Faille, nicknamed 'Bod-dough', was found on the last morning of the year 1639, at the out end of the Eary Beg in Glen Auldyn, not far from his own house and on his own land.

The circumstances of his death and the telling of it provide some interesting glimpses of the life and beliefs of people in Lezayre three hundred years ago.

According to custom, the Coroner of Ayre, William Kissage, obtained the Deemster's token for the impanelling of a jury of six who immediately assembled with Coroner and parish Lockman at the spot where the undisturbed body lay. Their conclusions were delivered to a Court held at Milntown on January 3rd, 1640, before Ewan Christian, Edward Christian and Robert Quaile.

At that time the fortunes of the house of Milntown were approaching their zenith. The most powerful Manx family since the beginning of the fifteenth century, the Christians retained the favour of the Earl owing to their great influence in the country, rather than from any love he bore them. Ewan had been Deemster since 1605 and, in spite of the activities of his son 'Illiam Dhone', held office till his death fifty-one years later. At the time of the trial he was Deputy [i.e. Deputy Governor], a post from which the able but restless Edward Christian of Maughold had been relieved not long before. The third member of the Court, Deemster Robert Quaile, died in 1644.

The Coroner's jury, through their spokesman, Ewan Kneale, de-posed that portions of the dead man's clothes, including his band (neck cloth), were wet, though he lay on dry ground, after a dry, frosty night. Near by 'a little bogge of water' shewed plainly the impress of a man's body and the ground was bruised as by the body of a man cast down upon it. Grass of the bog was upon Mac a Faille's stockings, and the wool of his clothes 'raysed' as if by a wool card, by dragging along the ground.

The jury, who apparently pursued their enquiry without direction from the Coroner, caused two men, John Kinread and Ewan Casement, to handle the body in turn. Nothing happened nor was considered likely to happen, for they were not implicated.

Then they called upon Gilnow Casement, who was 'much suspected for the murder', to handle the dead man. As soon as he turned him as the others had done, Mac a Faille bled pure blood from the nose, a phenomenon attested to by various members of the jury.

When Edmond Casement was asked to do as his brother had he turned pale, as if ready to die, and, on his touching the body, the bleeding was repeated. There was a general belief that such a reaction pointed to the murderer, and the jury required no further confirmation of their suspicions. But if the judges were less willing to accept this manifestation as a proof of guilt, the statements of the other witnesses must have turned their doubts to conviction.

These depositions are noteworthy not only for their dramatic quality, but also for their literary form which suggests that some part of the evidence, at any rate, was given in the Manx idiom and set down in English. This is what might be expected, since much of the business of the Common Law Courts was conducted in the native language until the third decade of the nineteenth century. Lezayre, too, was one of the parishes, which protested strongly at various times in the seventeenth and eighteenth centuries against the use of English instead of Manx in the Church service.

The stories told to the Court at Milntown show that there was an extraordinary lack of concealment on the part of the criminals and their relatives before and after the commission of the crime—as if the tragedy was fated and inescapable, though the murder was cold-blooded enough.

'An ill hour upon Gilnow, an ill hour was ordained for him!' cried his mother.

For some time before the event William Mac a Faille knew he was in danger and walked under a cloud of fear. He had had a quarrel with Standish of the Ellanbane regarding a church seat, which had disquieted him, 'but there are others', he told John Corlett, 'who go about to destroy and kill me.'

Corlett asked him who they were. William seeing two kinsmen of Gilnow approaching said, 'I will tell thee another time. They come upon us: I cannot tell thee now.'

At the root of the trouble was Gilnow's desire for Mac a Faille's wife and land, a craving that was not to be thwarted. Katherine had been living apart from her husband for five years and had returned only three weeks before to the Eary Beg. One night when there was a gathering at Cannon's miln, Gilnow's mother prayed that he should forgo the company of Katherine Mac a Faille, but he answered that he would not leave her and that it would do her no good to dissuade him from her.

To Edmond Corleod he said at that time, 'It may be that the ground the Nary Beg which William Mac a Faille now possesseth, may come to me, and it is not known but I may have it.'

On December 19th a young woman named Margrett Foster was going to Kirk Bride and Gilnow came into her company. He spoke of his relationship with Mac a Faille's wife and Margrett said to him, 'If thou have given a false oath it were better that thou had given all the world if it were thine, and better for thee to suffer in punishment than to forswear thyself.'

He answered evasively, and began to talk of ratsbane and a herb called *nahau*,[1] a name Margrett did not know but supposed to be micklewort. Shocked by the sinister implications of this talk she exclaimed, 'Thief! If her husband were dead thou would marry his wife!' Whereat, she says, 'he smiled and said nothing.'

Kathrin Casement, a cousin of Gilnow, was at the Eary Beg on December 20th. William Mac a Faille was ploughing and his brother Edmond drying malt, when Gilnow appeared. He sent to the miln for ale and went into the chamber[2] to drink with his cousin and William's wife.

His last visit was on December 30th and some days later Kathrin Casement told John Kinread 'By God I may swear that Gilnow Casement and whosoever was with him murdered Mac a Faille, for he was at this house three times that day', and that she had wondered and asked him what brought him so often to the house:

'I get anger for thy coming,' she complained.

Then Gilnow Casement said, 'Who is angry with thee? Is it Boddough? I will take order with him,' and presently coming out of the chamber he invited Mac a Faille to come that night to his mother's house to take part of some meat they had. Essabel, William's sister, was afraid for him and wished him not to go, but he said, 'I think they will do me no hurt and therefore I will go.' At nightfall he went out of the house.

That night his wife Katherine 'after his going out became very pensive and oftentimes sighed and leaned her head upon her hand which she used not to do, and afterwards she sent for Kathrin Casement when she was in bed to know of her mother if her husband was gone'.

But William did not return.

---

[1] *Yn aghaue vooar*, the great hemlock.
[2] The parlour known as *shamyr*, or *cuillee*.

In the night Gilnow and his brother Edmond came to the house of young John Crowe, the parish Lockman. Gilnow remarked on the scanty fire, and the Lockman thought some evil occasion brought them, for they were not in the habit of coming.

On the following morning old John Crowe, going up into the hills, met Gilnow's aunt, Christian Casement, who asked him what the people were doing below. Thinking she feigned ignorance he answered ironically, 'They are taking a beast which is fallen.' Then again he said, 'Knowest thou what they are doing? Boddough is killed and lieth dead in yonder place. God send that some near unto thee be not challenged.'

She answered, 'Doth thou say that Gilnow did it?'

He replied, 'I say it not, if thou say it not.'

'I did not', said she, 'see Gilnow since yesterday.'

Amy Mac a Faille said that she was in the house of Emill Mac a Faille on January 3rd, the day of the Court at Milntown, when Edmond Casement came in. His sister, the wife of the house, said, 'An ill hour on you if you killed Mac a Faille! Why left you him not in the water, that people might think himself had done it?'

Edmond answered, 'If they have no better proofs than yet is had, they can do us no harm, for, sure, some must swear that we did it or else it cannot be proved.'

At this time Margaret Casement, mother to the supposed murderers, was saying to John Kinread, 'My two sons are gone down to Milntown.'

He said, 'The Deputy will cause John Lace who is now there to shew the picture of the murderer,' whereupon the grieving mother cried, 'God forbid! An ill hour upon Gilnow, an ill hour was ordained for him!'[1]

Thus by his own indiscretions and the unguarded talk of his people was the rope twisted for his hanging.

[1] Apparently Lace, who was a doctor, was credited with magical powers.

X

CHURCH AND CLERGY, 1600–1800

It is generally accepted that the Manx parishes were created in the twelfth century in the time of the Norse kings of Man. The districts about to be formed into parishes already contained on the average ten keeills or chapels, used by the Celts and the early Norse Christians; and one of these, chosen for its importance and the convenience of its site—which was generally near the sea—became the parish church. Although not every parish at the outset was equipped with accommodation for the incumbent and land for his support, they all had cemeteries and received endowments from the old ecclesiastical lands. In 1221 the Manx King Reginald was asked by the Pope to make up deficiencies, and provide a grant of free land for the priest's house where it was lacking.

RECTORIES

It has been suggested that at first there may have been sixteen parishes, later increased to seventeen when one of them was divided into two to make Santan and Marown, but this is not certain. All of them were Rectories, each with its *persona* (i.e. the 'person' or parson of the parish), and each enjoyed the whole of its endowments and income until the episcopate of Bishop Reginald in the twelfth century, when one third of the parochial tithes was granted to the Bishop for his own maintenance by an agreement made with the clergy.

But this state of affairs did not long continue. At various times, during the Middle Ages, the Manx kings and other patrons of livings made over churches and lands to monasteries—to Rushen Abbey, the Priory of Whithorn in Galloway, the Abbeys of Bangor and Sabal in Ulster and the Priory of St. Bees in Cumberland. When a religious foundation of this kind gained possession of a church it nominally assumed the functions of rector and appointed a *Vicarius* or substitute, who had to manage his parish on a third of the total revenue. He was therefore known as a 'Vicar of Thirds'.

Some vicars did not have this fixed income, but had to be content with a smaller stipend at the discretion of the patron—as in the case

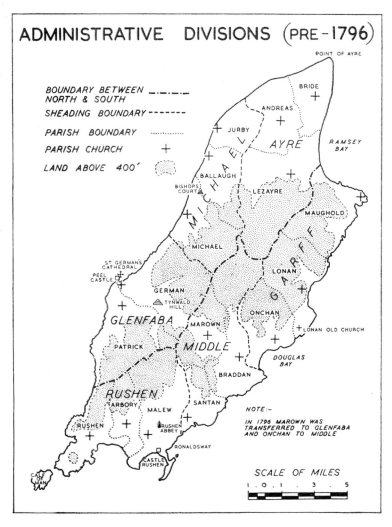

ADMINISTRATIVE DIVISIONS (PRE-1796)

BOUNDARY BETWEEN NORTH & SOUTH

SHEADING BOUNDARY

PARISH BOUNDARY

PARISH CHURCH

LAND ABOVE 400'

POINT OF AYRE

BRIDE

ANDREAS

JURBY

AYRE

RAMSEY BAY

BALLAUGH

BISHOPS COURT

LEZAYRE

MAUGHOLD

MICHAEL

ST GERMANS CATHEDRAL

PEEL CASTLE

LONAN

GERMAN

TYNWALD HILL

ONCHAN

GLENFABA

MAROWN

LONAN OLD CHURCH

PATRICK

MIDDLE

DOUGLAS BAY

BRADDAN

RUSHEN

ARBORY

MALEW

SANTAN

NOTE:—

IN 1796 MAROWN WAS TRANSFERRED TO GLENFABA AND ONCHAN TO MIDDLE

RUSHEN

RUSHEN ABBEY

RONALDSWAY

CASTLE RUSHEN

CALF OF MAN

SCALE OF MILES

1 . 0 . 1 . 3 . 5

THE TRADITIONAL ADMINISTRATIVE DIVISIONS OF THE ISLE OF MAN
(Reproduced from R. H. Kinvig's *History of the Isle of Man*, 1950)

of Jurby and Lezayre, whose incumbents were called 'Vicars of Pension'. They sometimes revolted against the uncertain conditions of their appointment. In 1654, when Sir Edward Crowe was presented by the Lezayre parish quest for absenting himself from church and neglecting the duty of preaching, he protested that he had had no pay from the proctors. 'Neither', he declared, 'do I intend to serve any longer for the same stipend.'

It is true that sometimes compensation was given to a parish in return for carrying off a substantial part of its income. For example, it was customary for a Manx boy from Kirk Maughold to be given free education in the school at St. Bees. The Rev. Thomas Howard, a rector of Ballaugh in the nineteenth century, was the last to be accepted on such grounds. But this kind of return for benefits received obviously gave no relief to the unfortunate Vicar.

The austere nature of his celibate life in pre-Reformation times is hinted at in a Manx Spiritual law of 1417 which prescribes what property of a deceased Vicar of Thirds must be passed on to his successor.

It names a pair of bed stocks, a cupboard, a board and trestle, a chair and form, a pot or pan, a roasting spit, a chain from which to hang the pot over the fire, and finally, a spoon, if he had one. Forks had not yet come into use in the fifteenth century, and a knife is not mentioned because every man, clergy and lay, carried a knife or dagger at his girdle.

One can, however, read too much into this scanty list of the household equipment due to a newcomer; and it must be remembered that the famous Synod, over which Bishop Mark presided at Kirk Braddan in 1291, found it necessary to issue a sumptuary law restraining the Island clergy from going about in worldly attire. They were ordered to wear the *capa clausa* or closed cassock, a gown of sober colour falling below the knees; and particularly on those solemn feast days when they would be most tempted to cut a dash. The open cloak and other ostentations were strictly forbidden; and disobedience was to be punished by the confiscation of the offending dress, and its sale in aid of the building of the cathedral of Kirk German.

At the end of the Middle Ages the English Church, through the spoliation already mentioned, had lost a third of its rectories, but the Isle of Man proportionately had suffered much more severely; only three out of the seventeen parishes retaining their original status: Kirk Andreas, which was generally reserved for the Archdeacon whose office carried no stipend, Ballaugh and Kirk Bride. The Reformation brought no relief to the hard lot of the clergy, for the Lord of the Isle eventually got possession of the Thirds formerly taken by the monks, and the vicars were as badly off as ever.

PARISH CLERK

One parochial office which has disappeared in modern times was that of Parish Clerk. In pre-Reformation times he belonged to the most important of the four minor orders of the Church and acted as assistant to the priest. In the Isle of Man no details of his functions are recorded until after 1600.

Then the position was held by a layman, who was still an assistant to the priest, and enjoyed a position of profit, having the use and produce of the portion of Church land known as the Clerk's glebe, and receiving certain perquisites. A competent Clerk was a great aid and comfort to the parish incumbent. He attended on the priest, robed him for service and accompanied him upon visitations of the sick and other business of the parish. He took care of the vestments and church vessels, and cut the bread for the Sacrament. John Clague, Vicar of Rushen at the end of the eighteenth century, who has left a full account of the Clerk's duties, says that he also saw to the baptismal font which was to be filled 'with fair water once a month'.

He led the congregational responses and, what was important at a time when only a small proportion of the country people were conversant with English, he read the psalm for the day, line by line, in Manx, the congregation then singing the line with him.

In Santan, as late as 1798, there were great complaints of the Clerk's failure to follow this practice. 'It is well known,' said the churchwarden, John Moore,

> 'that the custom of reading the Manx metrical psalms of David, line by line, has been always practised in this church, and was thought to tend much to the comfort and edification of the unlearned, by enabling them to sing with the spirit, by singing with the understanding—whereas the present mode of John Crebbin in reading out the first two lines only of the psalm or that part which he intends singing, and often sings two, three or four stanzas, can tend no more (with submission to the court) to the comfort and edification of the illiterate, than if he sang them out in high Dutch, or in any other foreign and barbarous language.'

Save in a few special cases such as Kirk Andreas, where the Lord of the Isle had the right of appointment, the parish clerks for a long time were elected by the votes of the parishioners. Their choice was limited, for there were only a few men in any parish possessing the required qualifications. In 1671, Ballaugh chose John Corlett of

Ballakeoig, and the parishioners in submitting his name for the Bishop's approval, justified their action by saying, 'John Corlett of Ballakeoig is the ablest and fittest man in this parish for this place by reason of his learning, good carriage, vicinity of the minister and propinquity to the church.'

In the nineteenth century before the disappearance of the office its prestige had declined—perhaps because of the rapid increase in the number of literates. But in previous times it was an attractive appointment for those with good voices and the requisite amount of education. Its glebe and other emoluments formed an agreeable addition to the slender income of a Manx landowner, and one often finds, particularly in the seventeenth and the first half of the eighteenth century, the office occupied by the Captain of the Parish.

In fees, the Parish Clerk received fourpence—the *Groat shesheree* or 'Ploughman's groat'—for each plough which during the year had turned a furrow. Where there was a dwelling-house with a fire but no plough, he received the *Ping jaagh*, the 'Smoke penny'. He also got a head-penny from each parishioner, and fees and gifts came to him for christenings, marriages and burials.

Wills were generally written down by the parish minister or the clerk, who was expected to appear at the *Aaght-oie*, 'the night of lodging,' a phrase equivalent to 'Wake', a word not used in Man. There he read, line by line, an appropriate psalm, followed in the singing by the mourners.

The funeral procession was led by the Clerk who again read the psalm line by line. At one time the custom of circling the Church Cross, sometimes the Church itself, three times clock-wise, was practised—a ritual survival of pre-Christian days. In one parish, Kirk Bride, the mourners halted at a holy pool, the *Dem ny marroo*, 'the pool of the dead,' to sprinkle the bier with the water.

A church enquiry in 1666 reported that a 'death bell' stood on the altar of Kirk Andreas, and its removal as a superstitious relic was immediately ordered. In conformity with ancient practice, the Rector, bell in hand, had met Clerk and funeral procession and led it from the churchyard stile, tolling the bell as they proceeded.

WOODS OF BALLEIRA

When the Parish Clerk was a substantial owner-farmer he sometimes exhibited the independent spirit of his class, and overstepped the limits prescribed for him. In 1665, for example, Henry Woods of Balleira, Parish Clerk of Kirk Michael, in the absence of the Vicar, took upon himself to administer the Holy Sacrament and duly did penance for his presumption. He appeared for an hour at Castletown

Cross in a white sheet and with a white wand in his hand; and falling on his knees desired all good people passing by to take example from his downfall. This penance which was accompanied by the recital of his offences and a promise of reform was repeated at Douglas, Peel and Ramsey; and finally at the Church Stile of Kirk Michael, where he knelt during the whole of the morning service.

Henry Woods was not the only member of his family to display unorthodox tendencies. His grandfather, John Woods, had been Clerk half a century before, and had apparently come under the influence of the extreme Puritanism which played such an important part in the religious and political developments of the seventeenth century. In 1616 he refused to fulfil some of the customary duties of his office—in particular, attending the minister in the Chancel and reading the First Lesson there. He demanded that the Communion Table and Bible be moved down into the Body of the Church where he sat, and where alone, he said, he would execute those services, and not in the Chancel.

On the Sunday preceding his appearance before the Spiritual Judges he made his way into Kirk Michael Church, armed with sword and dagger. 'Whereat', says the account, 'the Minister of the Church, Sir Hugh Cannell, was dismayed and made afraid, for that he did especially contest him in maintenance of his own wilful demeanour offensive to good devotion amongst the Congregation.'

He was luckier than his grandson in not having the Sword-Bishop to pass judgment upon him. He was fined forty shillings, which was reduced to ten shillings, 'in hope', said the Court, 'of his better Demeanour and Conformitie of life hereafter.'

One Braddan Clerk, Daniel Curghey, achieved notoriety by tearing leaves out of the parish register to oblige an alien Douglas merchant, who wished to falsify his marriage record. But the Clerk appears in a more favourable light in a pathetic little story of domestic tragedy, with its atmosphere of piety and superstition and human kindness. In 1714 he was out walking with his wife to Mullen Doway (now Union Mills), when Thomas Oates's wife Isabel came to him and asked for the loan of a Bible to lay under her husband's head to cause him to sleep. The Clerk asked her how he was, and she answered that he dreamed that he was dead. The night before, he had said that he would go three times about the house and pray for the pardon of his sins.

'What needs that?' said Curghey to the sick man. 'Go your ways to your bed and pray there.' Thomas asked them if they would pray with him. They said they would and so they joined together in prayers. Later Isabel came out of the room and clapped her hands together, crying, '*Losta lome!*[1] Yonder man says that he is beside himself for want of sleep!' In the night he broke through the thatch of the low-roofed little cottage and next day was found dead in the Black River [The Dhoo].

He had been sick for some time with a disorder of the head, and his neighbour John Gelling had taken him home and, with his servant, ploughed for him. He was said to have been of good life and conversation; and the sympathetic jury called together by the Coroner of Middle, found his death had been caused by his disorder and by the river; so avoiding a verdict of *felo de se*, which would have entailed the forfeiture of the dead man's property to the Lord, and his burial in unconsecrated ground.

The office of Parish Clerk sometimes persisted in a family for generations, and in one parish the Clerk's glebe had been attached so long to an estate which had provided a succession of Clerks that the wardens had difficulty in establishing the rightful ownership. One remarkable instance of family succession was quoted at the death of Margaret Cannell in 1831. She was widow of John Cain, Parish Clerk of Kirk Michael; and her great-grandfather, grandfather, father and brother had all occupied the post in turn. Her son Thomas was Clerk in 1831.

In the course of time, with the diminishing financial value of the office and changes in its functions, it was often an extra duty for the parish schoolmaster. In 1840 Rector Howard of Ballaugh advertised for a schoolmaster for the parochial school, 'who is also required to fill the situation of Parish Clerk and to be able to fill the duties of Clerk in Manx and English.' There is no mention of a popular election but the one chosen had to be approved by the Bishop.

THE CHURCH

The Church was the social as well as the spiritual centre of the Manx parish. At the Parish Cross which stood outside every churchyard fence people gathered after service to exchange news and hear the Sumner make public announcements; there, warning was given for attendance at the Spiritual and Civil courts; and there, too, were held the annual fairs.

The Manx of past times disliked any break in the practices of their ancestors. *Mannagh vow cliaghtey cliaghtey, nee cliaghty coe,* they said—'Unless custom is indulged by custom, custom will weep.'

This reluctance to sever relations with the past is seen plainly in the history of the churches. The sites they occupy appear to have

[1] See page 24.

been sacred places from time immemorial, and were chosen by the first Christian missionaries because of the veneration they had already aroused in the minds of the people.

The late Canon Quine drew attention, too, to the influence of tradition on the form and proportions of the ancient Manx parish churches. Nearly all have now disappeared but there is evidence enough to show that in plan they resembled the medieval church of St. Trinian. They were rectangular and without transepts, the length being approximately three times the breadth. These traditional proportions are to be found in Old Kirk Lonan which is fifty-four feet by eighteen. Kirks Malew, Andreas, Bride and Maughold were originally of the same proportions; and when Ballure Chapel was re-built in 1743, its dimensions, either by accident or design, followed the tradition, and were fifty-seven feet by nineteen.

The absence of transepts and the stark simplicity of the old Manx church sometimes made doubtful the position of the boundary between the Chancel and the body of the Church. It was important to know the dividing line, since the patron or owner of the appropriated (or Impropriate) third of the tithes was liable for the repair of the Chancel, and the parishioners for the rest of the fabric.

In 1663 when the repair of the Church of Kirk Andreas was being considered and the division was in doubt, a jury of two clergy, two churchwardens and two soldiers, representing the interested parties —clergy, parishioners and the Lord as patron—was appointed to hear the evidence of the ancients, and find out 'the distinct division betwixt Church and Chancel'.

There was a pre-Christian belief in the Scandinavian countries that evil came from the north. This superstition is found in the Manx expression *Bee er dty hwoaie!*, 'Be on thy guard!' which is literally, 'Be on thy north!' north being synonymous with danger. And in the early Celtic church building the architect, actuated by the same superstition, made as few openings as possible in the north wall. The Manx churches perpetuated this custom. Old Kirks Malew and Marown had no window on the sinister northern side; Kirk Lonan and Kirk Michael, one small window. The present windows of Old Ballaugh Church are of fairly recent date—not earlier than the eighteenth century—and take the place of two small openings of earlier times.

The early Manx keeills were thatched or roofed with *scrahyn* (sods); but the Episcopal records imply that the parish churches were slated by the end of the sixteenth century, and that it was customary to whitewash them periodically inside and out.

SEATS

Medieval chapels and churches were not provided with seats for the congregation. In the case of the Manx keeills their small size makes it probable that the building itself was often reserved for the officiating priest, whilst the worshippers knelt outside. After the Reformation the floor space in a Manx church was divided up into portions which were allotted in country parishes to the occupiers of quarterlands, crofts and intacks; in other words, to land and not to houses, as in England. Generally the seat holders were responsible for the erection of their own benches; and this sometimes led to trouble when a bench was shared between two landowners. The fact that the seats were private property made their owners sensitive to any uninvited intrusion into them; and their resentment led to scandal.

Much the same sort of trouble arose in the towns. In 1669 there was a squabble during service time in St. Mary's, Castletown, over the possession of a seat. Two prominent women, members of Castletown society, were involved. One pricked the other several times with a great pin to induce her to move, and tore off her kerchief and scarf 'to the great offence', it was said, 'of the congregation.' And no doubt they agreed with the victim of the assault when she cried out, 'Good Lord, deliver me from such rude bears!'

In Kirk Arbory in 1718, when there was disagreement between two parishioners over their adjoining pews, the man and woman concerned went separately and secretly to Church, and ripped out the opponent's pew.

Many burials took place within the churches, the quarterland owners being interred below the seats owned by them. But the most desired place was the chancel, and for this a special fee was charged. Richard Fox, Vicar of Lezayre, who died in 1679, even requested in his will that he should be laid to rest beneath the altar.

As a result of these inside burials the floor was often uneven and the body of the church unpaved; and during Bishop Wilson's episcopate the Ecclesiastical authorities adopted a policy of strong discouragement when such interments were sought. It was expressly laid down in 1714, for example, that the newly built Church of St. Patrick should not be used as a burial place or a school room—these being the two main causes of the dirty, dishevelled condition of some of the parish churches.

PEWS

Pews which had already appeared in England in the sixteenth century were introduced into Man in the eighteenth. This late adoption was partly due to the expensiveness of the imported timber and the unprosperous condition of the Island. The churchwardens found difficulty even in getting some sort of uniformity of repair of the plain unbacked benches, and more than once complained that they were propped up on big stones.

A general lack of money and resources reduced the decoration and upkeep of the churches to the lowest level. Here there were no wealthy village squires and other magnates with a proprietory interest in the parish church, and with the means to embellish it; and the Manx churches never developed the elaborate high-screened enclosures—often reserved in English country churches for the local overlord—sometimes furnished with fireplace, sofa, table and curtains, and a servant bringing in sherry and light refreshments between prayers and the sermon.

Some differentiation in Manx churches did occur in the eighteenth and nineteenth centuries with the more general introduction of pews; and as these, like the benches they supplanted, were provided and paid for by their occupants, the size of their estates was sometimes reflected in their more spacious pews.

But the Manx countryside viewed any attempts to introduce such social preferences into a place of worship with the greatest distaste; and the churchwardens and chapter quest quickly raised their voices in protest. In 1804, for example, when the Milntown pew was re-made, the Lezayre wardens immediately objected to it because it did not conform in height to the common level, to the great annoyance of those sitting behind; and brought the matter before the Vicars-General.

When a request for special treatment was made in 1663 by James Christian, a member of the same powerful family, it was received very coldly by the Lezayre wardens, who failed to move in the matter. Their lukewarmness was rebuked by Bishop Barrow. The Bishop, accustomed to more strongly marked social distinctions in England, issued a peremptory order to the wardens to provide James Christian with a seat suitable to his quality. History does not say how the Lezayre men, with a vision of the dungeon at Peel before their eyes in case of disobedience, responded to the command.

THE CIVIL WAR

The Civil War (1643–1651) imposed a great strain upon the material and spiritual resources of the Island, and the Manx Church shared in the general decline of public and private morale. It had, in addition, its own peculiar difficulties. The diocese, for example, suffered greatly from absentee bishops and archdeacons. Even so great a friend of the Manx as Bishop Phillips divided his time between North Yorkshire where he was Archdeacon of Cleveland, two English livings which he had received, and the diocese of Sodor and Man; and, what was worse, for seventeen years, from 1644 to 1661, there was no Bishop at all, and during a part of that time the revenues of the Bishopric were apparently used by the Earl of Derby for his own purposes. It is to the credit of the Parliamentary régime under Fairfax that during his Lordship (1651–1660) the income in question was used for the benefit of education and the clergy.

The general indiscipline in the first half of the century was reflected in the conduct of many of the parish clergy, who often failed to live up to their professions and fulfil their primary obligations to the extremely patient and long-suffering people in their care. Nevertheless, when viewed against the background of their turbulent and intolerant age they display themselves to quite as great advantage as their contemporaries in neighbouring countries.

But they were the creatures of their time and environment; often hot-tempered and rash in action, like Sir Silvester Crowe, Vicar of Lezayre, who, when a political controversy flamed out in violence in a parish alehouse in 1612, and weapons were brandished, was the first to draw his dagger; and of William Cosnahan, Vicar of Kirk German, a black shepherd of the flock, who, enraged on receiving an order to appear before the Ecclesiastical judges, Sir Robert and Sir Thomas Parr, to answer for various misdemeanours, horrified his listeners with a frightful medieval oath; 'By God's blood,' he roared, 'I will not be censured by any Sir Robert or Sir Thomas, Sir Jack or Sir Jill!'

For such outbreaks, the Church had a potent antidote—suspension from office with the loss of emoluments, and confinement in the Bishop's prison at Peel for a period whose length usually depended upon the quickness with which the offender found sureties for future good behaviour. Sir William Cosnahan like many of his brethren before and after his time secured a mitigation of his punishment by submitting a petition in which he expressed abject contrition for his offence, gave a promise to reform and, describing the calamities brought upon his innocent wife and children by his wrongdoing, begged humbly for a reinstatement.

SINS OF OMISSION

But it was the clerical sins of omission which most tried the tempers of the parishioners, who were prepared to overlook even grave faults of personal conduct, if their pastors performed their duties with reasonable efficiency, and provided the services which were so universally and so eagerly desired.

H

It is difficult to reconcile the contradiction sometimes found in the virtuous clergyman of the time and his conscienceless failure to feed his flock. There is, for example, an agreeable letter from young Robert Allen, curate to his father, Thomas Allen, Vicar of Kirk Maughold, members of a family which in the seventeenth and eighteenth centuries provided the parish with five vicars of good reputation and sober life. It was written to Vicar-General Robert Parr excusing his absence from the Ecclesiastical Court; and runs,
'Mr. Parson Parr,

'My love and dutifull respects tendered.

'These are to desire your excuses for my absence from the Ecclesiastical Court and to shew the reason; my father and mother are both at Castletown, so that there is nobody at home but myselfe to take care of any thinge in my absence. Neither have I a horse, and the way longe for I could not well goe and come in less than two days in which time my parents might bear losse through the neglect of servants.

'Thus I only desire your excuse for this time, and at the next Ecclesiastical Court, God permittinge, I will attende.

'Vale

'Yours to comande

Robert Allen: April 5th, 1642.'

There, one is disposed to say, is a good type of young man, the worthy son of a virtuous father, anxious to carry out his everyday obligations.

But, five months before, the churchwardens and chapter quest of Kirk Maughold had produced an indictment at the Chapter Court which clouds this vision.

They complain, 'There is no Manx sermon in our Church; not for so much as one in the year, for the edification of the people, who understand no other language; the want whereof is a great grief to the people. There is no catechising or only a little at Lent; the sick are not visited; the parties dying without prayers, exhortations and the Holy Communion, though much desired by the sick. Children weak and strong have to be taken to other parishes for their christendom and to pay for it.'

The Vicar, they go on to say, has ploughed and sown a part of the churchyard which is rooted up by swine, its gates having been broken down by the Vicar's cattle. They further declared that he had not gone in procession round the parish—a formal annual perambulation which was regarded as being of great importance by countrymen, since it was accompanied by a religious service and the blessing of the fields and their growing crops.

The Maughold Wardens' presentment names some of the most important matters affecting the relationship of parishioners and pastor. Seventeenth century Manx people were, as Bishop Lloyd said, very religious, and believed unquestioningly that their eternal salvation depended on their observance of the teachings of the Church. Failing to give them the spiritual solace afforded by the normal ministrations of the clergy, deeply disturbed them. This failure, as we have seen, was sometimes due to the inadequacy of the incumbent; but it sometimes arose from the slowness of Bishop or patron in presenting to the living.

Owing to this, Lonan was left for a long period without a minister. In 1680, when Sir Thomas Thwaites was appointed he was asked to serve also the vacant living of Kirk Onchan. Thus cheated once more of their regular services and led by the Moores of Baldromma, the exasperated Lonan men held a mock funeral of the absent Vicar. They covered a bundle of hemp on the church bier with a black blanket used for funerals and brought it to the vicarage door, making a great noise, 'as if it were by way of lamentation,' for half an hour. After singing psalms, they carried the bier to the Church door and tolled the bell.

The culprits were punished for what their indictment described as 'impudent insolencies'.

THE MANX LANGUAGE

Again the country people wanted the services in Manx, the language they all understood. Bishop Barrow's answer to their demand was to introduce schools for the teaching of English. But the native language died hard, in spite of the indifference of the Anglicised townspeople and other sections of the population. Bishop Wilson wrote, 'The English is not understood by two-thirds at least of the island, though there is an English school in every parish; so hard is it to change the language of a whole country.'

It was in his episcopate in the first half of the eighteenth century that some of the clergy, prejudiced perhaps by the emphasis on a classical education in the schools at Douglas and Castletown, began to cold-shoulder their native tongue. There is a suggestive passage in a letter as early as 1742, in which Vicar-General Matthias Curghey, Rector of Bride, asks the Ecclesiastical judge to reprimand his young and erring Parish Clerk.

'I do not object', he says, 'if you . . . slip [him] some words in Manx, which may not please all nice and prejudiced palates. . . .'

In 1763 Bishop Hildesley expressed astonishment at the indifference and disapprobation which he met with in his endeavours to circulate religious reading in the Manx. 'This', he exclaimed, 'I believe is the only country in the world that is ashamed of, and even inclined to extirpate, if it could, its own native tongue.'

But the Manx Bible for which he was so largely responsible and in the translation of which the parish clergy all took their honourable share, gave great satisfaction and happiness to the country people of his time, and long afterwards their reception of the translation is typified in the Bishop's own story of the Kirk Michael woman listening with joy to her son reading the Manx and crying out in exultation, 'Until now we have sat in darkness!'

THE FISH TITHE

It would be too much to expect that any fixed ecclesiastical levy would fail to breed grievances, but the fish tithe aroused especial dissatisfaction owing to the fact that when a fisherman landed his fish over a third of the catch disappeared in dues to the Lord and his officer, the Water Bailiff, and to the Church. As some recompense the Water Bailiff provided harbour lights, and the parish clergy visited the harbours and creeks during the fishing season, to conduct services for boats about to sail for the fishing grounds.

The Clergy complained bitterly of the Fish Tithe evasions, and the dificulties of collection. Sir Thomas Parr, walking down from Malew vicarage to Castletown one day in 1691, saw a boat fresh in from the sea with dogfish in it. He asked the owner, John Elsmore, for his tithe. Elsmore refused; and taking up a dogfish said, 'Sir Thomas, if you want a fish at home, here, take a *gobbag* along with you, but I would not have you take it as tithe.'

'And', said a witness, 'Sir Thomas going away from them, the wife of Elsmore, coming to the boat, said, "You do better pay him tithe, for Sir Thomas knows the law better than you do." Whereupon Elsmore said, "I care not a jot for him or his laws!" ' A rash assertion which his subsequent experience in the Ecclesiastical Court made clear.

In 1733 John Cosnahan, Curate of Rushen, complained that the boat masters did not, as in other parishes, openly divide the fish, but concealed and panniered up their fish before they landed, so depriving him of tithe. The fishermen, he said, did not fish grey fish, but caught lobsters which they sold at three and four shillings a dozen. The minister got no consideration for these, 'though', he said, 'they, too, grow of God's providence from the sea.'

By the middle of the eighteenth century the fish tithe had ceased to be collected, but in 1770 the Vicars-General were instructed to find out the legal position, and obtained a declaration in their favour from the Island Courts. Some of the Kirk Michael fishermen however made a costly appeal to the Privy Council. They lost their case and were ruined, but the fishermen persisted in their refusal to pay the tithes, which were never again exacted.

THE CLERGY

The country clergyman, in addition to his parochial work and the superintendence of his glebe, found change and relaxation in attendance at the Church Courts; and in friendly gatherings in farm houses where the countrymen sat over their cups of home-brewed ale, and discussed intelligently in their native Manx the current events and problems of the day.

There is a brief glimpse of one of these meetings at the house of John Teare of Loughcroute in Jurby in 1672. The Vicar, William Crowe, is there with a number of neighbouring farmers. They are comparing Island Bishops of whom they have knowledge. The formidable Bishop Barrow is still alive, and all save one unite in praising his educational policy, Gilbert Skally of the KerrooCroie admiring its scope in giving a chance of schooling to the children of all classes, the poor as well as the rich. But Patrick Clarke of Bretny, Serjeant of the Bishop's Barony, considers Bishop Phillips better than Barrow, against whom he has a grievance, arising from his duties as Serjeant. He said the Bishop had done him wrong and had denied him justice and the law.

The Vicar was thereupon forced for his own protection to take official notice of Patrick's indiscreet talk and report him to the chapter quest for his scandalous aspersions of the Bishop. But when he appeared in court the judges mercifully accepted the plea that his good sense had been affected by the ale he had drunk, and let him off with a fine and admonition.

Isaac Barrow, the Bishop who had won the praise of the Jurby men, succeeded the amiable Bishop Rutter in 1663 and played a great part in giving fresh energy to the debilitated Church and its ministers. One of the ablest of the long line of occupants of the See of Sodor and Man, Barrow proceeded to discipline the faltering clergy with a ruthlessness which spared none, from the Vicars-General to the humblest Church officer.

His first impression of his Manx brethren was that they were very illiterate and completely ignorant, but this sweeping statement is not borne out by the evidence of William Blundell who visited Man in 1648, and wrote in his History, 'I did not converse with anyone but that I found him a scholar and discreet;' and Governor Chaloner who in 1655 said, 'Considering the ministers here are generally natives, and have had their whole education in the Isle, it is marvellous what good preachers there be.'

SIR JOHN CRELLIN

These more optimistic estimates get some support from the results of a questionnaire sent to the wardens of the parishes in 1666. In the parish of Kirk Arbory the Vicar was Sir John Crellin whose people had put on record their approval of him long before the coming of the reforming Bishop. Of him his churchwardens reported in 1665—

> 'He observes holydays, fasting days, Ember weeks and yearly perambulations. He instructs children diligently, preparing them to be confirmed.
>
> 'He never neglects to visit the sick nor baptise any children.
>
> 'He preaches true and sound doctrine to his congregation in knowledge, faith and obedience.
>
> 'Our vicar is, in our apprehension, sober and unblaimable in his life. Neither doth he accompany any vitious or excommunicate persons, neither is hee a drinker, a swearer, gamester or quarreller.
>
> 'As for his apparel it is but baire, though grave; and according to the fashion of the country, and the colour poore. As for his behaviour in any kinde, he is affable, without scandal, but as it becomes a minister. . . .'

The reference to the unadorned and faded clothes of this Manx Vicar of Wakefield recalls the fact that when he died his earthly wealth in money amounted to half a crown; and his greatest household treasures, in addition to his books, were a chest, a press, and a half share of a silver spoon.

Among other favourable reports in the answers to the Bishop's enquiry regarding the parish incumbents was one from Kirk Maughold. Robert Allen, the letter writer of 1642, was dead, having been succeeded by his son Thomas, who was Curate for the time being, but a year later was made Vicar, a post he held for sixty years.

Of young Thomas the Wardens say, 'The Curate is sober as becometh, and his apparel is fitting according to his abilities; which himselfe in that kind wee cannot say anything by him but good.'

One old grievance emerges, however—the misuse of the churchyard. The wardens say,

> 'The churchyard is well fenced and yet not without beasts (as swine) to annoy; and other beasts come there, which only eat the grass, and with rubbing [act] prejudiciously, the windows being low.'

CHURCH YARD

In former times the Churchyard, so far as its grass was concerned, was looked upon as an adjunct of the Glebe, and the parish incumbent often pastured his horses and cattle there. Any expression of doubt as to the propriety of such use appears to have surprised the person concerned. When Henry Allen, nephew of the long-lived Thomas, was presented by his chapter quest in 1744, for making a gap in the churchyard fence, his tart letter to the Ecclesiastical judges reveals his resentment at the charge made against him. He wrote,

> 'I find myself presented for my too much freedom in the churchyard. ... This is the eighteenth year of my being Vicar and I thought I never took any other freedom in it than my predecessors did, time out of mind. As they did, I had my milch cows grassed in it every morning in summer and then driven to the glebe; but last summer I made free to open a gap in the churchyard fence in a convenient place, to drive my cattle through it for a shorter passage to the glebe, ... without making undecent passage through the graves; and before presentment I had the gap shut up in better order than before.'

Apparently public opinion, which had been long opposed to the custom was growing more critical of the use of the churchyard for pasturage, for in 1759, the Kirk Michael Chapter Quest arraigned the Vicar, Vicar-General Wilks, for a similar offence. But the practice continued, and in 1836, an observer saw twenty cattle grazing in Kirk Maughold churchyard.

Neither the custom nor the attitude of the Clergy was confined to the Isle of Man, however, and there is the story of the nineteenth century Archdeacon of an English diocese, who found that a Rector had sown the unoccupied part of the burial ground with turnips. The Archdeacon admonished him saying that he must not let him see turnips there again.

'Certainly not, Sir!' replied the innocent Rector. 'It will be barley next year.'

AGRICULTURE

Agriculture was the obvious means of adding to a country vicar's emoluments and one sometimes finds him farming much more land than the glebe contained. At the beginning of the seventeenth century Sir John Oates, Vicar of Kirk Onchan had a team of six oxen for the working of his land; and he had a boat at Port Onchan which was used for inshore fishing and at the right season went after herrings.

Sir John Huddleston, Curate of Kirk Andreas between 1660 and 1674, had apparently a prosperous farm. He had four draught oxen for the plough, ten other cattle, six horses, seventy sheep and four pigs; and eleven stocks of bees; and he also had a fishing boat.

The clergy had to do a good deal of travelling, and, like the quarterland farmers, invariably owned a riding-horse with saddle, and a pillion for a female companion. Among the indispensable articles of dress belonging to the wife of a clergyman or well-to-do farmer of the period were a riding-cloak and hood. Without a horse the only means of land travel was walking; for there was little or no wheel traffic on the uneven highways until the last half of the eighteenth century.

As late as 1763 Bishop Hildesley, who had driven in his coach by way of Peel to Castletown for the funeral of Deemster Taubman, was unable to return the same day, owing to a rainstorm which made the roads and river fords impassable.

SIR JOHN HUDDLESTON'S HOUSE

Some indication of the size and furnishing of the house of one of the most prosperous clergymen in the last half of the seventeenth century is given in an inventory, of 1674, of the goods of the curate of Kirk Andreas, Sir John Huddleston, already mentioned. He occupied the Rectory house which was rebuilt in 1666, the year of the Great Fire of London, and part of it still survives. There were at least five rooms—the *thie mooar* or 'great house', the parlour, chamber, closet and upper chamber. The parlour and chamber had iron grates.

The *thie mooar* was the centre of family life, and had an open hearth with hanging chain, from which to suspend the pots. A cupboard in the Kirk Andreas house contained a store of pewter ware, weighing sixty-five pounds. The curate's earthenware consisted of some bottles and eight white dishes standing upon a dish-board. There were also eighteen wooden bowls and trenchers. There were brass pans among the cooking utensils, and the candlesticks were of pewter.

Three little spinning wheels for flax and hemp, and two big ones for wool, stood ready for the use of female members of the household with any unoccupied time. The house furniture included two tables, made up in the ancient way with movable boards and trestles, a small table, two cupboards, a press and two chests. There were stools but only two chairs. Cushions and a settle provided the rest of the seating.

Two bedsteads with feather beds stood in the parlour, and one with curtains in the upper chamber. The inventory mentions green curtains and carpets—including some of Kidderminster—but rushes were the usual floor covering, and the carpets were probably used, not for the floor, but for covering beds and tables.

BOOKS

There is no mention of books. Huddleston was apparently much better off than most of his brethren and might be supposed to have a small collection of the theological works of the time, and perhaps he had disposed of them among his friends before his death. Sir Thomas Thwaites, Vicar of Lonan, may have done the same, but he was in less prosperous circumstances. He died in 1686, and the only literature he presumably owned at the time was some old books valued at ninepence.

Books were scarce and expensive, and as Bishop Barrow said, almost impossible to buy out of the small incomes of the impoverished country clergy.

Sir Charles Coole, Vicar of Santan, who died in 1658, owned thirty volumes, all theological. His contemporary, Sir John Crellin, Vicar of Arbory, possessed seventy-one, sixty-eight of which were theological, the remaining three consisting of a volume of poetry by Chatelard; the popular seventeenth century satire, 'Hudibras'; and the third volume entitled, 'The Mystery of Witchcraft,' a subject which often occupied the attention of the Church Courts until the third decade of the eighteenth century.

At a later time, Bishop Wilson, who was familiar with the disabilities under which the clergy worked, made provision for parochial libraries of theological books and for addition to a library in Castletown. This, founded in 1669, numbered more than 1,000 volumes, and was eventually housed at King William's College, where it was destroyed in the fire of 1844.

CLOCKS

Pictures, musical instruments and clocks, were still rarer adornments of Manx vicarages in the seventeenth century. The late Mr. Daniel Clarke of the Nappin, Jurby, when he was ninety-one years of age, told in Manx, an artless story of unknown antiquity, given to him by his grandfather, which illustrates the scarcity of timepieces; though it was primarily a simple commentary on the vagaries of human nature, and, frail and unsubstantial, by word of mouth had been passed down the centuries.

'Long, long ago,' he said, 'on a frosty moonlit night in Winter, the Archdeacon sat dozing over the warm turf fire in his Rectory at Kirk Andreas, with his manservant Patrick sitting on the other side of the *chiollagh*. At length he roused himself, and wishing to know how far the evening was advanced, he said to the servant,

'*Jean siyr, Pharic! Gow as jeeagh my vel yn eayst harrish y thie 'n ollee!* "Make haste, Pat! Go and see if the moon is over the cowhouse!"

Upon which Patrick, hating to leave the warmth of the chimney nook, grumbled, "Aw, your Reverence, and what can I do with the moon if it *is* over the cowhouse?" '

The lack of timepieces, apart from hour-glasses and a sun-dial in the churchyard, gave importance to the Parish Clerk's duty of what was known as the ringing of the 'Three Bells'. Failure to perform this regularly on the Sabbath and in due time, caused much indignation in the parish he served and might lead to the delinquent's appearance before the Spiritual Judges.

Though all Manx parishes at one time or another produced some-one nicknamed *Mun-laa*—'Noon'—because of his extraordinary ability to recognise the time to stop work for the mid-day meal, the average parishioner was not so gifted, and, in the absence of a signal, might not only miss his desired participation in the Church service, but also expose himself to Ecclesiastical censure for non-attendance. The first warning bell was therefore rung at eight o'clock in the morning, the second at nine, and the third before Service began at ten. Similarly for the Evening service—'evening' being the translation of the Manx *fastyr* which may also mean 'afternoon'—the first bell was rung at one o'clock, the second at two and the third before the service at three o'clock.

CLERGYMAN'S WIFE

The life of a clergyman's wife two or three hundred years ago was somewhat circumscribed. Except for the occasions when she mounted a horse behind her husband to visit friends, she did not travel out-side her own parish, and her ordinary days were busily occupied in attending to her family, and in supervising and sharing in the many activities of the house—combing and spinning of wool, carding and heckling of hemp and flax, the brewing of small beer, the making of butter, bacon, salted mutton and beef, salted herring and cod-fish, looking after the poultry and bee-hives, milking sheep in the sheep fold, and making sheep's and goats' cheese.

In the outspoken seventeenth century the clergyman's wife some-times refused to keep strictly to her role of housewife and allowed her tongue to wag too freely. In such a case she discovered that her social position did not save her from the consequences of her indis-cretion.

In 1637, for example, the wife of the Vicar of Kirk German was brought before a Church Court for saying that a certain Peel woman was a witch. She paid for her offence by doing penance at the north stile of St. Peters in Peel, with a bridle of leather in her mouth, whilst her husband's congregation filed past her out of Church.

A complaint of another kind was made in 1669 against the English-born wife of Charles Parr, Vicar of Kirk Lonan. She was presented by the Chapter quest for not coming to church. Her attitude before the Court was that of a contemptuous newcomer. 'The Minister's wife,' she said, 'not having the service of the Church read to her in English and not understanding the Manx, absents herself till the parish will allow half the service to be read in English; and then she will duly observe the service.'

If the Spiritual Judges were taken aback by her nonchalance, they soon made her realise that a change of mind on her part was preferable to a stay in the bleak prison of Castle Peel; and she quickly decided to reform her ways.

SIR THOMAS PARR

Among the notable clergymen of the last half of the seventeenth century was Vicar-General Sir Thomas Parr, whose strongly marked idiosyncrasies make themselves apparent in quaint entries in the Register of Kirk Malew, where he was Vicar from 1641 to 1691. He was a man of good life who faithfully performed his obligations to Church and parishioners. But he was humourless, with a niggling cantankerous vein in his character, which sometimes brought him into conflict with his flock and his brethren.

A complaint he made against a churchwarden in 1674 is revealing and typical:

> 'Sir,' he writes to the Ecclesiastical Judge, 'som of our wardens take great bouldness and regard nothinge that I say but will doe as they please, flighting and undervalueing me; the cover of the pulpit and cushion [that] was made two yeeres and wanted but a fringe; and the thrid of the same being culloured before Christmas, the workman Chas Voas came to Wm. Carrowne, warden, for bonds to pay for the same; haveing the money in his hande [he] would not pay nor come to the Church to see the cover put up; he refused and said he would not neglect his owne worke and when the workman tould him that I would have it done for Christmas he sayd, "What care I for Sir Thomas I care not for him. I will do nothinge for him," and disdained me very much.
>
> Thomas Parre.'

He was for a long time at cross purposes with the vicar of the neighbouring parish of Kirk Arbory, who was a Scot named Sam Robinson. How he got the living is not recorded, for he was doubly unsuitable, not only because he could not speak Manx—an indispensable qualification for the incumbent of a Manx parish then and for long afterwards—but also because he was not a good exemplar of important Christian virtues. The Kirk Arbory people complained that he did not preach either in Manx or English and that when he tried to read a homily in the native language they were unable to make out what he was saying.

His wife was successful in picking up a little Manx, not all of the right kind, which she used irritatingly in wordy battles with Mrs. Parr, and once when her husband was suspended for his conduct, she cried, '*Lane y mollagh* (A full curse) on the parish!' as the Kirk Arbory wardens plaintively protested, 'exclaiming against the parish that did them noe harme but bore too longe with them.'

On one occasion in 1675 Robinson appeared to get the better of the argument with the Vicar-General, who had the reputation of being fond of money. Sir Thomas had supplied the church of Kirk Arbory when its vicar was in disgrace, and in due course asked the parish sumner to claim his fee. Robinson asserted, quite untruthfully (as it turned out) that it had been demanded during service time, and wrote to the Vicar-General with a show of virtuous indignation:

'Sir Thomas,

'If you were as serious in studying the gift of the Holy Ghost as you are upon the contrivance of money I hope I should not be disturbed with your orders upon the Lord's Day in time of service, nor the people neither; however I shall only make application what was said to Simon the Sorcerer, Acts VIII, 20, and leave it to be read at leisure; and for further confirmation be pleased to consult with the new Catechism, p. 166. If I have done you any injury I begg your pardon and rest

Yours

Sam Robinson.'

Robinson took the oath of allegiance to the Island Lord and laws and became a naturalised Manxman, but retained to the end the defects of character which had alienated his Arbory flock. He was suspended for the last time in 1708 for calling the highly respected Deemster Parr a Church robber, and died four years later.

He had survived into an age which frowned on the boisterous social interchanges of the century that was past; and if the occupants, male or female, of the eighteenth century vicarages and parsonages chose to disagree with their colleagues and their parishioners they usually conducted themselves in a genteel manner according to the temper of the times.

STIPENDS

Bishop Barrow who had found so many weaknesses in his diocese fortunately did not stop at criticism and penal remedies for the sickness of the Church. He says that the salary of a parish priest was only £5 or £6 a year, and that sometimes as in the cases of the Vicars of Kirk Santan and Rushen he was reduced to keep an alehouse for addition to his income. The Bishop was well aware of the effect of poverty on the outlook and actions of the average man. With great energy he proceeded by various ways to increase clerical salaries, and by 1686 every parish priest was assured of at least £17 per annum, which appears to have been considered a competence at that time. In addition he raised a fund to provide an income for an Academic school in Castletown with four free scholarships for boys intended for the Church.

A free Grammar school established in 1707 provided a similar education in Douglas; and most eighteenth century Manxmen in public life were educated at one or other of these schools Shortly before the Rev. Philip Moore died in 1783, he was able to declare with pardonable pride that, with four exceptions, every clergyman serving in the Manx Church at that time had been trained by him at the Douglas School. 'Two things above all,' he says, gave him satisfaction, when he viewed his life in retrospect, 'that I had a capital hand and concern in the Manx Scriptures, and was instrumental in the education of several ingenious, sensible and pious young men.'

Philip, like his elder brother Edward Moore, was educated at Douglas. Both entered the Church, and both in their early years of manhood exhibited the defects of their times, and the easy-going complacency of the sceptical eighteenth century. When curate of Marown Philip got into Bishop Wilson's bad books by masquerading one night in the ruins of St. Trinian's to scare the country people, and then show them how wrong they were in their belief in the famous Buggane. But his escapade irritated rather than changed the Marown people in their superstitions. In maturity however he acquired a reputation for scholarship and virtuous living, and became the valued friend of two great bishops—Wilson and Hildesley. He was incidentally the most noted Manx pluralist, being at once Chaplain of Douglas, Master of the Grammar School, Chaplain to the Bishop, Private Chaplain to the Duke of Atholl, and Rector of Ballaugh and Bride in succession.

Obviously he could not fill these positions simultaneously with reasonable efficiency; and he aroused the anger of his Ballaugh parishioners by his failure to provide the services for which they were tithed. And in 1762 when similar complaints of neglect came from Kirk Bride, even his intimate and indulgent friend, Bishop Hildesley, was compelled to remind him that 'We must not think to enjoy our preferments without care and trouble'.

EDWARD MOORE

Edward Moore in the first years of his curacy at Kirk Andreas was also adversely criticised for negligence of duty, but later, appears to have reformed, and joined his brother as a valued assistant of Bishop Wilson. He became a Vicar-General and spent the last years of his life as Vicar of Kirk Michael. He left behind him an interesting little account book which he kept at Kirk Andreas for several years from 1727, and which throws some light on life there.

In addition to the barn, cow-house, and ox-house, there were a lime-kiln, drying kiln for corn and malt, and a brewhouse. The work of cultivating the glebe and some other fields was done by a man-servant and boy, hired by the year. The man's wages ranged from 20s. per annum in 1728 to 33s. in 1733, together with food and lodging. When hired he received earnest money to seal the bargain, the amount varying from 2d. to 12d. In addition a *dhooragh* or present was also given—generally a pair of old breeches.

Boys naturally got much less. In 1733 John Christian was hired for 9s. per annum and a pair of old breeches; and when advances had been made to his father for clothing there was not much left—a petticoat (short coat), cost 1s. 2d.; russet breeches, 1s. 9d.; a hat, 1s. 2d.; a buckle for his neck-cloth, 3d.; shoes, 3s.

The domestic staff at the Rectory consisted of a maid who got 20s. a year, and earnest money of 7d. when she was engaged. On several occasions a girl was hired to assist the maid. In 1730, for instance, Ann Moore was engaged for 8s. a year, but as in the case of the boy most of the sum disappeared in 5 yds. of stuff for her gown; 4 yds. of linen, 1s. 10d.; a bodice, 1s. 2d.; 1 yd. of material for an apron, 10d.; a total of 7s. 11d., leaving 1d. for luxuries for the whole of the year.

Apparently conditions were not very attractive, or perhaps the curate was not fortunate in his choice, for his hired servants, domestic and outside, did not remain more than a year or two.

The clergy had the privilege known as 'Bridge and Staff'; that is to say, a servant who had come to them voluntarily, could not be 'yarded' by those privileged officials—the Deemsters, Moars and Coroners—who until 1777 had the legal right to conscript for their service one or more servants who took their fancy.

A good deal of casual labour was employed on the glebe, the pay, with food, varying from 2d. to 5d. a day. Threshing with flails went on at intervals throughout the year, as corn was needed for food, at 2d. a day. It was done by two workers—sometimes women—who stood opposite to one another at the threshing floor, and struck alternate blows with their sticks at the heads of the corn lying between them. The grain was winnowed, and then dried on the floor of the kiln.

Edward Moore grew wheat, rye, barley, oats, hemp, potatoes and pease; and in his notebook names the fields he grew them in. One called the *Faaie-ny-Oalan*, 'the field of the Holy Wafer,' according to tradition was consecrated, and always used in the Middle Ages for growing the wheat for the sacramental bread; but the notebook shows that barley and rye were sown in it during Moore's occupation.

Twopence with food was the daily wage for various labouring work like hedging, breaking lime-stones to burn in the kiln, thatching turf stacks, setting potatoes and gorsing the folds. The folds or *booilltyn* were temporary small enclosures in which cattle were kept for a week or two until they had eaten the grass and had manured the ground. Cutting turf in the Archdeacon's turf *lag* below the Guilcagh, drying malt, and harvesting corn and hay, were paid at the higher rate of 4d. per day.

THE MELLIA

In 1728 Edward writes in his notebook: 'Aug. 29th we cut down the last of the glebe corn and had the melleh brought in;' the Mellia, of course, being the last sheaf of corn cut, and decorated with ribbons, carried in by one of the workers to grace the table at the harvest feast. He sets down the number of stooks of corn and pease as being 384 of 12 sheaves each, and the number of working days to cut down the corn and bind it was 81 at 4d. a day, a total cost of £1 7s.

He also gives the result of the harvest in 1729, the 'Melleh' taking place on the same day of the month as in the previous year—August 29th. The number of stooks has increased from 384 to 426, and, with a full heart, he writes, *Laus et Gratia Deo optimo et maximo!* 'Praise and thanks to God best and greatest!'

CONCLUSION

The two centuries under review produced not only individual divines of note like William Walker, James Wilks and Philip Moore, but also remarkable examples of families with a long history of service to the Church.

Thomas Allen, a Puritan clergyman from Norwich, was the first of six of his family to take Orders, all but one following in succession as Vicars of Kirk Maughold from 1625 to 1754, and maintaining the tradition for piety and sober living created by the founder of the family.

At least eight descendants of Robert Parr of Parville in Kirk Arbory who died in 1645, entered the Manx Church. Five Cosnahans, Vicars of Kirk Santan, lie under the famous great stone in the parish churchyard; and the Crowes and Curgheys of Lezayre and the

Norrises of Ballanorris in Kirk Arbory appear as often in the lists of parish incumbents.

Nearly all the eighteenth century clergy had benefited from the humanistic education afforded by the schools at Douglas and Castletown, and Bishop Hildesley found them, as he told the Archbishop of York in 1762, 'Almost without exception a very sensible, decent set of men.'

The eighteenth century saw a great increase in the material prosperity of the Island, and the clergy shared in the growing amenities of life, though for a period between 1735 and 1757 a claim made by the Duke of Atholl deprived them of a large part of their income and reduced some of them to destitution. Even as late as 1832 Governor Smelt could write that only four church livings were worth more than £100 a year.

But the position of the clergy in the national life during the seventeenth and eighteenth centuries is not to be measured by the size of their emoluments. In the greater part of the two hundred years under consideration none of the other learned professions enjoyed the respect of the Manx community. It was the clergy, generally, who taught in the schools, the few lay schoolmasters being, for the most part, failures from other occupations.

The medical profession was still struggling towards a modest respectability; but had not yet rid itself entirely from the imputation of charlatanism of which it had been accused in former times.

There were no professional lawyers until the middle of the eighteenth century. 'It is but of late years', wrote Bishop Wilson, 'that attornies and such as gain by strife have even forced themselves into business.'

A great responsibility, therefore, of providing spiritual and intellectual illumination for the people, rested on the Church; and if, at times, its ministers, following the way of human nature, may have deviated a little from their appointed course and the light burned dim, in the result they exercised a supremely important influence for good upon the life of the Manx community.

XI

THE DUNGEON OF ST. GERMAN'S

Few places in the Isle of Man can have witnessed more tragedy than the prison crypt under the chancel of St. German's Cathedral, with its cold stone walls and roof, its perpetually damp floor, and its darkness—in ancient times relieved only by fitful gleams of light from a narrow embrasure opening on to Peel Bay.

In 1722, when Governor Horne was at pains to rebut charges of arbitrary and oppressive conduct and of illtreatment of prisoners in Castle Rushen, made against the Lord's officers by Bishop and Keys, he found a ready *tu quoque* in the Bishop's prison, which, he told the British Government, 'is a most horrid dungeon or vault under the graves of the dead in an old church in a small island in the sea'.

The mournful cry of a Long Jury shut up in 1680 does not, however, suggest better conditions in the Lord's prison at Peel. They had failed to agree, owing to the dissidence of three of their number, and were confined until they came to a unanimous decision.

> '. . . Which disagreement of the said three occasioned much trouble and hasard of life to the petitioners (writing out of the Peele) being several days kept in close prison without either meat drink fireing or candlelight, ready to perish, their feet hands and bodys oftimes being swoln with cold, and all unable to suffer the present affliction. . . .'

The Governor accepted the petition, and the three jurymen who had so perversely refused to vote with the majority were punished with fine and imprisonment.

THE CRYPT

According to experts the prison-crypt of St. German's was built after Bishop Simon erected the chancel in 1229, and may have taken the place of an earlier crypt built at that date. The floor of the chancel was raised to accommodate the roof of the new chamber.

A staircase of eighteen steps within the thickened south wall of the chancel leads down to the prison. This is thirty-four feet long and sixteen feet broad, and is barrel-vaulted, with thirteen ribs springing from pilasters on either side.

When *débris* was cleared away in 1871 an arched doorway was discovered, leading to the rock outside the castle walls below the chancel window. A third doorway on the north side of the crypt opens on to the remains of the Bishop's quarters. Light is admitted through a loophole five feet high and six inches wide.

Romantic inventions which have claimed the dungeon as the prison and haunting-place of the fifteenth century Duchess of Gloucester appear to have no foundation in fact.

One, indeed, can imagine this place of sombre memories visited, not by the ghost of the magic-making Duchess, but by the presences of some of the multitude of long-forgotten Manx men and women who despaired and agonised here, and whose piteous abject prayers for release, blotted sometimes, one fancies, by their tears, are hidden away in the ecclesiastical records. For the historical interest of the crypt is not in the unsubstantiated stories of English State prisoners, but in the fact that it was the symbol of that carefully ordered discipline, enforced by fear, which the Church developed in the Middle Ages, and which the Manx and other churches retained with modifications after the Reformation.

Over the proceedings of every Manx Spiritual Court, and in the imagination of every offender, loomed the sinister shadow of the crypt of St. German's. Only a short stay within its walls was sufficient to bring the average transgressor to resolve, as one petitioner in 1742 put it, 'never to be guilty of the like trespass again and admonish others to beware thereof; and his reflections thereon, together with his Darksome prison, puts him in a serious thought of his Darker crime'.

For the chill of that dismal abode sapped the courage of the most defiant spirits; though William Callow, of Ballafayle, and several others of the Kirk Maughold Quakers, fortified by their fervent beliefs, bore its rigours without shrinking; and occasionally an obstinate man with a grievance would pit his powers of endurance against the unrelenting dungeon.

In 1712 William Fargher, of Skibrick, refused, on some point of principle, to pay his accustomed tithes, and was committed to St. German's until he found sureties for his compliance. For eleven long months he fought a battle of which the result was certain. Then, broken in body, he admitted defeat.

THE SPIRITUAL COURTS

The right of committal to St. German's belonged solely to the Bishop and was delegated to the judges sitting in the Spiritual Courts. These, briefly, were of three kinds: Summary, dealing with matters relating to the wills of deceased persons, tithes and other Church dues; Chapter, in which breaches of discipline were 'presented', and probate granted; and Consistory, to hear appeals.

The Courts were competent to try all cases relating to marriage and infringement of the orthodox sexual code, witchcraft, profanation of the Sabbath and other holy days, non-attendance at Church and school, cursing and swearing, slander, drunkenness, and fighting and the spilling of blood in the churchyard.

In addition the Courts supervised the estates of minors and orphans. They retained their testamentary jurisdiction until 1884. To judge from the records the work was done conscientiously and with humanity, and with an integrity at least as great as that to be expected from the contemporary Civil Courts.

The two (sometimes three) Vicars-General (Mx., *personyn*) did the bulk of the judicial work, in which the Bishop or his deputy, and the Archdeacon or his official also took part. Until 1824 a Vicar-General was invariably a clergyman. He generally held the Rectory of Ballaugh or Kirk Bride, hence the title of *person* or parson, and was assisted in his parochial work by a curate, sometimes called the 'Parson's Clerk'.

The Courts when on circuit were generally held in the parish churches, though sometimes in secular buildings when the former were not available. John Woods, the Episcopal Registrar, writing of a Court held in Douglas in March, 1709, says, 'This day about 3 o' th' clock in the afternoon, the Court-house loft was so throng'd that it fell down into the Stable, with the Officers, Registrars and People; but very few were hurt by it.'

THE GENERAL SUMNER

The principal executive officer of the diocese was the General Sumner (Mx., *Ardsunder*). He was responsible for enforcing the decrees of the Spiritual Courts and appointed a subordinate sumner in each of the seventeen parishes of the Island. The alternative title, 'Apparitor,' was sometimes used, and in 1702 Ewan Christian of Lewaigue styled himself 'Apparitor General or General Sumner'.

The General Sumner sent out orders and citations from the Bishop, and in some cases took out letters of administration for intestate estates. He was employed on special missions in which the sumner of the parish involved was likely to fail. In 1664, for example when Bishop Barrow embarked on his campaign against the Quakers he addressed an order to John Christian in the following terms:

'General Sumner,
'you are required to repayre to the houses of the schismatiques in the parish of Kk. Maughold commonly called Quakers and to give

particular charge to every one of them ... to joyn with their neighbours in the publique worship by Law established ... and to returne to mee, the names of such as refuse and the reasons of their refusall, that if they appear and continue refractory they may be proceeded against by excommunication, according to the Canon of the Church and the Lawes of this Island. ...'

When a number of the non-conforming Quakers were excommunicated John Christian had the duty of escorting them to St. German's and then handing them over to the temporal power.

APPOINTMENT OF GENERAL SUMNER

The General Sumnership was an office of profit and was bought by the holder. In 1661, Ewan Christian, of Lewaigue, compounded for the position which had previously been held by his kinsmen John and Robert, for £50. On one occasion in the eighteenth century the Lord of the Isle received £15 for a lease of the office for twenty-one years.

The Bishop's claim to appoint an official filling such an important post in his administration was strongly challenged on two occasions. In 1612, the Countess of Derby, the *de facto* ruler of Man, issued a precept claiming the right. The clergy did not hide their hostility to the proposed change, and several were committed to Castle Rushen or otherwise punished for indiscreet criticism of the Countess's action.

The Bishop's nominee, Pat Foster, persisted in collecting the perquisites of office and was successful in Lezayre. In Kirk Michael he met with opposition and was accused of breaking down the 'cheeks' of house doors and cudgelling those who refused to yield up their tithe cheese. These and other irregularities brought about his arraignment in the Civil Courts. In 1627 the Bishop's right of appointment was restored.

During Wilson's episcopate when the conflict between the civil and ecclesiastical powers came to a head the Lord's claim was revived. Thomas Corlett, of Ballakeoig, who had been appointed by the Bishop in 1712, was supplanted by William Christian of Jurby, in 1727, and thereafter all General Sumners received their commissions from the Lord.

THE PARISH SUMNER

The Parish Sumner's duties were very varied and the office was sometimes combined with that of parish clerk or licensed parish schoolmaster.

When a death occurred the Sumner swore four prizers who made an inventory and valuation of the deceadent's estate; and he summoned all the interested parties to the Spiritual Court dealing with the case. With the consent of the Vicar and churchwardens he gave 'a call', as it was termed, of lost and found property, of meetings and fairs. This he did both within the Church, and at the Cross, which formerly stood near the entrance of every parish churchyard.

He collected fines imposed by the Church Courts, and customary payments which had fallen in arrear. In 1746 the Kirk Braddan Sumner was sent round to levy the payment of the 'ploughman's groat', due annually to the Parish Clerk, which had lapsed for some years. Sometimes a farmer stacked his corn before the tithe had been taken—either rebelling against the collection, or because his stooks had been kept standing an unreasonable time. The Sumner was sent with two companions to throw down the stack and cast out the tithe.

His most conspicuous duty was to sit at the chancel door during service and drive out any dogs which came into the church after their owners. It was, as the churchwardens of Kirk Arbory remarked in 1665 'a difficult thing to do', and all through the seventeenth and eighteenth centuries every Manx parish complained at one time or another of the Sumner's failure to deal with the nuisance. In 1735, the Curate of Kirk Andreas asked the Court if the Sumner was not obliged to attend funerals, since the noise of barking dogs drowned the voices of those taking part in the burial services. It was ordered as an alternative that the owners of intruding dogs should be presented.

A great part of the Sumner's fees came from the tithe-gathering. From each farmer he received a principal cheese; i.e. of the best made, monthly from May to October, or alternatively, butter from twenty-four hours milk, six times during the same period.

He also received from each farmer a sheaf of corn tied by a band the length of three long straws—in Manx the *boandey-sunder* or sumner's band. In the nineteenth century this was often commuted for three ordinary sheaves or a money payment, at the option of the recipient.

When he was engaged in gathering the wool tithe with horse and sack he received a choice lamb and a fleece out of the tithe. If it was necessary for him to inspect cattle, sheep and goats, for the purpose of discovering the just tithe, he received payments at the rate of 1d. or 2d. for each cow, 2d. out of eight sheep, and 2d. out of four goats. His fee for escorting an offender to prison was 4d.

THE CHAPTER QUEST

During the many centuries in which the Manx Church courts exercised disciplinary functions, the Sumner's occupation was not an idle one.

Annually he arranged for the swearing-in of his parish church-wardens, and also impanelled the chapter quest of four 'honest and sufficient men', who, with the wardens, met every three or four weeks under the chairmanship of the Vicar or Rector, and were bound by oath to report and present persons alleged to have been guilty of a breach of the Canon law.

Thus every parish had a body of nine or ten men whose duties tempted them to spy on all the activities—however trivial—of their neighbours. For example, in 1742, a girl in Kirk Andreas was seen stooping at the church stile. She was charged with gathering dust to make a charm. In fact, she was recovering the beads of a broken necklace. A woman knocking a ball to her little child with a *cammag* stick, another steeping beans, a Foxdale miner baking a *bonnag*, were all arraigned for Sabbath-breaking.

In retaliation the parishioners tried to catch out the watchers and were sometimes successful, as when J.B., of Jurby, was presented in 1714 for weaving on the loom on St. Matthew's day 'with the door shut on him, being one of the chapter quest at the very same time'.

In practice the efficiency of the system was bound to be affected by the restraints which govern the conduct of the individual in small communities. As time went on the quest men were increasingly reluctant to perform their office. But even if they hesitated to destroy the goodwill of their neighbours by excessive zeal during their year of office, they had a great respect for oaths, and in the result the quest must have exerted a steady pressure on the life of a parish, encouraging resentment, suspicion and fear.

The great contempt in which Manx country people still hold the *skeet* or prying person is in part a legacy from the Church courts. Ironically enough the Spiritual Courts punished the inquisitiveness which was to some extent a by-product of their own methods. In 1670 (to take two from many instances) M.C. was presented 'for goeinge from house to house with stories and fables, backbitinge people, emulatinge and speaking of their goods'; and in 1714 D.G. 'for listening at Pat Stephen's door and for bearing tales'.

The smallest offences, sins of omission rather than commission, were often dismissed after admonition, on a promise of reformation, as with T.C., of Kirk Braddan, in 1720, who slept always in the church during Prayer time.

Robert Kissag's sorrowful excuse for inebriety got him off lightly in 1761: 'When he gets a sup of ale or liquor,' he explained, 'it takes impression on him and puts him out of his regular course . . . his misfortune was to have taken a sup extraordinary at times.'

More serious offences were punished by one or more penances at the church. Where the crime was regarded as grave, or there was a doubt of the offender's performing his penance, he was committed to the Dungeon until he gave proofs of contrition, in the form of a written plea for mercy, and provided two sureties for £3 that he would carry out his obligations. So constant was the demand for sureties that it is probable some people in Peeltown made a trade of signing the bonds. On releasement a prisoner paid 6d. to the keeper of the prison and 4d. to the porter at the gate.

THE GARB OF PENITENCE

The Sumner was responsible for the appearance of the penitent correctly dressed for the performance of his censure. Usually this took place at his parish church, but sometimes the punishment was much severer.

In 1645 the Vicars-General sentenced an incorrigible offender

'to penance in the churchyard and at the church door of every parish church and every markett crosse within this Isle of Mann in habitt and manner followinge:

'He shalbe ready at the ringinge of the last peale to morning prayers to begin his penance, bareheaded barelegged and footed, in his doublett and hose without a shirt, his outward habitt covered with a linnen sheet all over, with a little white wan in his hand, and there and then at the going in and comeinge out of the parishioners, and at the markett crosses for the space of 2 houres beginning at 9 of the cloack and continuing untill 11, to stand with his schedule on his breast and repeat after the minister. . . .'

When a penitent came without the essential white sheet, the Sumner lent him one for a fee of 4d.

An unusual form of penance imposed for slandering the dead is found in the early part of the seventeenth century. In 1619 it was decreed that Pat Kelly, of Ballaugh, should go to the grave of Donnold Christin deceased, and kneeling there ask the forgiveness of God and Donnold's kindred for calling his son the son of a dog. This was to be done on the Sabbath day, before the congregation. Similarly Pat's sister was ordered to go to the grave of William Caine, of the Glen, and ask God forgiveness for her innuendo in saying that William had died of the grease of the grey mutton. Apparently he had been suspected of stealing the sheep.

BRIDLE AND STOOL

The parish Sumner had charge of the 'bridle' which was put round the tongue of a person convicted of evil speaking. According to Waldron the Manx bridle was a noose of leather and not so formidable as the kind used in Britain. It was considered to be a gesture of contrite submission if the offender himself placed the instrument in position. In 1714 most of the parish bridles had disappeared and Bishop Wilson ordered that one should be carried in circuit by the General Sumner 'as a terror to people of ill tongues'.

Occasionally there are records of whipping as a punishment—and in the episcopacy of Richard Bridgman there was the unusual case of a woman receiving twelve strokes of a rod. She had said that the Virgin Mary used charms.

In 1668 a ducking stool was bought for ten shillings, the commuted penance of Philip Christian, of Douglas. It was to be set up at or near the town—probably at the market-place, the scene of some of the notorious boat-drawings in which boats were used to drag offenders across the harbour and back. This penance appears to have fallen into disuse, and was revived in Wilson's time. It aroused great public resentment, garrison soldiers had to be called in to coerce the boatmen, who refused to provide either boats or rowers; and the last drawing, ordered in 1734, was not carried out.

EXCOMMUNICATION

The final means of punishment in the hands of the spiritual judges was that of Excommunication, by which the offender was excluded from the spiritual consolation of the Church, and from normal relations with other Christians, who were forbidden to have any intercourse or dealings with him, save in extreme necessity.

In 1722, Mary Hendricks, of Douglas, who had been excommunicated for scandalous conduct, wrote, 'Your Lordshipp's poor and distressed petitioner is reduced to great extremity and want, being forced to wander from place to place in a miserable destitute condition, being that every person, though of never soe great acquaintance, are in noe ways willing to give your poor petitioner either releife or lodging, soe long as she remains excluded out of the Church. . . .'

When an offender obstinately refused to submit, the Church washed its hands of him and passed him over to the Civil power, with resultant forfeiture of body and goods.

Even in death the anathema of the Church still operated. John *Noe*, of Lezayre, the last to suffer excommunication, died miserably in 1825. Local tradition says that the funeral party was held up at the grave-side until a messenger received permission from Bishopscourt to proceed. After adjoining to a near-by house to consider the position and drink ale, mourners and bearers went resolutely back to the churchyard, and interred the body of the unfortunate man without further parley.

COMMUTATION

One discreditable legacy from the pre-Reformation Church was the commutation of penance for money by the better-off sinners, who thus escaped the humiliations and hardships suffered by their poorer brethren. The money obtained was devoted to useful purposes such as the making of roads and bridges.

The lively and likeable Archdeacon Rutter, later Bishop, had no scruples in encouraging the iniquitous practice, which was at last abolished at a Convocation in 1703, though fines were still imposed for non-attendance at church and school.

> 'To my much esteemed good friend Sir James Moore, Vicar-General,' Thomas Norris—Deemster some years later—wrote in 1649, 'Our bridge here att Castletowne goes on apace and many workemen att it, and I believe that you and all good people will bee great helpers of so good a work. I pray you what moneys you have collected send it by this bearer according to the Archdeacon's note.
>
> 'I am informed that one Christian, a rich man of your parish or Kk. Conchan will come or should now bee on your booke. I pray look after him for all . . . will be little enough. . . .'

In the Middle Ages the villainy with which the English Sumner was credited in connection with Commutation—the exaction of fees from the innocent and blackmail from the guilty—brought his office into contempt and hatred, and in Chaucer's tale, the Sompnour, when he met a stranger, passed himself off as a bailiff, to avoid the odium attached to his proper title:

> 'He dorste not for veray filth and shame
> Say that he was a Sompnour, for the name.'

Nothing is known of the Manx Sumner's behaviour before 1600, and there is no evidence of bad conduct in later times, but his duties were not likely to make him popular with his fellow parishioners.

Doubtless factors which induced the Manx to accept without much active protest the censures of the Spiritual Courts, were not only that they were apparently backed by Divine authority, but that they tempered justice with mercy, and that punishments were often mitigated on petition.

Offenders sometimes made vigorous protests against their sentences, like Thomas Carroon, who cried out to his judges that there were no laws which threw a man into the fire sooner than the laws of the Church. But Bishop Wilson expressed the general policy of the Courts when he wrote in 1729, 'I am not forward to break the bruised reed or quench the smoking flax, but bless God for the faintest prospect of repentance.'

In addition the Church Courts were not noticeably respectors of persons. If the crofters and the landless were presented, so too were members of the more substantial classes, and obscure men saw, not without some complacency, the great ones of the earth—high officers of government, clergy, parish captains and prosperous merchants, and their women-folk—all humbling themselves in the motley and tragic procession to the prison of St. German's, and the penitential sheet.

THE RECORDS

The records of the Spiritual Courts date from 1600, earlier accounts of their proceedings having long ago perished through neglect and damp. Those remaining are very incomplete but are full of interest and many extracts have already appeared in print.

It is unfortunate that the Registrars were almost exclusively concerned with the frailties and aberrations of the Manx and not with their Christian virtues; so that there is danger of forgetting the great majority who lived useful blameless lives and escaped the notice of the Chapter Quest.

The reader has also to bridge the gulf in thought and practice which separates us from the two centuries covered by the disciplinary records. It was a boisterous age, when men still carried arms, were passionate in their resentments and quick to strike. The general level of social restraint and tolerance, even among the educated classes, was much lower than now. In the early part of the seventeenth century an irate Vicar of Santan pulled an offending parishioner by the beard, and the senior Deemster drew blood on a clergyman who gave him the lie.

In 1649 Major Calcott of the Nunnery, with his mother Margrett, waylaid the Vicar of Kirk Braddan, on the ground of some grievance, and assaulted him, both of them suddenly striking him, pulling him by the hair and, says the account, 'spilling his blood in aboundance.'

Among the attractions of the records are occasional examples of the expressive diction of the period—used sometimes in condemnation or in righteous anger or with dignified regret.

In 1734 a Conservative living at Braust in Kirk Andreas spoke contemptuously of new altar vessels, 'to the offence of some serious Christians,' says the presentment, 'though a laugh to the more prophane.' And the Vicar-General adds a note: 'The defendant is now dead and must answer the Judge of all the world.'

In 1637 a penitent woman of Kirk Malew who had made a violent attack on Bishop and clergy at a friend's house and had been reported in consequence, in her recantation was made to begin,

'Whereas I Kathren Robinson, contrary to all humanity, have cast a grievous obliquy and matchlesse aspersion upon the most sacred ministeriall function in saying that a blacke coate could not be an honest man, and further, have most impiously and uncharitably damned them all to the Devill. . . .'

A century later the Vicars-General draw a spirited picture of a type which disturbed the equanimity of the judges from time to time, and tempted them to use the too easy remedy of the Bishop's dungeon:

'John Corlett y Valla having at our Chapter Court here in Lezayre behaved himself after a rude turbulent and audacious manner, to the disturbance of the causes in Debate and without any Regard had to the Reverence due to Magistrates was thereupon repeatedly enjoyned Silence, and admonished of his late Fine for a crime of this nature.

'When with Insolence and Clamour he reply'd If he was fined again he was able to pay it.'

Scattered through the records are letters from the clergy, often apologies for not attending a Court. In these yellowing pages the personalities of long dead writers spring to life again, to demonstrate the varied but unchanging quality of human nature.

Here is Matthias Curghy, Rector of Kirk Bride, pleading that he is 'indisposed with a Grievous Toothach', and here, in 1715, is kindly John Taubman, of Kirk Lonan, decrepit and near the end of his days, airing his Latinity and pleading consideration for the parish schoolmaster: 'Pray let poore Killip be encourag'd about the schoole, and pray remember me to all your clergy. *Precipue*', he adds, with a sly dig at masterful Bishop Wilson, 'Especially let my sacerdotall obedience be alwayes acknowledg'd to my Right Reverend Lord Bishopp—*verba sapienti satis.*'

Here too is the revealing downrightness of a Vicar of Kirk Maughold, commenting on a seating dispute two centuries ago:

'Gentlemen, Lest our Right Rev. Ld. Bishop should be surprised by the overmuch assurance of our mountaineers, contending for a sitting place in the Church, to their liking, Be pleased to observe to his Lordship that our Font stands in the antient door of our Church, to which and the passage from it no particular man had ever a Right of sitting.

'Therefore, if they needs must be pleased, in that case let them find it elsewhere, since the Font now stands in the most convenient place in the Church.

I am Your affectionate Brother,

Henry Allen.'

Finally, here in 1678 is a letter from Charles Parr, Vicar-General and Rector of Ballaugh, to illustrate the depths to which both he and his pastoral office were degraded for the purposes of Church discipline.

In a matter-of-fact communication to the keeper of the prison, and without a hint of compassion, he gives instructions for the disposal of two of his parishioners—one unhappy woman to be taken by force to the Dungeon, and the other from prison to Ballaugh church for public humiliation. He writes:

> 'Pray acquaint our sumner, who is one of the prisoners, that Corraige's daughter doth not make her penance as she engaged to Hen Young, and that he bring Young down with him, to bring her to prison. Mind him also of the other woman that is in your party, that he is to bring to this church to make penance. . . . If you can procure a fresh herring-mackerell and send it by the sumner I would satisfy you for it to the full.'

MARRIAGE

The Manx Church was very active in the detection and punishment of sexual irregularities, and exercised powers of divorce of marriage, though these appear to have been used only on rare occasions.

In 1637, a Ballaugh farmer based his plea for divorce on his wife's admissions. According to custom the matter was published in the parish church so that an opportunity might be given to opposers to present their objections. Nothing being advanced against the application the plaintiff obtained the divorce. The guilty party forfeited her interest in the estate and was inhibited from marrying in the natural life of her husband.

The Courts also intervened to straighten out other matrimonial difficulties, the Sumner being called in to perform the duties of the modern welfare visitor. In 1644 the Archdeacon and Vicars-General ordered that 'N.M., of Santon, shall fit and furnish his wife from Tagart . . . with a suit from top to tow accordinge to his and her . . . eynce and callinge, and this without fayle to be done before tuseday the 12th of December and thereof . . . neighbours (whereof the sumner is to be one) to see that she shall be well used in foode bed and other necessaries. . . .'

Of J.K., of Lonan, it was said in 1714 that his wife had a very uneasy life with him. He was therefore ordered to bring her home and use her civilly or else to allow her son for his care of her, at the discretion of the Court. Otherwise he was to be committed to St. German's by the Sumner or a soldier.

One Pagan marriage custom which survived in Scotland until the eighteenth century was that of Handfasting, or pledging by word and hand—by which an unmarried man and woman made a trial-contract to live together for a year, after which they might separate at the option of either party, or regularise the union by formal marriage.

The Bishop of the Isles presided over an assembly of Highland chiefs at Iona in 1609, which condemned the practice. But it died hard, and in 1772 Pennant wrote that Handfasting had been one of the features of the annual fair in Upper Eskdale. A similar custom existed in Ireland. It is not surprising, therefore, to come across an example of a Manx experimental marriage in 1641, when it is said that 'R.M. and B.C. of Kirk Arbory are presented for being handfasted this whole year and more, and doth not marry.' There is nothing to show that Handfasting was commonly practised in Man after 1600, when the records begin.

One pleasing little wedding custom is revealed in a Kirk Michael presentment of 1735, according to which Adam McBooy had been charged to perform his censure for a breach of the Sabbath. When he appeared at church he was asked by the Sumner if he had come to submit himself, and answered that he had not, 'thus greatly offending the congregation.'

The threat of St. German's speedily produced explanations for his conduct. In a petition asking for forgiveness he said that he was not positively refusing to submit. The sole reason for taking upon himself to choose his own time was that he had been 'bridegroom's man', and, as was usual at such a time, came with the wedding party to church on the following Sunday.

Whether he and the other bridegroom's men carried the willow rods they had borne in the wedding-day procession, to show their dominance over the other sex, does not appear, but, according to Adam, they still wore their festival garments on this second visit; and, as he reasonably suggested, it was too much to expect him, on such an occasion, to endure the mortification of covering up his holiday attire with the sheet of penitence.

COMPURGATION

The Manx Church custom of Compurgation was the subject of much debate during the period in which it was practised. It was the solemn ceremony used when a man wished to prove a debt owed by a deceased person's estate and for which the creditor had 'no bill, bond or other evidence'; or when he wished to clear himself of a charge involving the deceased and had no definite evidence to advance in proof of his innocence.

On the direction of the Spiritual court he repaired to the grave of the dead man, accompanied by witnesses or compurgators prepared to swear to his integrity. He then lay on the grave on his back with an open Bible on his breast and the compurgators kneeling on either side; and he then declared on oath that his claim was just or that he was innocent of the accusation.

The civil power contested the right of the Church to dispose of the case in this way, and in 1609 an Act of Tynwald was passed declaring the illegality of the procedure. But the ecclesiastical judges refused to obey, and the custom continued to be practised until the beginning of the eighteenth century.

One notable instance of its use took place at Peel in 1654, when Mrs. Radcliffe, alias Caesar, wife of Samsbury Radcliffe of Gordon, Captain of Kirk Patrick, appeared at St. Peter's church to swear that she was not guilty of irregularities imputed to her. Six clergymen, including the Vicars-General, were present together with two laymen; and Elizabeth was accompanied by six women compurgators. They swore to her good behaviour and credibility, and she then took an oath that she was guiltless.

Thereupon the author of the charges was tried and sentenced to fourteen days in St. German's prison. After this she was to appear in the white sheet of penitence at every parish church in turn during service time. At each she knelt and placing her finger upon her tongue, said: 'Tongue, thou hast lied!' and then asked forgiveness of the Church and the injured woman. In addition she had to wear the leather 'bridle' on her tongue for an hour at the market crosses of Douglas, Castletown and Peel.

The exceptional severity of the punishment was no doubt due to the fact that the trial took place during the Cromwellian control of the Island, and that sentence was given not by an ecclesiastical judge, but by the Lieut.-Governor, Matthew Cadwell.

PROFANATION OF THE SABBATH

Profanation of the Sabbath was throughout the seventeenth and eighteenth centuries the commonest offence and not easily forgiven. Even the kindly Bishop Hildesley vented his wrath upon an old man of eighty-two caught travelling on a long journey to visit a sick relative. And he himself tells how returning from service at Kirk Michael in 1767 he met a man on horseback with his wife riding pillion. They dismounted and, kneeling by the wayside, asked for his blessing. But the Bishop without, apparently, enquiring the object of their journey, admonished them for their breach of the Sabbath, and sent them on their way unhappy and unblessed.

Breaches of the holy days were very varied in character. Men were presented for grinding snuff; for selling sickles near the Cross at Rushen church; making bee-hives and horn spoons; gathering sand-eels; grinding on the *wherne*; Richard Wilson, the famous master of Peel Mathematical School for travelling, in 1780, on his worldly business with a surveyor's chain on his back; a Ramsey banker, as late as 1808, for digging potatoes in his garden.

In 1737, according to the Chaplain of St. Matthew's, a party of thirteen met on Sunday 'in a disorderly and tumultuous manner at the Nunnery Mill dam to swim, and passed the day there in Idleness and Folly'. They were committed to gaol.

One curious case, foreshadowing the activities of Manxmen in California one hundred and fifty years later, was that of William Caine, of Kirk German, in 1716, who 'worked with his spade and dish upon the Lord's day, seeking gold in *Traie bane* (White Strand)'.

In 1713, an English custom was performed in Lonan, when some people rode the Stang on the Sabbath. The Stang was a pole upon which, when strong feeling was aroused by a wife or husband beater, the culprit was carried in procession. In Lonan it was the wife who was accused of ill-treating her husband. When the case was tried she magnanimously forgave those who had paraded her by proxy.

The transgression of Steven Kneen, of Kirk Andreas, in 1679, has interest apart from the charge. He presented against himself, as a conscientious quest man, 'that coming from the mill at St. John's Chapel upon a Saturday at night, his horses failed by the way, whereby he was so long hindered that 'twas sun-rise on Sunday morning before he got home.' He was excused.

His wearisome journey with creel-laden horses to St. John's was due to the Lord's monopoly of the mills. At that time the Lhen Mooar miln could deal with only a part of Kirk Andreas corn. No other mill could be built in the parish without the Lord's licence, and the unfortunate farmers who owned the rest of the crop had to carry it for grinding, along the ill-kept horse tracks to St. John's and the South.

THE BOOMING TRADE

In the eighteenth century the rapid development of Manx trade with foreign countries, and of contraband traffic, led to an increase in breaches of the Sabbath. In 1738 the Vicar of Kirk Maughold writes that at Ramsey 'the daring wickedness of running Brandy into North Brittain, etc., . . . is continued uncontroulably. . . . Now, of choice, they go abroad on Saturday that they may have a fairer opportunity of securing their loading, while others are retired in a due observance of the day'.

Wine and spirits brought into the Isle paid only a penny per gallon duty, and this fact gave rise to the Booming trade. For when vessels sailing from British ports appeared in the offing, Douglas traders went out in their boom (or 'bum') boats, loaded with liquor, and sold it to the ships at much lower than the English price. The handsome profits were an irresistible temptation, and numbers of prominent merchants, like William Fine and Lewis Geneste, were called to account for opening their cellars and going a-booming instead of attending church.

The barbers and wigmakers were another class of people whose Sabbath activities were sometimes, as a Douglas indictment put it, 'a great offence and scandal to the town.' The best known tradesmen —John Tobin, Roger Lewellin, and Turner Ingoldsby, with half a dozen others—figure more than once in the Courts between 1730 and 1760. The Castletown and Ramsey barbers apparently escaped censure, but there is mention of one Dan Colvin who in 1775 was caught dressing wigs on Sunday in sophisticated Peel.

One pictures the barber's apprentices hurrying through the narrow Douglas streets on a Sunday morning, with dangling wigboxes, on their way to deliver newly-dressed wigs. Soon, well powdered, these will adorn the heads of prosperous citizens sedately walking to Douglas Chapel; or sometimes, if the bridge over the Bright River is in repair, to Kirk Braddan—all models of propriety and outward virtue, despite their connivance in a breach of the Spiritual laws.

Later, when Service has begun and censorious churchwardens are safe indoors, the master barbers issue from their retreats with basins and other implements of their trade, to visit patrons who have disregarded the call of the Chapel bell. This irregular behaviour was considered the more culpable since it happened during Service time.

AMUSEMENTS

Convictions for Sabbath-breaking throw light upon some of the ways in which Manx people amused themselves. Probably the most general recreation—apart from visits to the fairs held several times a year in each parish—was social gatherings of friends and neighbours, for talk, cards, music and dancing, in one another's houses and particularly where there was an ale licence.

Alehouses were patronised by every class, including the clergy, though there was a feeling that they should avoid places where the drinking was often immoderate and led to strife. Bishop Russell's injunction to Manx Clerics in 1350 that they must not 'stand and drink [in inns] beyond a single draught, nor tarry', was echoed at the end of the eighteenth century when it was laid down that a clergyman should stay in an alehouse no longer than his honest necessities required.

The attacks to which a minister's prestige might be exposed in such resorts is shown in the story of Sir Thomas Thwaites, Vicar of Lonan, when he visited a Ballaugh house in 1669, and sat drinking with others who remembered his boyhood on his father's croft in Ballacrosha.

PEEL CASTLE AND CATHEDRAL, 1795

The Chancel, above the Bishop's Prison, was still roofed at this period

'Here's to you, Thautah!' said John Quarke, growing insolent with liquor, and eager to remind him of his modest origins.

Quarke's play on the Vicar's name (which the Manx always found hard to pronounce) and *toot*, the Manx for 'simpleton', aroused the Vicar's anger.

'Sirrah,' he exclaimed, 'hast thou no better manners? Get you out!'

'Do not sirrah me,' Quarke replied, 'for I was born of a woman as well as thee,' and called him a beggar's son and said that he was drunk.

Sir Thomas answered, 'What if I come of never so mean a kindred so as I do well myself?' But he went on to destroy the effect of this just retort by demonstrating his sobriety. Standing on one leg, he took a cup of ale and drank it off. He retained his equilibrium, but lost his dignity.

Violins and viols are the only musical instruments mentioned, and the fiddlers who played at the gatherings generally went in twos and travelled long distances to fulfil engagements.

Playing was strictly forbidden on Sundays and other holy days. The definition of 'Sabbath' varied from time to time. At one period it stretched from sunset on Saturday to Sunday at sunset, or to Monday morning. Saturday evening was always debatable ground and the fear of punishment must have damped the fun of many a social gathering.

In 1780 when Robert Corlett, of Peel, was charged with permitting a puppet showman to exhibit and play his puppets on a Saturday night in his house the Court dismissed the case on proof that the show ended before 10 p.m. John Shimmin, a well-known fiddler of Kirk German, who, after frequently encroaching on the Sabbath limits, disappeared from the Island for some years, on his return in 1723 was immediately clapped into St. German's for his past offences.

Many mills had licences to brew and were often meeting places for young people. In the seventeen-thirties Baldwin Mill more than once came under severe Church censures for entertaining fiddlers and dancers during forbidden times.

In 1799, Richard Daly, an 'emigrant' as newcomers were then styled, was sent to prison on the complaint of Hugh Stowell, Chaplain to St. George's, for playing billiards on Sunday.

The out-of-doors games mentioned most often are bow and arrows, quoits, kit-cat or cat and trap, and nine holes. *Cammag* (spelt *cammack* in the eighteenth century), like bowls, is not often met with; probably because it could not easily be played without detection. Quoits are sometimes given the Scottish name of 'pennystane'. Cricket appears in 1803.

K

One game perhaps imported from Ireland and called 'Throwing the Bullet' was played along the Kirk Malew highways in the early eighteenth century. Each competing team of two was provided with a ball of stone or iron. A course was fixed along a road, and the partners threw their ball alternately and with an underhand movement. The ball was picked up for succeeding throws at the place where it had come to rest. The game was won by the team which completed the course with the smallest number of throws. The danger to passers-by when the 'bullet' was being thrown, must have made it unpopular with the general public.

An unattractive amusement of the same period was the ancient contest of 'Clubbing the Cock'. A live bird was set down and tied to a stake. The players paid the owner of the bird for the right to take turns in throwing at it until it was killed. Presumably the player who threw the killing stone took the cock.

The bird, as in similar games in Scotland, may have been a beaten and injured gamecock. Cockfighting was carried on in the Island, and a Kirk Onchan man was presented in connection with a fight in 1790.

Evidence of duck-baiting—a popular English pastime in the eighteenth and early nineteenth centuries—is also found. A pinioned duck was set loose on a large pond, and dogs were unleashed to catch it, whilst their owners laid wagers on the result. In 1725 three Douglas traders were presented for 'swimming a duck' with a dog on Sunday.

These barbarous sports evoked no protest from the Church, which ignored the bird and concentrated its attention on the people concerned—like the Puritan in Macaulay's much-quoted epigram, who reprobated bear-baiting, not because it gave pain to the bear, but because it gave pleasure to the spectator. The question which the Spiritual Courts asked was whether the killing had taken place on a Holy day.

One Sunday in 1791 a dozen youths with thoughtless cruelty drove and rode a pig to death. The judges expressed disapproval of the destruction of private property, and then, apparently insensitive to the animal's sufferings, directed that the offenders were to attend Douglas Chapel for the chaplain to make them aware of their heinous sin of profaning the Sabbath.

A petition of the same period to the famous Doctor Castley, Master of the Academic School in Castletown, gives a further glimpse of the strange insensitiveness of the average person of the time. The Academic Scholars asked 'that you would be pleased to grant us this day's play, upon account of the fair at Ballasalla, particularly as there is a man to be flogged there, an uncommon sight, which therefore raises up great curiosity to see it. A granting of which shall infinitely oblige your dutiful and loving scholars'.

OPPROBRIUM

The Courts were sympathetic to complaints of abusive or libellous language, and sometimes meted out severe punishment for offences of this kind. In 1714 a woman who called a person of weak intellect, *caillagh holaanagh*, that is, a feeble-minded old woman, was given seven days' imprisonment. When a Douglas merchant, after exchanges in Court, called the parish clerk of Kirk Michael a blockhead, he was immediately committed to St. German's.

The use of animals' names as opprobrious epithets was banned by the Church. The Spiritual Statutes singled out 'dog', in particular, and prescribed as punishment for its misuse the wearing of the bridle at the Cross or seven days' penance. But in spite of the Church's frown, or perhaps partly because it was forbidden, 'dog' has remained almost the only animal name commonly used by the Manx in a derogatory sense—as in the phrase, 'a hard dog.'

In Jurby the word 'porpoise' was used in *screbbin gy perkin*: 'a scabby porpoise', and a girl in 1742 called her red-haired rival, *muck jiarg*: 'a red pig'. But such epithets are rare. 'Donkey' is never used, probably because the animal was a stranger here until modern times. In 1803, however, the Vicar of Kirk Conchan was presented for calling a troublesome parishioner, 'a mule,' which, like 'donkey', was an exotic name in Man.

Smaller creatures like the *carnoain*, a beetle, sometimes provided words of contempt. A Kirk Arbory woman called her victim a 'grub'. 'Thou *caillagh ny growag!*' she cried. 'Thou grub of an old woman, and of the grubby kind didst thou come!'

In 1757 J.K., of Kirk Braddan, called his neighbour a *sniegan*, the Manx word for 'ant'. The Chapter Court, remembering favourable Biblical comment on the little insect's activities, solemnly declared that *sniegan* was 'a word of no great scandal', and dismissed the case.

THE END OF DISCIPLINE

As time went on there appears to have been some amelioration in the conditions of confinement at St. German's. According to Waldron, who wrote in the first quarter of the eighteenth century, the Peel garrison soldiers of his time were accustomed, out of compassion, to give the prisoners more tolerable quarters in the Castle.

A case recorded in the Kirk German parish register also suggests that chosen offenders were allowed a limited freedom of movement outside St. Patrick's Isle. In 1742, there is an entry concerning 'Mr. John Nicholson from Dublin, being here under confinement, but had the libberty of the town. . . .'

After the death in 1772 of Bishop Wilson's successor, Mark Hildesley, there was a rapid decline in the activities of the disciplinary courts, and an increasing number of blank parish presentment sheets handed in to the Registrars. In 1799, Paul Crebbin, Vicar of Kirk Santan, with a levity which would have shocked the Vicars-General of an earlier age, wrote across his return, 'Churchwardens in abundance, but no presentments!'

The Dungeon was used as a prison for the last time in 1780, but the Spiritual Courts exercised powers of committal to the civil prison in Castle Rushen and of excommunication until 1825.

After that date no further cases are recorded, and the system of penance by coercion which John Wyclif, more than four hundred years before, had declared to be wrong and anti-Christian, came to a belated and unregretted end.

XII

THE GREAT ENQUEST

The Sheading Jury known as the *Bing Vooar* or Great Enquest, played a notable part in the regulation of many activities in Manx social and economic life and—as Mr. R. B. Moore points out in his learned and fascinating paper on Juries in the Isle of Man[1]—so far as its juridical functions were concerned, was in importance second only to the Twenty-four themselves.

It consisted of twelve men drawn equally from the parishes of the sheading, and sworn in before the Deemster at a Sheading Court. Its term of office lasted six months, at the end of which a new jury was chosen to take its place. The insular ecclesiastical Baronies—Bangor and Sabal, St. Trinian and St. Bees, the Bishop's Barony and the Abbey of Rushen—had each its own Great Enquest; and when a dispute involved the interests both of the Lord of the Isle and a Baron, a combined Grand Enquest of twenty-four was called together.

When the verdict of a Great Enquest was disputed and a newly appointed Enquest came to the same decision as its predecessor, this was held to be conclusive. If on the other hand, the Enquests disagreed, a Grand or Long Jury of twenty-four was selected from the Sheadings nearest the scene of the dispute, to examine into the matter and report to the Court.

A person desiring an enquiry into loss by robbery, etc., made the gesture known as the *Laue my hooit*—'the hand of my suit,' or handsuit—in which he formally gave his hand to the Coroner, as an assurance that he, the plaintiff, would pursue the case. The Coroner then applied to the Deemster for a warrant authorising him to summon the jury. Until 1770 the warrant took the form of a token made of a small piece of thin flat slate, on which the Deemster had scratched his initials; and the ease with which a forged token of this primitive kind could be used to impose on illiterate country people occasionally led to abuses.

In one ancient version of the oath taken by the Enquest there is a curious intrusion of the phrase, *corp ny kimmagh*: 'the body of the

[1] *Proc. N.H.A.S.*, Vol. V.

offender'; as though that, too, was sworn upon. This is reminiscent of an incident which occurred in the seventeenth century, involving the usual reluctance of Manx jurors to arrive at a verdict entailing capital punishment. When a Jury of Life and Death passed upon felons at the Court of General Gaol Delivery in 1688, they acquitted two of the prisoners against the evidence, and were immediately fined and committed to Castle Rushen.

They hastened to petition Governor Heywood for release and forgiveness. They blamed, as they said,

> 'their ignorance and shallow understanding. Now your poor petitioners do humbly make bould to offer to your worshipps consideration that it was not through any wilfulness or partiality that they proceeded . . . but had been led aside by the notion of a customary law which the vulgar sort of people in this Isle do pretend to set up in matters of the nature; that is to say, that no fellon is to be condemned unless the witnesses do positively swear upon his hands flesh and bones.'

The field of enquiry with which the Great Enquest had to concern itself was extensive and varied. It was its duty to present people who, as an alternative to drastic punishment, had agreed to depart from the Isle and had returned without permission; to enquire into the way in which the Sheading officials—Coroner, Lockmen and Moars —and the Forester and Water Bailiff's deputy, performed their duties; to examine charges of inefficiency against millers, weavers, shoemakers and other craftsmen; to present poachers of deer and other game in the Lord's Forest and Warrens, and of salmon in the bays and rivers.

Among other subjects of investigation were the burning of ling, gorse and turf on the hills; the concealment of felons; the keeping of diseased horses; the unlicensed export of wool and cattle; the operations of alien pedlars; the fencing of the mountain commons; the taking of wreckage; misuse of the turf lands; the rotting of flax in running water; the maintenance of fairgrounds, markets and pinfolds.

BOUNDARIES AND ENCLOSURES

But in the first half of the eighteenth century the Enquest was more and more engaged with the definition of land boundaries, and the examination of new licences to enclose portions of the commons. The greatly increased interest in the land sprang directly from the land settlement of 1703, agreed upon by the Lord of the Isle and the representatives of the Manx people.

For generations the landowners, great and small, had been threatened by the loss of their ancient rights and the conversion of their property into leasehold. The 1703 agreement, often called the 'Manx Magna Carta', put an end to the attempt initiated by the Great Earl, seventy years before, to reduce the independent farmers and crofters to tenants on sufferance.

When the danger was past, a demand at once arose for more acres; and in the next fifty years thousands of licences were granted to applicants wishing to enclose unoccupied land adjoining their holdings—mainly in the hills, though waste land was to be found elsewhere, in the lowlands and in Douglas and the other towns. A licence did not become effective until it had received the approval of the Great Enquest, which heard witnesses, inspected the projected enclosure, and was satisfied that the grant did not interfere with rights of way, water and access to turf ground.

Until the beginning of the eighteenth century the enclosures did not arouse much attention. They were usually small in size and made no very appreciable reduction of the mountain grazing grounds on which the people had right to pasture cattle, sheep, goats and pigs. But alien adventurers appeared on the scene. The Maguires of Dublin and a Liverpool alderman named Poole, prevailed upon the Governor to issue licences for the enclosure of great stretches of mountain.

In Santan where Maguire was given land extending north to Ashole, now known as the Mount, the grant violated the rights of many farmers who were cut off from access to their turbaries. When they protested, their petition for an Enquest was rejected and twenty-five landowners who used forbidden ways to the turf grounds were cast into prison. In 1723 when the same speculators acquired a great strip of mountain land between Eary Kelly—now called Druidale—and Slieu Dhoo, which deprived the Ballaugh men of their rights of pasture, the angry countrymen assembled with staves, and bloodshed was narrowly avoided.

The new enthusiasm for land acquisition and cultivation gave value to land hitherto thought lightly of, and frequently sold on easy terms. In the seventeenth century, for example, Kelly of Raby in Kirk Lonan parted with the land called the Grenanes for three pounds sterling and a quart (i.e. two pounds) of wool. There were, too, numerous areas of uncultivated ground, particularly in the little glens forming natural farm boundaries, where there was no definite dividing line.

It was a common statement in such cases for a witness to say that in past times he or his father had seen the animals of the farms adjacent to a glen feeding in it *fud y chelley*, that is indiscriminately. But this was only one aspect of the problems produced by the fact that much of the land was unfenced. As late as 1770 it was said of

Jurby that 'few or no good fences have been erected there, save only temporary fences which are . . . made up in the summer to keep each neighbour harmless; in so much that the same hath been until late always open commons in the winter to pass and repass on each other as their occasions require'.

The land around Douglas was without hedges as late as 1730. In a dispute over a right of way through the Hills and Ballaquayle to Tromode Mill it was stated that horses and cattle had freely used the way, since there were no stiles or fences of any sort to obstruct their movement.

There were of course some enclosures permanently hedged in the fifteenth century; and, in 1583, an order issued by the Deputy (Governor) and Council made it lawful for a landowner to put up permanent fences. He was also protected from any action for damages his neighbours might take for loss of common pasturage during the winter months.

The growth of permanent hedging was, however, very slow, and until well into the eighteenth century, the fences usually to be seen in many parts of the Island were those of the temporary folds, which were surrounded by a low and unsubstantial hedge only one sod thick and topped with branches of gorse. In them the farm animals were confined for short periods during the summer months, the temporary fences being thrown down in the autumn. Permanent fencing in a neighbourhood often began with a fenced *loan* or lane by or through several estates, along which animals could be driven without fear of damage to the unenclosed fields nearby.

Sometimes a *loan* of ancient formation was so wide that its stretches of grass provided food for a poor man's cow. In 1697, a woman, resisting an attempt to evict her from such a grazing ground near Kentraugh, and pleading that it was rented ground, and therefore could not be granted by licence, said to Governor Sankey that her mother had paid a half-penny or penny rent out of grazing it. The Governor's reply was eloquent of his character. 'And what cares my Lord Derby about your halfpenny or penny rent?' he said with contempt.

LANDMARKS

Among the difficulties confronting a Great Enquest summoned to settle a boundary dispute was the absence of plans. In the last half of the eighteenth century a number of schoolmasters appeared who were expert in land-surveying. But by the end of the century the cultivable area of the Island was permanently fenced, and surveyors had no longer to deal with the vague outlines of inadequately marked open fields.

Where hedges were missing, streams, rocks, stones and trees were useful landmarks; though trees disappeared with the passing of time. And when, as in 1721, a Ballaugh boundary in Glion Voirrey was fixed by reference to 'a thorn tree in the middle of the bank on the Carmodil side, now fallen', the decision of the Enquest must, sometimes, have left doubts behind it. Stones, among the commonest marks used, were occasionally moved by unscrupulous people; and a boundary strip of grass or *skeem*, customarily up to six feet in width, was at the mercy of the neighbour's plough. In 1793, when Bishop Crigan issued directions for suitable prayers to be used in the long neglected parish perambulations, there was still a practical application for the curse which he included in the service: 'Cursed be he that removeth his neighbour's landmark.'

The large white boulders of quartz, relics of the glacial age, served admirably as marks. Such a one is mentioned in 1715, when the Enquest defined the boundary of Ballacarnane, and Ballana in Kirk Michael, and a witness walked the dividing line down past the Spooyt Vane to a big white stone in Glen Beast, 'where', he said, 'a man might stand on Ballaleigh, Ballana and Ballagranane, and join hands over the stone.'

In 1645 the famous Illiam Dhone, owner of Ronaldsway, had a dispute with Christopher Kennish of Arragon Beg, concerning their boundary by the Santan Burn. Kennish violently opposed the Receiver when he attempted to walk on the Arragon, or east side ('in the opening of the gill coming up to the Broo Vollagh where the thorn tree is now,' said a witness in 1722). Illiam refused to be driven back by the owner of Arragon, and marched down the east side of the Burn to a rock with a hole in it. There the Enquest took the depositions of witnesses, and decided against Christopher, recording that the boundary was on the height on the Arragon side of the stream, and then down to the holed rock which also marked the limit of Santan and Malew.

SWEARING

In stating their case to the Enquest the contending parties depended largely on the testimony of those with the longest knowledge of the place of dispute. 'Costain tracked no way before us by any ancients,' said one Great Enquest in rejecting a claim. Hearsay evidence was not rejected, and the demeanour of the old people—whether they showed hesitation or doubt—was closely watched by the jurymen. The witnesses gave their evidence on oath. 'They walked before the Enquest,' as the phrase was, treading where they asserted the way ran; and knelt before Coroner and Quest to swear that they had spoken truth.

When an important point in the track was reached the witness fixed the attention of the Jury upon it by touching it. Pointing was not enough. A witness walking along the alleged *mere* or boundary of the Nunnery and Ballakermeen in 1670, came to a prominent bush, beat it vigorously with his stick and declared that it marked the end of the junction between the two properties. In Kirk Bride in 1721, when Ewan Christian of Ballaghenny wished to disclaim responsibility for a drain which was near but outside his land, he walked with his son and heir Donald to the boundary hedge in the Loughan Vooar. There they pressed their breasts against the hedge and swore that none of their ground lay beyond it.

Now and then an unscrupulous witness tried to ease his fears of the supernatural consequences of perjury by a pretence of telling the truth. In 1680, C. owned a farm on the Santan Burn. He laid claim to a *claddagh* or meadow on the Malew side of the stream, which he said was part of Santan; and duly walking before the Great Enquest, swore that, in tracing the boundary of the *claddagh*, he had been walking on Santan soil. He was granted the meadow; but, after his death forty years later, it was divulged that he had put Kirk Santan soil into his shoes, and so, in his perambulation before the jury, was literally standing on the earth of that parish.

This was not the only predatory exploit of C., for he was said to have done much wrong to Cooill Cam; and would have done more, said William Harrison, but the three Fargher brothers of Cooill Cam came with sticks to oppose him, and beat him back again over the river. A story of the same shoe and soil trickery has been handed down in Jurby.

The report of an enquiry, held in 1733 to determine the Braddan and Santan boundary, is full of interest. At that time the Crogga stream was called the Awin Argid—the Silverburn—and John Kneale, a 'very ancient man' known as the 'Bishop of Santan', accounted for the name with a story of buried treasure. The boundary followed the stream to its source on the flank of Ashole or Anjole, now the Mount. John Moore of Ballnahown told how when a boy he had taken part in a parish perambulation of the boundary, but was not sure of it at the north end; for near Ashole he went in quest of a hare with other lads and so did not see the end of the perambulation; and he and his companions were admonished by the Vicar, John Cosnahan.

Great rivalry existed between the two parishes. Thomas Oates of Santan when a boy had been warned by his father not to cross the river to pull ling, for if he did, it would be taken from him by the Braddan men. And an amusing story was told of Kneale, Ballacostain and John Stephan of Braddan working together in the Curragh Cutchal near Knock na Shawk (Hill of the Hawk); and how when they left off work to rest themselves they went a-trouting; and Kneale would not let Stephan fish on the Santan side of the stream, nor would Stephan let Kneale fish from the Braddan bank.

Before Isaac Barrow came in 1663 to strengthen the discipline of his diocese, pre-Reformation customs still survived along the banks of the Silverburn. On Sundays, after the last service of the day, the young people of the two parishes met at the Aah Meanagh—the Middle Ford—near Knock na Shawk, and had competitions in archery; and there were games and dancing.

HIGHWAYS

In this present age of excellent roads it is difficult for us to picture the state of the main roads during the time of which we are speaking, and the difficulties of transport. Until the eighteenth century was well on its way, the chief highways remained as they had always been, uneven grassy tracks, for the most part unusable by wheeled traffic. And the secondary public ways were often so little distinguishable from the ground through which they wandered, that Enquests were called from time to time to define them.

It is hard for anyone going nowadays along the fine wide road running from the Bayr ne Creggey (the Craige road) through Jurby past Sandy Gate and Ballamoar to Ballaugh, to imagine it so obscure that a Great Enquest was called in 1726 to trace its course, and the mistress of Ballahasna tried to stop travellers journeying on it, on the ground that there was no road and no right of way past the farm.

It was not until the end of the seventeenth century that there was a systematic attempt to make the main public ways tolerably safe for travellers. The orders issued implicitly reveal their defects. They were to be at least twelve feet wide, with trenches to drain them. Where they had been encroached upon by building or enclosing part of the way, the offending buildings were to be demolished. Punishment was prescribed for those who made the grass-covered roads dangerous by cutting sods and placing heaps of rubbish on them.

A Sheading Court of Glenfaba was held at Peeltown in 1682 'to consider', it was said, 'of the many complaints made touching the uneasiness and unpassableness of the highway betwixt this town of Peel and the town of Douglas, both for ridinge and carriage of goodes, both on horseback and by draught, which is very obnoxious and obstructive to traidinge and the general good of the country.'

The Captains of Kirk German and Kirk Marown were therefore ordered to bring their parish militia companies to Lag y Vollagh [where the telephone kiosk stands today], the boundary of the two parishes. Here, under Greeba, rocks were broken and removed, and the ground levelled for the passage of riders, horse carriage and draught by sledge, and if need be—a rather unlikely event—by cart. From Greeba the Kirk German company worked back to Peel under the supervision of the Constable of Peel Castle, whilst the Kirk Marown men moved towards Douglas, directed by the Captain of that town.

The parish companies addressed themselves to road-making in no very cheerful mood. They got no pay, there is no mention of a food allowance, and fines and punishment were promised for those who failed to attend the muster.

With the improvement of roads after the passing in 1712 of a Highways Act, which provided for regular repairs and highway surveyors, wheeled vehicles gradually came into use, though much remained to be done to make travelling on the roads reasonably safe.

In 1770 a petition from farmers of Michael and German complained that the highroad through Baaregarrow and Cronk y Voddy was in several parts so steep and unsafe 'that it is with great difficulty that any cart or wheel-carriage can pass or repass on the road'; and they offered to give land and do the hedging or ditching of a newly planned road at twopence a Manx yard ($37\frac{1}{2}$ inches). Even as late as 1811 an offender, summoned to appear before an ecclesiastical court at St. John's Chapel, made a successful excuse for his non-appearance by pleading the depth and danger of the way from Douglas.

TRANSPORT

The earliest method of transport, and a very common one during the seventeenth and eighteenth centuries, was carriage on a man's back. Even last century men and women with full creels slung from their shoulders would set off from the North side before daylight, and crossing the mountains, drop down Baldwin to Douglas market; and later in the day, their produce sold, they walked up the long valley to Injebreck and re-crossed the hills for home.

Goods were also carried on horseback in creels fastened to a pegged saddle called a 'straddle'. Hay was made into long packs slung on either side of the straddle, and big enough to hide the tough little Manx horse between them. Four ropes or straps were used to a pack, with a fifth to secure it to the harness. It was for this kind of work that horses were mainly kept, oxen being employed for ploughing.

Horses offered to land travellers the only alternative to walking. Every farmer owned a riding horse which carried him to church, market, to the sheading court and to musters of the parish companies; and his wife on her journeys from home sat behind him on a straw-stuffed *pollan* or pillion.

Before roads became good enough for wheels, the trail-car and the *carr* or sledge were used for drawing goods. The trail-car was made of two poles placed parallel and four feet apart with cross planks to form a platform. The poles at one end made shafts for a draught animal, the other ends of the poles trailed on the ground. When in use the platform was on the slant and the cargo carried had to be secured with ropes. The *carr* was a sledge on runners with a box or flat platform. In the early period of the use of wheels instead of runners it was called a 'wheel-car'. In 1759 there is the rare mention of a horse-litter, used for the bringing home of Edward Christian, Lewage, drowned in flood-time at a ford of the Santan Burn.

RIGHTS OF WAY

Three hundred years ago the passionate desire, which nowadays drives people out from the towns and from the social and architectural tedium of the suburbs into the by-ways to savour the delights of the countryside, had not yet been born. The Manx towns were very small, the houses were interspersed among gardens and un-rented pieces of ground, and merged insensibly into the open fields.

Even when rapidly growing trade between Man and foreign parts caused a demand in Douglas for more houses which blotted out the gardens and unoccupied land, the townspeople were not completely divorced from the sights and sounds of the country. Cattle lowed in cow-houses, and pigs grunting and rooting in the lanes brought fines upon their careless owners, and poultry fled before the feet of the passers-by.

In Castletown, in 1694, an ill-balanced party of three drakes and a duck, belonging to Governor Sacheverell, waddled from his lodgings at the Bagnio House in Arbory Street into the market place, and shared the meal given by Mrs. Halsall to her birds. Then they disappeared. Mary, Mrs. Harley's maid, said that her mistress had enticed them into her house near the Cross by throwing corn at the door, but later she confessed that she alone was responsible and had killed and cooked a drake. A witness testified to the great outcry that arose at the Bagnio when the Governor found that one of his precious flock was missing; and one sees in his firm signature appended to the order sending Mary to the whipping post that in his righteous indignation he had allowed his feelings as a duck-lover to blot out the calm impartiality of a judge.

PATHWAYS

Owing to the bad condition of the high roads the lesser pathways, which were often much more easy to negotiate than the main thoroughfares, assumed a great importance in the life of the community, and were often the subject of enquiry by the Sheading Quest. They covered the countryside with a network of communication lines, which were, however, limited generally to use by particular groups of people and for specific purposes.

A landowner cut off from the high road or *raad mooar* by another man's land could claim a right of way across it, on condition that he had no way to the *raad mooar* on his own land; and that the wanted path was the nearest route and did no harm to his neighbour. The need for provisions of this kind is evident from the petition of a crofter who went to live at Croit y Crowe in Ballachrink, Jurby, in 1738, and found that he was completely cut off from a public road. Asking for an Enquest he made great play of the fact that his only established right of way was a burial way, along which, he predicted, he and his family would be carried before long, if they were to be imprisoned on the croft.

There was a great diversity in the rights conceded to applicants, the chief being ways to church, mill, market, water, mountain and sea. The church ways which according to their use were also known as christening, marriage, and burial or corse ways, have survived longest in memory, but in the present century most of them have gone out of use and been forgotten.

There was a wide-spread but erroneous belief that a track, once followed by a burial, became a legal right of way. In 1740 Pat Howland of Knock Orley in Bride fell into dispute with John Christian of Ballakey who claimed a way across Knock Orley, saying it was a church way which had been used for burials. The Great Enquest, however, disallowed the claim, pointing out that Ballakey came to the highway, and that there was no great inconvenience for Christian to go there on his own land. Special church ways, known as Visitation ways, were allowed to the clergy going about on their parochial calls, and were never disputed by the landowners.

Along the mountain ways cattle, sheep, pigs and goats were driven to and from the hill pastures; and turf and ling were brought down on horses' backs. One Ramsey turf road ran from the neighbourhood of the present-day electric station up the *lhergy* of Ballacowle and on until it reached the fell-dyke or mountain hedge. A man occupied in carrying turf in 1720 from Barrule to Ramsey by way of Lhergy Ballure was able to make four journeys a day with his creel-horses, receiving twopence a load for his labours.

Port and strand ways were used for the carriage of fish and wrack, the sea-weed being spread on the land as fertiliser. A limestone way through Clucas's ground at Port St. Mary enabled farmers to draw the stone; and in many other places on the coast, limestone pebbles were carried away to be burnt in the numerous little kilns which sprang up in the eighteenth century, when the importance of liming fields had been realised.

THE USE OF RIGHTS OF WAY

Most ways could be used all the year, some only during the summer months, others in winter; some only in frosty weather between Michaelmas and Lady Day; others when an alternative route was deep in mud. Quine of Ballaleaney in Kirk Lonan claimed two separate ways on Kneale's land—one to mill and market, the other to church. The Enquest directed that he was to go on his own land from March to November, and on Kneale's land from November to March. Kelly of Kirk Patrick had the liberty of driving his cattle through neighbours' land to the shore on a fine day, to feed on seaweed.

Karran of Creg Lea in the same parish was granted a wrack way and the right to draw wrack from the harbour of Port Massoule (now Niarbyl Bay), with two horses yearly. In 1725 it was said that the usual harbour way to Port Soderick, which ran through Ballamona and Ballashemark, was a common driving way in the winter half, but only a horse by the halter in summer.

BREADTH OF WAY

The breadth of the way was adjusted to the kind of traffic permitted. A Kirk Santan track starting at Kiondroghad 'and on by the top part of William Bridson's hedge in Ballaquiggin, was of such a breadth that Quaye of Ballcregga might lawfully pass with a boll of corn on horseback'. In return Quaye had to keep the way in repair and provide any necessary 'shutts' or gates.

A path two yards wide was considered sufficient for the passage of a horse with a *carr*—either sledge or trail-car—or with a pack. Some paths were known as leading ways: tracks through open fields, along which one horse at a time must be led. Thus a Malew path was ordered to be for church and mill and a horse by the head. When there were several horses crossing his land at Ballalough, Thomas Craine of Boollie Cleay in Kirk German, made the owner tie them head to tail in a string, before allowing them to pass, and thus prevented them from feeding on his grass or corn.

A driving way on a neighbour's land was generally given on condition that the users hedged it so that the driven animals would not be able to trespass on the open fields. By a law of 1577 such a road was to be eighteen feet wide. This was a more generous width than the generality of highroads possessed, and the juries were not always disposed to grant it. An example of the Quest's reasonableness is found in 1694, when Cannon of Ballana asked for a leading and driving way to the mountains. 'Though', they said, 'the statute orders the like way to be eighteen feet broad, yet in our consciences we think ten feet sufficient, and so do allow it to be, this being the next way and least hurtful we could get through Quayle's land.'

Where the driving way was not hedged in special precautions were to be taken. In 1658, for example, when the springs of Ballastole were dried up in the summer, Nicholas Christian was permitted to drive his cattle to a watering place in the Ballure river, on condition that he provided two cattle herds to prevent the animals from damaging crops in the open fields of Christian, Ballure.

Sometimes when no legal right of passage existed the privilege was paid for. In Jurby, in 1711, Jony Birrag, a cottager on the West Nappin, gave yearly to Mylecharaine of the Doologh the spinning of a pound of hemp, for permission to pass to the Curraghs; and Ballaugh farmers crossing Ballakinnag to the shore to get limestones paid a yearly fee to the owner of the land.

Rights of passage with animals were restricted to the farmer of the quarterland, the occupants of any cottages on the estate being forbidden use of the way. The reason for this was that in spite of the very limited amount of grazing at their disposal the small agriculturists persisted in keeping more animals than they were able to feed, and were tempted to drive them slowly along the trackways, grazing them on their neighbour's ground as they went.

This practice became so common that in 1676 Tynwald set up a Fodder Jury of four in every parish to examine into the amount of live stock kept by the farmers, but especially by the crofters and other small landowners. The jury had power to sell an animal which the owner's ground could not support.

PINPOUNDS

The numerous unenclosed fields made trespass easy and in the summertime sheep and cattle herds, often children, were regularly employed by the farmers. The unsubstantial fences of the temporary folds or *booilltyn* offered feeble resistance to hungry animals in search of green pasture, and much irritation was caused when they escaped to feast on a neighbour's crops.

One trespass for which the countrymen had no redress came from the Lord's deer which descended from the hills to feed in the fields

GROUDLE MILL

From a painting by J. M. Nicholson, 1875

of the unfortunate farmers; and, according to feudal custom, had a free run for six weeks every year. One can sympathise with Quilliam of Kirk Patrick, who in 1714, saw a great stag and five other deer standing in the middle of his corn, and shot at them with his musket, wounding the stag. He was imprisoned and heavily fined for his offence.

As time went on deer poachers and neglectful Lord's foresters rid the farmers of this particular annoyance. The deer herds were reported to be very much decayed in 1696, and in the next century they disappeared. A greater trouble was trespass by animals put out to graze on the hill commons and escaping by way of unrepaired gaps in the fell-dyke; or those wandering from their folds or guardians on the lowland farms.

The parish pinfold was therefore an essential feature of country life of the period. The Lezayre pound of the seventeenth century was typical. A rectangular walled enclosure, it was forty-two yards in circumference, each of the forty-two quarterland farms having the building and upkeep of one yard of the wall. The lesser landholders— the crofters and intackholders—were responsible for the door and lock. The keeper of the pinfold or pinder was appointed by the parish captain and four men of the Great Enquest, and received half of the fees.

Much bad feeling was produced among the people concerned, and attempts at rescue were sometimes made, as strayed animals were being driven to the pound. Robert Cottiam of the Renabb described in 1716 how he saw Margaret Cashin approaching a Kirk Lonan pinfold with ten strayed cattle; and their owner, a farmer's wife Katrine, 'sitting on the side of the pinfould door, having a stick in her hand, striking at the other side of the door, and swore that the Divil a wan of her goods should go into the pinfould this night.' And Katrine had her way, though a subsequent fine in addition to the pounding fee dimmed the pleasure of her victory.

DISPUTES

The disputes which took place over questions of boundaries, pathways, etc., were not always conducted peacefully. The Nunnery Lake, the flat land, behind and including, the present timber yard and railway station, was claimed by the Nunnery, though said by Moore of Pulrose and others to be unoccupied land. In 1660, the servants of Hugh Moore, the Water Bailiff, came to the Lake to dig clay for mortar, and to cut the long thin sods called *scraghyn* for roofing under the thatch. The servants were driven off, upon which Moore came alone, and Margaret Calcott, the mistress of the Nunnery, sent

L

her nephew Richard to deal with the intruder. A fight took place on the river bank, in which the Water Bailiff was defeated; and, bruised and bleeding, made an ignominious retreat to Pulrose.

In 1740 Dan Cowin of Lanjaghan sought a church way through the Abbey Lands. When, however, 'the old woman of Lanjaghan', as a witness described her, came riding down the valley to church she was stopped by Thomas Lewn of Ballacreetch. In the argument that followed she fell from the horse, and was hurt. Lewn was apparently considered to blame for the mishap, and was called upon to beg her pardon in the presence of Bishop Wilson, 'seeing', to quote the account, 'it was Sunday when the incident occurred', and he therefore came under the Canon Law.

One of the liveliest battles occurred in Lezayre in 1738, between Arthur Cowle of the Kella Beg and the owner of Ballabrooie. Cowle, like his opponent, was a man of lively aggressive temper, and ten years later was engaged in a right of way squabble with an Englishman named Drake living in the Kella Mooar. Drake and a female companion drove over the disputed road in a one-horse shay (chaise) —perhaps the earliest Manx reference to this light vehicle, and a sign of improving roads. Cowle blocked the way and seized the horse's bridle, the shay overturned, and the occupants were thrown out. Cowle denied being the cause of the accident, and in felicitous language declared that, on the contrary, the shay horse 'went quietly and calmly, with jollity, and a seeming good composure of mind'.

Cowle's dispute with Ballabrooie sprang from his construction of a dam for his Kella mill. The owner of Ballabrooie appeared on the scene with his son and menservants, and started to break down the dam bank. When Cowle advanced along it his opponent splashed him with water and he retreated. But his wife, a worthy descendant of the women who saved the day at Santwat, cried out, 'Stone the ould thief! He should be cut off from Church and Churchyard!' and entered the battle, part of which was fought waist-deep in the water.

Meanwhile the Amazon's obedient husband had floored his chief enemy with a stone, and was soon engaged in combat with the Ballabrooie's son who was armed with a spade handle. The menservants appear to have watched the antics of their infuriated employers with the detachment one might expect from men enjoying a meagre wage of thirty or forty shillings a year; and they only intervened when the fighting tended to become really dangerous.

The four principals, all badly damaged, appealed for redress, and were fined equal amounts by the impartial court; though Cowle had, in addition, to pay for the cure of the Ballabrooie's broken head.

MILLS

Mills and millers played an important part in the Manx country-side, and were often the objects of the Enquest's consideration. By law only those mills licensed by the Lord and paying his dues were allowed to function. Every landowner was assigned and said to be tenant to a particular mill, and could not legally have his corn ground elsewhere; though sometimes influential farmers found a way to escape this restriction.

In ancient times, for example, the farms of Balladoole and Balla-cagen were attached for grinding to Grenaby mill, having a mill-way which passed through Bymaccan (Ballanorris and the Friary) Balla-maddrell and Ballavarkish. The way was said to be long and vile; and so the owners of the two farms bought Knock a Vullen, a piece of ground near Grenaby, and gave it to the miller, in place of the fees due to him.

Thereafter the two farms could grind where they pleased, and Balladoole got a licence for a mill of its own. In 1697 old William Maddrell of Ballamaddrell, giving evidence relating to the history of the Balladoole mill, drew a pleasing picture of the social ease of inter-course which existed and the simple jokes that gave them pleasure when the countrymen met at the mill to talk and to drink cups of the miller's home-brewed ale. 'Sometimes', said William, 'in company with old Major Stevenson, Richard Kneale, William Kneale and others, in the house of old Ewan Hingley (he was eighty-five), and being merrily disposed, one of the company called Ewan "Miller", by reason he was miller of Balladoole Mill. But with a twinkle in his eye the old man replied, "I am not the miller, but my Master, the Major here, that pays a shilling a year Lord's rent out of the mill." '

MULCTURE

The anxiety shown by the Lord's officers and millers in seeing that the tenants attached to a mill should bring their corn to it, arose from the fact that the miller received one-twenty-fourth of the grind in payment for his services. The miller's *foilliu* or mulcture was an enduring object of the farmers' suspicions. Yearly every miller took an oath to deal justly with his customers, but this act did not banish doubts bred by a long tradition attributing shady practices to him. And indeed a number of cases in the records suggests that there was sometimes reason for suspicion.

There was the extraordinary behaviour of the miller of Mullen Oates, Kirk Braddan, in 1733. Grain and meal were measured with a government-stamped *kishan*—a wooden measure holding eight quarts. When taking mulcture, the miller of Mullen Oates had his sealed *kishan* standing in a larger one; and when the sealed *kishan* was filled he stroked the overplus above the rim so that it fell into the large *kishan*. He then poured the contents of the sealed *kishan* into the large one which he kept. He thus got not only his lawful share but also the amount heaped above the rim.

In 1738, Henry Taylor's little boy was sent to Colby mill with corn to grind, and on his return said to his aunt, 'Aunt, the miller took *foilliu* of the wheat three times!' upon which the aunt, almost struck dumb by such perfidy, is reported to have cried, 'How, child?' and thereafter lapsed into dazed silence. It is a story which suggests that there may have been good grounds for the traditional tale of the Blackbird of Baldwin mill.[1]

Long ago the miller of a Baldwin mill, going to Douglas on business, left orders with his son to take the *foilliu* from flour ground for Awhallan. When the father returned he went to the Awhallan sacks and, eyeing them covetously, easily persuaded himself that his twenty-fourth share had not been taken. He thereupon began to measure it off again.

Then he heard a *lhondoo* or blackbird which had suddenly appeared and alighted on a trammon-tree branch overhanging the mill door. Its song was so loud and insistent that he paused to listen, and, to his amazement found that the bird was not only singing in Manx— everybody knew the *lhondoo* could do that—but that the song was about himself.

Vel oo cheet, vel oo cheet? 'Art thou coming, art thou coming?' it was crying to its mate.

Jeeagh er y myllar, jeeagh er y myllar! 'Look, look on the miller!'

> *Ta'n myllar ny Boaldin drogh mitchoor,*
> *T'eh'n maarliagh smoo er ooilley'n ooir.*
> *Daa cheayrt y goaill eh jeh'n foilliu,*
> *Ta mee ginsh Awhallan er my loo!*
> *Ta mee ginsh, ta mee ginsh,*
> *Ta mee ginsh Awhallan er my loo!*

> 'The miller of Baldwin is a bad rascal,
> He is the biggest thief on the earth.
> He is taking the *foilliu* twice,
> I shall tell Awhallan, on my oath!
> I shall tell, I shall tell!'

So deeply was the miller's conscience smitten by his interpretation of the blackbird's song that he immediately put back what he had

---

[1] Collected by Mr. W. Cubbon.

taken from the Awhallan sacks; and for months afterwards was engaged in surreptitiously restoring to mill tenants some of the flour and grain of which he had plundered them in former times.

In 1723 the miller of Ballasalla was punished for taking one-sixteenth of the grind as his perquisite—fifty per cent more than the legal amount—and he was also presented for doing bad grinding which produced *groblagh* or lumpy half-ground meal. The evidence in this and other cases makes it clear that people bringing corn to the mills generally looked after the grinding themselves, after the miller had set the millstone to what was called the right tune. The amounts of corn brought by the least prosperous of the country people were often of small bulk, corresponding to the daily grinding done on the quern or hand-mill, and were symptomatic of an impoverished countryside, visited from time to time with stark famine.

A Maughold jury in 1696 heard the story of how the *fer-thie*, 'the man of the house', was sick; and how he died, while his mother and the maid were threshing sheaves with flails to get food for the cattle and his wife had gone to Cornaa mill, to grind a little corn for the day's bread.

The mills were scarcely ever adequate to the demands thrust upon them, and much hardship was thus caused to country people, who were entirely dependent upon the flour made from their own grain. When the position became unbearable permission was usually given to a tenant to take his corn to another mill free to handle it. Sometimes it was suspicion or dislike of his miller that prompted a farmer to carry his grain to other mills eager to earn their *foilliu*; as in 1683, when the holder of the Nunnery Mill complained that country millers were coming stealthily by night into Douglas with creel-horses. These they loaded with corn for grinding in their own mills, and then brought it back in the same way, thus robbing him of his lawful dues.

HAND-MILLS

The millers had always to face the illegal competition of the quern or *myllin-laue* (hand-mill), a pre-historic survival which, in the seventeenth century was still to be found in nearly every country house; and severe measures were taken from time to time to limit or stop its use.

In 1610 the Coroner of Garff was ordered to seek out the hand-mills, and smash the upper stones. In 1648 the parishioners of Bride, Andreas and Lezayre, were ordered to bring their querns to the Lhen Mooar or Sulby mill. It was made a concession that an owner might ask for the return of his mill when the Lord's mills were unable to do all the grinding required. In Kirk Andreas seventy-seven querns were surrendered, and apparently had been in use in the houses of the most prosperous landowners—including the Curate and the Parish Captain—as well as in the cottages.

The Kirk Bride men were the most aggrieved, since they had no water-mill at all in the parish, and in normal times were forced to bring their corn to Sulby. They begged for the return of the querns, 'Praying', they said, 'for Christ Jesus' sake that wee may have them againe as our ancestors had before us.'

In an Island community always more or less actively struggling to break the numerous feudal bonds which restricted its freedom, it was not likely that the ban upon the querns would be entirely successful. The lawbreakers had to work circumspectly, for the spirit of the times in Church and State bred the tell-tale, and the hand-mill in action made a great noise; but it was still being used in the eighteenth century; for in 1722 William Hogg, the miller of Groudle, threatened, in a great rage, to break the quern of one Phillip Clague, a crofter, on the ground that Phillip not only ground his own corn on the *myllin-laue*, but also permitted others to do the same.

REPAIRS

The country-people were bound by law to perform various services relating to the mill assigned to them for grinding. They were called on to repair the mill, clean out the mill-stream and dam, and to carry new mill-stones. In 1697 the owners of Ballaquayle and Ballakermeen, now part of Douglas, were 'tenants' of Tromode Mill. They sent sledges to repair the mill-race, provided straw and *suggane* (straw rope) for thatching the mill roof, and helped to transport new grinding stones from Douglas harbour.

The duty of keeping the mills in repair was not viewed with enthusiasm by the farmers; and when long periods elapsed between repairs, they were tempted to disclaim responsibility, and the Great Enquest was called in to settle the dispute. Much of the uncertainty in the seventeenth century regarding customary obligations was caused by the lack of documentary evidence, a want partly due to the scarcity and dearness of paper which discouraged the making of copies, but more, perhaps, to the slip-shod keeping of the records.

In 1669 the Lhen Mooar Mill made a call on the inhabitants of Kirk Andreas to assist in the transport of a new stone from the port of Ramsey. Only twenty-two people gave help. One hundred and twelve refused on the plea either that they were not tenants to the mill, or that it was not a custom, and were fined.

An Enquest found that all the normal obligations save one—the cleansing of the mill race—had been established. In the matter of proving who were the tenants attached to the mill, the conduct of the parishioners revealed the determination of the objectors and their care for the due observance of old rules. When the three partners in the mill were about to give evidence as to the names of the customary tenants, and put their hands on the book to swear, the parishioners present stepped forward and took their hands off; and demanded that the ancient tenants to the mill should be proved by lawful witnesses and not by the mill-owners themselves.

MARKETS

The markets were another object of the Great Enquest's investigations. Each of the four town markets was controlled by a jury of four which examined complaints of forestalling, that is, buying before the opening of the market; regrating (buying goods at a fair and selling them on the same day at another fair at a higher price); overcharging and the sale of faulty goods. Forestalling was regarded as a serious offence, and it was ordered that no goods should be sold before the ringing of the market bell, so that everyone should have an equal chance of buying food and other commodities often very hard to obtain.

The Lord's officers caused bitter resentment by breaches of this regulation. In 1692 there was a brush between John Wattleworth, a garrison soldier, and John Rowe, who held the outstanding position of Controller and (on occasion) Deputy Governor. He was one of a number of imported officials of the period guilty of arbitrary behaviour.

One morning between the hours of eleven and twelve the Controller came down into the Marketplace at Castletown and asked for a parcel of malt that was for sale. When those who stood by the Market Cross told him that it had already been sold to Turner Calcott, Rowe summoned John Wattleworth—who, like the other garrison soldiers, could be called on to perform certain civil duties—and ordered him to go and carry the malt back again.

Wattleworth asked, 'Why should I go? For the malt was bought after the Market bell was rung.' Rowe replied, 'I bid you go and fetch it.' Then the soldier answered, 'I will not fetch it, but I will go and bid Turner Calcott to send it back.' And, says the account, 'as John Wattleworth was going away from them he turned about and said that he did not know after the Market bell was rung but that Turner Calcott had as great a right or privilege to buy as the Comptroller had'.

In rebuking Rowe for his flagrant breach of the Market Laws, Wattleworth showed considerable courage, not only in jeopardising his soldier's place, a position much sought after, but in running the risk of being indicted under the law of 1601. He appears to have escaped serious consequences from his outspoken speech, probably because Rowe was in the wrong and glad to let the matter drop.

WRECK

In 1538, when a Breton vessel captured by pirates was taken into custody by the Lord's officer at Ramsey, Edward Earl of Derby told Henry the Eighth's minister Thomas Cromwell, 'If there is any forfeiture of the said vessel it belongs to him (the Lord). It has been so used in ancient time since they were first Lords of the Isle.' The practice of claiming all wreck went even farther than the first rulers of his House. For, in 1422, when his ancestor, Sir John Stanley, King of Man and the Isles, sought the opinion of his Deemsters and the Twenty-four regarding wreck, they declared the ancient customary law to be,

> 'If any vessel or ship ar any other goods be imbayed within the Heads of Man above water or under water, it is the Lord's by his prerogative.'

The Lord's officers interpreted the law with the greatest strictness, and the rights of the original owners were generally ignored. Finders of wreck were enjoined, under penalties, to carry it to a point just above high sea-mark and no farther, to be received later into the custody of the Coroner or Water Bailiff. The country people, forbidden to take away the smallest piece of driftwood, felt no compunction in evading the law and cheating the Lord out of his plunder. When caught offenders were punished severely. A Jurby man, convicted in 1701 of making a false statement relating to wreck, was sentenced to stand in the Castletown pillory during market time with his ears nailed to it.

On no coast of the British Isles were shipwrecked people likely to receive a hospitable reception, and they ran as much risk of being robbed and knocked on the head by their own countrymen as on a foreign beach. But the Insular records tell of only one case where the unfortunates cast up by the waves suffered gross ill-treatment. The *Lucy* of London was driven ashore in Peel Bay in 1699, and the captain, Benjamin Holt, drowned, with members of his crew. 'Some passengers', says the account, 'were most barbarously and inhumanly stripped and their effects taken.'

A rigorous search of the countryside was made by coroners and lock-men, and some of the ship's belongings recovered. Two men walking on the Kirk Michael shore came upon the body of the captain, and later were found guilty of concealing various articles the list of which has a romantic Treasure Island flavour about it. It included a small bag of gold dust twelve ounces in weight, a little box containing one piece of bar gold, two Indian pendants, and a mourning ring, '*In memento mori*: A. H. 25.5.1694'; six guineas; three pairs of gold shirt buttons and pairs of gold and silver shoe buckles.

When the Governor heard of the wreck he ordered the Captain of Kirk German to call out the parish company and salve what they could of the wreck and cargo. The Captain, however, kept back some of the goods—notably a silk mant flowered with silver. He lost his commission and was discharged from the Keys—one of the few cases of a Parish Captain's loss of rank.

Eight years before the *Lucy* was lost, an English vessel came to grief off the coast between Dalby and Fleshwick; and the rumour spread in Rushen that various prominent women were in possession of some of the cargo. An enquiry was held at Bymaccan, and as a result Elinor Tyldesley, wife of the Captain of Kirk Arbory, was summoned to appear before the Controller, John Rowe.

But Edward Corrin, the soldier sent to the Friary, brought back a message from her that she was not in a condition to come, and was not coming if all the soldiers in the garrison were sent for her. Like her sister-in-law Dorathy, wife of Deemster Norris, she appears to have felt safe from the danger of penal consequences, although in possession of purple cloth and a black silk petticoat richly laced with gold, bought from a man of her parish.

The Deemster's wife came before the court for examination, and when questioned on the matter of concealed goods from the wreck, attacked the tell-tales, saying, 'The cutpurses of London when they cut purses are the first that cry, "Stop thief!" ' When asked what she meant by that, she replied saucily, 'You may take it as you will!' and, turning on her heel, she threw an insulting and most unladylike expression of contempt at the judges and swept out of the court.

After the Lordship became vested in the British Crown and it was no longer a question of anticipating the greedy hand of the Lord, public opinion became hostile to the old practice of carrying off wreck.

In 1834 a brig, the *John Fairfield*, bound from Liverpool to Cuba with a cargo of great value, ran on the rocks between Scarlett and Poylvash. In former times the Parish Captain would have sent out the Cross and set a guard upon the vessel. But it was not until it had been visited by large numbers of people and some looting had occurred that the High Bailiff of Castletown called upon the garrison to provide military protection. Unfortunately, a sentry challenging a boat which approached at night and, receiving no answer, fired his musket and killed the young son of James McHutcheon, Clerk of the Rolls, and the troops were then withdrawn.

A gang of looters immediately took advantage of the situation and, according to an eye-witness, there were 'scenes of outrageous and unparalleled plunder'. The leaders of the Methodist Connection of Castletown issued a public condemnation of the robbery and called for the return of the stolen goods. They expelled sixty of their members for disobedience.

Reporting to Whitehall, Attorney-General Clarke, an Englishman, made excuse for the Islanders. Writing of them in a tone of restrained commendation he said, 'After a knowledge of seventeen years, I think favourably of the pure Manx. They are somewhat litigious but not given to crime—and the practice of plundering wrecks I fear to be mainly attributed to the antient custom of the Lord of the Isle taking wreck with no sparing hand. "The Lord's wreck" is pregnantly referred to in old documents, and I never find anything in favour of the original owner.'

NAMES

The Enquest files record many hundreds of place names which have gone out of use since the eighteenth century. Names of fields predominate but there are many others of roads, fords, wells, streams, hills and glens; and some of them disclose forgotten history and tradition.

In 1723, for example, a dispute relating to the water supply of Ballamillaghyn in Kirk Braddan reveals that it was generally drawn from St. Mary's well in a Knock Rule meadow, from which one infers that the now nameless ancient chapel on Mount Rule was Keeill Moirrey, the Chapel of the Virgin Mary.

Two forgotten names—*Glonkillpatrick*, 'the Glen of Patrick's Chapel,' and *Cronk y Croghey*, 'the Hill of Hanging'—are mentioned in 1714 in connection with a pathway between Sulby and Glentrammon but the tantalisingly vague references leave the two places unidentified.

One name, Crowe, introduces a new complication in the interpretation of the name 'Ramsey', which was once assumed to be the Norse 'Raven's' or 'Hrafn's Isle', but this was discarded by philologists in favour of the Norse *Ramsá*, 'wild-garlic river.' The stream in question, now called the Lickeny, bounding the parishes of Lezayre and Maughold, is named *Struan y Craue*, Gaelic for 'Stream of the wild garlic', on the Ordnance Survey Map of 1873.

The agreement between *Ramsá* and *Struan y Craue* is, however, not so complete as could be wished for, for though a word similar in form and meaning to *craue* exists in Irish Gaelic, nothing like it is found in Manx vocabularies. Moreover in 1733 an Enquest file calls the Lickeny, 'Crowe's Stream;' and an official description of the Ramsey boundary in 1866 uses the same name. As the ancient Manx surname was, until last century, pronounced to rhyme with *craue* and the English 'cow', the town name still appears to remain of uncertain meaning.

A reference to the ancient route by which hill dwellers made their difficult way down Sulby Glen from Lhergy Renny, the Corrady, etc., raises a like problem with regard to the old name of Eary Kelly, 'Kelly's shieling.' The official scribe in 1724 took 'Kelly' to be *Kellee*, 'of a cock,' and so turned Eary Kelly into 'Cock Eary'.

In 1723 an Enquest witness recalled an old tradition relating to *Gat Beary*, 'Beary Gate,' a way coming down from the Beary mountain and crossing the highroad between Ballaspur and Ballig bridge, to drop into the Glen Mooar. It was along Gat Beary, he said, that the Kirk German farmers brought their creel-horses carrying customs turf to the Peel garrison, across the ford by Ballig and up by Ballachrink and Poortown. The old people remembered Cromwell's troops marching on Peel in 1651, and how as they neared St. John's they found the narrow track thronged with people. So the jack-booted English soldiers turned up at Ballacraine until they came to Gat Beary, and then followed the turfway by Ballig and Ballachrink.

THE ROAD OF MANANNAN

A hundred years ago the ancient road on the west side of the Tynwald—part of a way which crosses Glen Mooar and mounts the ridge of the Vaish—was called Follagh y Vannin. This was apparently a corrupt form of *Bollagh y Manannan*, 'the old road of Manannan.' Farther north it is now generally known as the Starvey road, but formerly its colloquial name was *Bayr ny Manannan* or *Managhan*, 'the Road of Manannan.'

Three miles along the road from Tynwald at one of the highest points of the ridge are the remains of a prehistoric earthwork recorded in the Files of 1735 as 'Manannan' and 'Manannan's Chair'. It is no doubt the place referred to in the Traditional Ballad as one of the two places at which bundles of green grass were offered up to the sea-god on Midsummer's eve. Some, says the ballad, went up with their rushes to the great mountain Barrule, but

> *Paart elley aagagh yn leagher wass*
> *Ec Manannan erskyn yn Keamool.*

Others would leave the grass below
With Manannan above the Apple Path.

Keamool later became *Bayr ny ooylyn*, the Apple Road, a track running up behind Lhergy Dhoo towards Manannan's Chair.

In more leisurely times the rhythmic Manx place-names tended to be long and descriptive. The watering place used by the people of Ballig near Garwick had the picturesque name of *Ushtey Bayr y Hroghad Saineen*, 'The Water by the Road of the Bridge of the Oxthong;' recording an incident forgotten long ago.

Occasionally Gaelic words absent from the dictionaries occur in Enquest evidence: *Durrag*, an opening in a mountain hedge big enough to allow the passage of a sheep; *asney* (1750), a damp hollow, probably the meaning of the place-name, *Hasna*, in Lezayre, which has puzzled students; *spaik* (1732), a horse-pack rope; *buncleighan* (1730), the mountain hedge or fell-dyke; *groblagh* (1738), corn spoilt by bad milling.

The exotic name 'Montpelier' was bestowed upon a part of the mountain land of Kirk Michael enclosed by the Maguire syndicate who came over with the blessing of the Lord of the Isles to exploit the Island in the seventeen-twenties. Montpelier fell into the hands of an Ulsterman, William Agnew of Donaghadee, who was responsible for its name.

There on New Year's morning of 1733 William Cannell is standing near his house. To him comes a man from Kirk German, nicknamed the Tinker, with a companion, and says he is on the way to Lhergy Renny for a mutton; upon which Cannell asks, 'Why not get one from Kelly na Heary?'

Then the Tinker frankly discloses the real object of his journey. He has heard of the wealth of Kewley of the Grenane in Lonan and plans to seize some of it that very night when the young people have gone after the fiddlers. 'Come along with us,' says the Tinker, 'and thou shalt get thy summer's bread, and it shall not cost thee a halfpenny.' Cannell, knowing the Tinker to be a dangerous man, pretends that he has a sore foot and cannot go so far. And the two men walk away, to dip down into Glen Crammag and up again, and he watches their dwindling figures move south-eastwards across the bare and windy slopes of the hills towards Clagh Ouyr and Lonan and the destined gallows.

CONCLUSION

The reputation of the Great Enquest noticeably declined in the last half of the eighteenth century, and this reflected the general deterioration in Manx traditions of social behaviour. Among the main local causes of this demoralisation was the Island's close connection with the 'Running' trade, for which it was a main depot and distributing centre, with unlimited quantities of cheap spirits for its inhabitants. In addition they were exposed to the bad example set by the numerous shady alien adventurers in contraband who infested the towns; and the broken down people of fashion and other refugees from justice who found asylum in Man.

In 1777 the Great Enquest was abolished as a result of many criticisms directed against its efficiency; but sixteen years later was re-instituted at the instigation of the Duke of Atholl who had been appointed Governor-in-Chief. He complained that the 20,000 acres of unappropriated land on which he claimed manorial rights had been extremely injured by the action of 1777; and encroachments on the land, the wrongful cutting of turf, burning of ling, etc., had been practised to a shameful degree since the Crown took possession of the Island, and particularly since the disappearance of the Great Enquest.

Summoned annually at Michaelmas, the Jury survived until the twentieth century, and finally was abolished by Act of Tynwald in 1919, when it was stated that it had rarely been asked to discharge any duties; whilst there was loss of time for the jurors.

In what was perhaps its busiest period, the first half of the eighteenth century, when it was frequently called upon, the Great Enquest was a cheap and efficient instrument in the settlement of claims and disputes. It consisted of men drawn from the then numerous independent native farmer-owners, with a long-inherited code of social conduct, and often a considerable knowledge of the common law. It was from this class—the firm core of the Manx nation—that the members of the legislature, judiciary and clergy were recruited; and the native merchants in the towns generally came from the same source.

There is a number of ways in which this ancient quest might still have given valuable service to the community at little cost, and it seems a pity that no attempt was made, by modification of the conditions and scope of its functions, to keep it in existence.

XIII

A MANX MERCHANT OF THE EIGHTEENTH CENTURY

In the latter half of the seventeenth century, as a consequence of the evergrowing trade between the western British ports and America, together with such fortuitous influences as the Great Plague and the Fire of 1666, there was some dispersal of merchants from the City of London. According to Bullock, at that time a number of commercial adventurers made a settlement in Man, having realised the opportunities of lawful and illicit trade offered by the Island's position and its low import duties.

Among the later immigrants was one Philip Moore, a citizen of London engaged in the Norway trade. He is said to have belonged to Wigtonshire, and in Man he founded a family known as the 'Moores of the Hills', the Hills being an estate near Douglas now swallowed up by the modern town. He died in 1728 and was succeeded by his son Philip, who was one of the Keys until his death in 1746. He had four sons—Philip, George, James, and John.

Philip III (1708–1788), the eldest, inherited the family business, whose nature was tersely described by the unfriendly pen of Thomas Heywood of the Nunnery. Commenting on the candidature of Philip's son-in-law, Thomas Moore, for the Deemstership, he wrote: 'Thomas Moore was not bred to the profession of the Law, but served an apprenticeship to one Philip Moore, a man in trade—if the late smuggling business can merit that appellation.'

GEORGE MOORE

George (1709–1787), the second son of Philip II, was the most notable of the family. A merchant from his youth up, he established a flourishing business in Peel, was a member of the Keys, and their Speaker during the trying period which followed the Revestment in 1765. He received a knighthood at the close of his public career.

Among the Bridge House papers now in the Manx Museum are Letter Books which once belonged to him and which form the chief sources for this account of one of the leading and most successful Manx merchants of the eighteenth century. The first foolscap volume contains correspondence closely written in various hands during the years 1750 to 1760, and for the most part relating to his business affairs. The second, a slim volume of a hundred pages, is mainly occupied by Moore's letters when he was in London in 1766 on deputation from the Keys. The last entry was made in 1780.

These two books covering only a small portion of his long life convey some idea of his interests and business activities during a quarter of a century, and enable the reader to sketch in, however vaguely and inadequately, a portrait of the writer.

Not all the features of this picture are attractive. But it does reveal Moore as a man who, in spite of certain defects of heart and mind, was a dignified representative of the shopkeeping and trading class of which he was a member—enterprising but prudent in his ventures, a man of integrity in his dealings with business associates, and a good citizen according to his lights.

The Letter Books do not record the date at which Moore settled in Peel. In 1733 he had married Catherine Callan, the daughter of a Dublin merchant, and his substantial interests in Ireland, including an estate at Donnybrook, took him annually to that country. In his younger days no doubt he took part in his father's business at Douglas, and on one occasion in 1736 he, with his brother Philip and other prominent merchants, was caught smuggling spirits into the town—a contemptible evasion in view of the extremely low duties levied by the Manx Customs,[1] and the standing of the traders involved. In 1750, the earliest date of the Letter Books, he had been established in the western port for many years, and had no further share in the family business.

As far as possible he avoided Douglas in his transactions, owing to the risks incurred by dealing with the alien merchants who swarmed there. He resented the presence of these intruders, not only because many of them were shady adventurers of uncertain financial stability, but because they were formidable competitors who did not hesitate to undercut in prices, and thus embarrassed him in his dealings with customers. Writing to Dan Mylrea in 1751, he says: 'Pity it is that no method has yet been taken whereby the trade of the Isle might be solely occupied by its natives.'

With the expansion of his business he found that it would be advantageous to have premises in Douglas, and in 1751 he bought property called 'Oats's Concerns', consisting of a house with a small garden and outhouses, and a seat in the Chapel of Douglas. 'I have now', he wrote, 'a house and cellars in Douglas, whereas I was in

[1] Before 1765 the duty on brandy and rum was 1d. per gal.; tea $2\frac{1}{2}\%$ of value; tobacco $\frac{1}{2}$d. lb.

want of both. With great difficulty such conveniences are there to be met with, for the town is so burthened with foreign curs dayly flying there that no manner of roome is unemployed.'

His main business interests were centred however in Peel. He was anxious to improve and deepen its harbour for the accommodation of all sizes of vessels, and he displayed characteristic energy in seeking financial aid, not only from the local merchants but also from Liverpool shipowners whose Guineamen somctimcs wcre forced to ride out a gale in the unprotected bay. His fellow citizens subscribed £500 of the £1,500 required, and his plans received the approval of experts brought over from England. But the scheme was frustrated by the jealous opposition of Douglas and the other Manx ports whose ruinous harbours were likely to suffer in competition with the projected alterations at the mouth of the Neb. It may be argued, as indeed it was at the time, that his exemplary enterprise on behalf of Peel had as its main object the provision of better facilities for his contraband ventures. What cannot be denied is that at all events he had the will and vigour to take the initiative.

THE ISLAND TRADE

The chief commodity in which Moore dealt was spirits imported into the Island and intended for sale to smugglers. He had been born into a society whose prosperity rested on the insecure foundations of illicit trading. Everyone in the Island, from the highest to the lowest, was affected directly or indirectly by a commerce which enriched a few, impoverished many, and corrupted the State. The official class, the owners of large estates and the merchants, for the most part condoned or participated in the traffic, and the Church as a whole displayed little sign of the will or the courage to attack an evil which was sapping the morale of the Manx people. The ecclesiastical courts condemned the porters who rolled brandy casks from cellar to quay on the Sabbath, and whilst the sinners repented in St. German's prison their employers dined with the Vicars-General.

Here and there, it is true, a voice was raised in support of Bishop Wilson, who throughout his episcopate had fearlessly denounced the contraband trade and drawn upon himself the abuse of its powerful supporters. In a sermon preached in 1735 he referred to the disastrous effects—idleness, drunkenness and thieving—produced by 'the sin of running goods, and', he said, 'defrauding the [British] nation of the rights and power of supporting itself. This we have borne testimony against ever since it first began in this place, but, God knows, to very little purpose'.

Moore was astonished and angered by the steadfast opposition of the Bishop. In the matter of trade the merchant had no lively sense of obligation to the sovereign State which pursued a short-sighted selfish policy towards its dependencies, raising tariff walls and placing restrictions whenever the interests of its own producers and manufacturers were threatened. He himself had experienced the irritations to which the system gave rise. On one occasion he was asked to buy some Loghtan sheep for a Durham peer, Lord Barnard. Twenty were obtained after some difficulty and shipped to Whitehaven. They were refused entry by the Customs, and five days later, when the animals were put on shore at Ramsey, nearly half were dead or dying of starvation.

Moore took up the position that his trade was conducted in conformity with the Insular laws and that if there was smuggling into Great Britain and Ireland, the chief offenders were natives of those countries. In 1750, when the English cruisers increased their patrols in the Irish Sea and appeared to threaten the safety of brandy landed on the Manx shores, he talked indignantly of 'measures levell'd at the privileges of the Isle'. Two years later he complained that the Episcopal crusader was still militant, in spite of his eighty-eight years, and working for the Duke of Atholl's disposal of his Lordship of Man.

> 'The Bishop', he said, 'is busying himself too much in these matters it's believed, and trade has received a very considerable stagnation from apprehensions of the Isle being to be alienated. We should follow the example of Jersey and Guernsey, where a much more extensive trade than we have is carried on without envy or noise. By exercising the like caution', he continued solemnly, 'we in like manner would establish a reputable character, our youth would have encouragement sufficient to stay at home and not look abroad to be employed.'

It is perhaps superfluous to remark at this point that Moore was as inconsistent as the rest of us; and, although he advocated employment for Manxmen, the captains and the crews (excepting some Manx apprentices) of his two vessels were Scottish, as were also his gardener and ploughman; and when he built a wherry at Peel he brought his carpenters from Ireland.

If the Bishop was only to be diverted by death from his attacks on the Contraband traffic, there were others of less standing who could be disposed of without much trouble. A letter from George Moore in 1754, when the Parish of Kirk German had lost its Vicar, is eloquent of the attitude of the Insular Administration and Judiciary.

M

'Dear Sir,' he wrote to the Comptroller, John Quayle of Bridge House, 'it is reported the Lord Bishop or the Clergy are minded to give the Rev. Mr. Gell a Presentation to this Parish . . . the Behaviour of Mr. Gell in all Instances and upon all occasions has shewn his Disposition to prejudice the trade in this Isle. Of such was the recd opinion in this particular of his Behaviour that the Governr interested himself formerly to prevt his being settled in this town to the end that being distt from the Objt of trade he might not have the opportunity of speculation or concern about it. I write this letter on purpose to intimate my fears of his settlemt in this town, and shd you acquaint the Dep. Governors to joyn their Influence with yours I am so well acquainted with our Governor's sentimts on this subject that I daresay you will hereby oblige him and in a most particular manner oblige

Yrs . . . . . .'

Mr. Gell did not become Vicar of Kirk German.

TRADING VOYAGES

During the period covered by the Letter Books, George Moore had shares in a number of ship ventures, but his chief interest lay in the fortunes of two vessels—one the *Peggy* of 150 tons burthen; and, newly built to his order at Boston, the *Lilly* of 120 tons. They were snows, two-masted ships popular at that period, and almost identical with the brig. He owned five-eighths of the *Peggy*, which was manned by a captain, mate, apprentice, and six other seamen. The *Lilly*, his own property, had a similar crew.

These small vessels voyaged across the Atlantic at all times of the year, braved the hurricanes and reefs of the West Indies, and passed through the Straits to trade with Mediterranean France and Spain. A typical voyage was taken by the *Peggy* in 1751. She sailed for North America with £800 worth of Glasgow-manufactured goods, including tartan and other cloth. These were disposed of at Boston, and the snow loaded with 3,000 quintals of salt fish and New England rum. A course was then set for Gibraltar and eventually the fish was sold at Alicant for a good price. This was used in the purchase of five thousand gallons of Spanish brandy, shipped at Barcelona, after which the *Peggy* sailed for home on the last leg of her triangular voyage. Another route was followed by the *Lilly* in 1752. At the end of May she called at Cork to ship £700 worth of Irish beef and butter in barrels. She reached Barbados at the beginning of July, and disposed of her provisions. With the proceeds rum was bought and landed at Peel in August. This particular voyage of three months did not meet with the vexatious delays which often detained ships at their ports of call. A third and shorter route was that in which the *Peggy* carried Welsh coal to Gibraltar and brought brandy from Cette in southern France on her return journey.

It will have been seen that a part of Moore's ventures was in trade which attracted no adverse criticism from the British Treasury. But the main objective of each voyage to which everything else was subordinated was a homeward cargo of spirits. His dealings in other commodities have often an air of amateurishness. On the subject of brandy and rum, however, he writes with the assurance of an expert and, as far as his temperament will allow, with enthusiasm. When he begins a correspondence with a Galloway man whose brother has a plantation in British Guiana, the first artless questions which come to his mind relate to rum: 'I take it the Rio Esquebo to be adjoyning of a part of Terra Firma,' he writes. 'Is sugarcanes planted there? or have they the mollasses from the Caribee Islands?'

In his trading expeditions much depended on the business acumen of the captain, who had to be given a wide discretion in choosing ports of call and in buying and selling the cargo to the best advantage. Moore sent letters which were picked up at arranged points and often modified the original instructions. These communications generally repeated certain simple words of advice in which he exhorted the captain or agent, as the case might be, to do everything in the most frugal way, and to conduct the business in hand with the same zeal as if it were for himself. Occasionally he supplemented this with a little applied commercial wisdom. 'On your arrival at Barbados', he informed the captain of the *Lilly*, 'make yourself acquainted with the prices of provisions and of Rum. You may seem as if you were in-different about buying Rum, lest your appearance might affect the price.'

He saw to it that the Manx apprentices on his vessels were not altogether neglected in education during the voyages. On one occasion he asked the captain to spend up to ten shillings on reading books with a little paper for writing and figuring purposes, their activities in this direction being supervised by the mate. Frugality in this and other matters was the note he always sounded, and in the case of the *Lilly* it appears to have had disastrous consequences.

The snow had lain for months at Antigua in the West Indies awaiting a cargo of rum, and had finally arrived in Peel with the hull below the waterline riddled by seaworms. Moore decided to have her bottom sheathed with copper, and in order that it might be done, as he said, in the frugalest way, she was sent to Boston. In addition to a cargo of Glasgow goods, Irish butter and linen, she took with her a quantity of brown paper, instead of the customary hair, for use as a filling between copper and hull. The owner further economised by shipping a crew of seven apprentices as mariners, thus reducing the total ship's wages to about three pounds a week. In spite of her condition the vessel survived the Atlantic crossing, and in Boston was joined by the *Peggy*. In the spring of 1755 the two snows set sail with cargoes of fish for the Mediterranean, and off Cape Cod were caught in a violent storm. The *Peggy* escaped, but the *Lilly* with her apprentice crew was driven ashore on the New England coast and became a total loss. The ship's company only saved their lives with difficulty.

Moore's apparent heartlessness in the ordering of the *Lilly's* last voyage, like some of his other faults, sprang inevitably out of the spirit of the paradoxical eighteenth century, in which the culture, beautiful clothes, and exquisite manners of the well-to-do insufficiently compensated for their complacent acceptance of political corruption and social brutalities.

It was a similar lack of sensibility to human suffering which accounts for the mantraps Moore set in his orchard to catch apple stealers, and for his directions in the sale of his slave Douglass, as though he was a bale of merchandise. 'I expect you have Disposed of my negroe Douglass,' he wrote to the captain of the *Peggy*, 'because his face I never want to see. If he be not sold sell him in Spain for what you can get for him.'

THE MERCHANT'S FAMILY

On the other hand he was an affectionate father and deeply interested in his children's welfare. He always remembered his family in his letters to captains taking the Mediterranean voyage, and they were instructed to supplement the cargoes of his beloved brandy with quantities of oranges, lemons, prunes, raisins, almonds, and nuts for the children. A list of articles and materials purchased for him at Continental ports hints at the fashionable display with which his wife and daughters dazzled the matrons of Peeltown—boxes of artificial head and breast flowers, fans, earrings and necklaces, silver tippets and Barcelona handkerchiefs, scarlet satin and crimson velvet, yellow lutestring and smooth silk paduasoy in various colours, pink and silver shoes, gauze dress caps and blow lace for ruffles. When his son Phil was twenty-one, he bought him a pair of French brilliant stone buckles and a blue satin waistcoat embroidered with gold.

His daughter Peggy acted as his book-keeper for a time, and some of her small beautiful script is to be found in the first Letter Book. In 1755 he wrote to a friend in Dublin, 'My daughter Margaret is gone off. She liked our young Comptroller [John Quayle of Bridge House] and I thought it the best way not to interpose; he's a very diligent young man.' In spite of Moore's not over-warm comment on the marriage, Peggy appears to have been happy, and her letters to her husband are touching in their expressions of love and devotion. It was her son, George Quayle, who in 1789 built the yacht *Peggy* which, a unique survival, still lies in its boathouse at Castletown. Another son, Basil, farmed the Creggans, where he continued his grandfather Moore's pioneer work in agriculture.

For his eldest son Moore nourished hopes of academic success which were not realised. His school career in Glasgow was unsatisfactory, and a letter of advice from his father on the eve of his entering the Glasgow College in 1751 was only a temporary stimulus.

> 'Dear Phil,' Moore wrote, 'The Time of your entering the college is very nigh and as it is the effect of your own inclination I expect you have used proper diligence to prepare yourself. The means for your improvement you must see that I am very carefull to consult nothing is wanting that I know of to contribute to it. Why I'm thus anxious arises from the knowledge I have of the usefulness of a good Education. This is what makes the Distinction in Mankind. To please me, your Friends, and in the End to please yourself is now in your power by duely attending your studys. If you neglect this opportunity I shall tell you what will be the Consequence. You have another Brother and may have more. When the time comes that Education is necessary I shall give him the same means of Education that I now give you and if he makes better use of his Time than you do whoever is most deserving you may be sure will be distinguished for having exerted his Capacity. . . . If you apply to your Studies I'm extreamly well satisfied . . . for it would be very trifling that you enter the College for the appearance of Education only and that thus I throw away my money to no purpose. . . . Your mama gives her Blessing your Sisters their love.'

A year later when Phil came home for his summer vacation his father soon discovered that the academic learning he had acquired on the banks of the Clyde was negligible.

> 'I find', he wrote, 'it will be very hazardous to lose sight of him, so that I'm minded to keep him here and not let him return to Glasgow where amusement has taken more of his time than study . . . he's more Inclinable to be a merchant than ever. This notion has all along been so grafted in him that I'm satisfied it is the reason he has given so small application to his studies.'

TOBACCO SPINNING

Phil commenced his business career at the age of sixteen with the purchase of half a chest of tea, but soon, in partnership with his father and another Peel merchant, John Callin, was engaged in a more ambitious enterprise—the establishment of a tobacco spinning factory. Tobacco had been manufactured in the Island since the end of the seventeenth century and Moore was not the first to spin leaf in Peel. Machines, operatives, and hogsheads of raw tobacco were obtained from Glasgow, and a beginning was made with six men, who received a total of five shillings a hundredweight on the 'leaf taking'—four shillings for five spinners and a shilling for the roller. The workmen were expected to give a small gratuity to a master so that the boys who waited on them might be taught to read. No 'Tobacco boys', Moore says, could be had if this instruction was not provided.

The entry of young Moore into business was a source of great satisfaction to his father in spite of the Glasgow disappointment, and soon he was buying rum in Belfast and visiting defaulting debtors in Galloway. His assistance was the more appreciated because all through his life the elder Moore appears to have been oppressed from time to time with fears of a decline in health. In 1754, when he was forty-six years old and on the return of Phil from Ireland, he writes: 'I was quite tired for want of him for I find this is not in my power to go thro the business with the application that it requires and gives me a proof of that Lesson that there is a season for all things.'

A year later he debates whether he should visit Dublin to obtain a doctor's opinion: 'I've severely left any Liquor stronger than water and am thinking that this habit may restore my stomach.' As credulous as any twentieth-century devotee of advertised nostrums he bought a supply of 'The original Balsom of Life', at three shillings and sixpence a bottle from Lombard Street, London. But despite his fears, the heady temptations lurking in the cellars at Peeltown, and the quack medicines of the City, he survived to the ripe age of seventy-eight.

SCOTTISH CUSTOMERS

The great stores of brandy and rum he kept in his sheds and cellars in Peel were, for the most part, destined for western Scotland, and from Kilfinan and Inveraray in Argyll to Kirkcudbright in the south there was scarcely a coast town or village of any size in which his liquor was not drunk, and his agents engaged in the not very remunerative and often difficult task of collecting his debts. They received a half of one per cent commission, and sometimes were sent a bag of a dozen bottles of spirits as a reward for zeal, or as a stimulus to greater activity. The Highland bills were the most difficult of settlement, though the Lowlanders were not far behind in their reluctance to meet their liabilities, and periodically his letters went out to his collectors telling them in oft repeated phrases that his occasions for money in Glasgow were urgent, and calling upon them to press for payment.

'It grudges me', he would write, 'whenever the payments are delayed to three months.' He was not unreasonable, however, where debtors were anxious to pay his dues. He had little of the litigiousness with which the Manx are credited and seldom pushed his demands to the point of court proceedings. Where there was evidence of a desire to make reparation he was willing to grant time or accept a composition, and in those cases always advised his agent to accept the first offer, for, as he was wont to assert, 'I have observed that the first offer made in such like circumstances have generally proved to be as good terms as could be thereafter obtained.'

When pushed to an extremity he wrote in another tone:

> 'The backward payments I now meet with from my Customers about Stranraer give me the highest reason to be displeased with my dealings with them, so that as they deserve no favour let me beg that for recovery of one and all my Debts you will use or cause to be used ultimate Diligence (i.e. distraint).'

Again he writes, 'Samson's and Kennedy's Bills I grudge much are so long unpaid; if you can, by fair or foul means try what can be done.' He must be acquitted of intentional irony when he uses an ambiguous alternative expression, 'fair or legal means,' for the limping prose of his letters, unilluminated by flashes of wit or humour, give little indication of the possession of that sometimes dangerous quality. Perhaps the best example occurs in a correspondence he pursued with the Rev. Anthony Halsall who was trustee of certain family funds. They were left by George Moore's father for a grandson, Peregrine Moore, but on his death in South Carolina in 1751 before coming of age his three uncles became entitled to the money involved—a sum of £380. Halsall would give no details of any effects in his hands nor did he show any great eagerness to pay out the legacy. After six months of fruitless attempts at settlement Moore brought the matter to a head by drawing a Bill on the reverend gentleman at thirty days' notice,

> 'to which', he said, 'I desire you will accordingly give Quittance to and payment in Terms of my Draft. This method I can have no doubt but that it will prove agreeable to you, for your sister complains of the Great Trouble the Multiplicity of Business not all properly your own has given you to the great Detriment of your health. By so much this therefore will lessen the Troubles and for both our sakes be agreeable.'

JAMES MOORE

His brother James, who shared in the legacy, was apparently a graduate of Trinity College, Dublin, and became proprietor of a school at Cavan. Tiring of his profession he sold his scholastic business. George's letter of approval had a sting in the tail and illustrates his sententious vein. He wrote:

> 'Foreign to the Purposes does any Engagement or Situation in Life turn, if the Circumstances cease to be agreeable or require a disagreeable attendance, which I have often thought with respect to yours, and if you found that this at last became unsupportable the Alternative you have chosen is laudable . . . my hearty warmest wishes but sorry I am no farther can I go to give you assistance. . . .'

James appears to have been a cheerful soul, and after making a tour of Scotland came to stop at Ballamoore for a time. 'Sweet Jimmy Moore', as George called him, with the affectionate contempt of the prosperous merchant for a brother who had not had the wit to choose a more lucrative occupation than that of a schoolmaster, had meanwhile been given a chaplaincy in the Army. It was a sinecure, as owing to his ill-health he was allowed to provide a substitute. Then one morning someone came to the War Office in a reforming mood and ordered all chaplains to join their regiments. James's was in North America where he had not the slightest intention of going, and he hurried back to Ireland to pull wires in an attempt to save his post. The letters do not reveal the outcome. He died in Ireland in 1763 and left legacies to Manx schools.

THE HAZARDS OF SMUGGLING

Moore firmly declined the risks involved in running his contraband goods to Argyll and Galloway, but when misfortune overtook the smuggler and the liquor was seized he was prepared to make an abatement of his bill. His customers sent word of their requirements, and boatmen of their own choice and hire took the casks on board for transport to the Scottish coast. There the goods were landed, generally at night, on some beach unlikely to be visited by inquisitive preventive men. The boatmen received payment from the carriers who met them there. Considering the hazards the wherrymen's charges were not excessive. On one occasion in 1752 the freightage of spirits loaded at Peel for Port Ballantrae was two shillings and twopence per cask. Manx boatmen disliked the weighty half-hogsheads and often refused to take them, preferring the much more easily handled anker casks containing from five to ten gallons. The vessels employed were light swift two-masted wherries with the stern as sharp as the bow, and easily manoeuvred in shallow waters. They were manned by crews of six.

Danger in one form or another was always lying in wait for the smuggler. Moore tells with sympathetic regret, in April 1754, how poor John McClure of Alloway freighted a Peel boat with a cargo of spirits for Scotland but was driven back from the Mull by a northerly wind, and in Manx waters met a Revenue barge from Ireland which promptly relieved him of his contraband and carried it off to Donaghadee. Some months later Hugh Kennedy, a boatman making for Galloway, was put back and forced to run aground near the Lhen Mooar, where he lost his life. The cargo floated out of the boat and eighty casks were brought to land. But according to Moore the rescued spirits were still in jeopardy, for the people of the Lhen were notoriously lacking in respect for such property insecurely stored, and he immediately sent two boats to bring it back to Peel and safety.

His son had an interest in a wherry which on her voyage out from Peel was seized at Ayr, a town in ill-odour with smugglers because of the distressing alertness of its Customs officers. A letter of October, 1757, in which Moore asked for assistance from a Glasgow merchant, is amusingly noncommittal:

> 'My son Phil is concerned in a wherry that was lately seized at Ayr . . . she was taken on her first trip, but had not a Drop of Goods on board and was intending to take some ankers and cables for Capt. Pat Montgomerie of the Peggy refitting here for Virginia and under charter for Ayr . . . there are two people who have sworn that Goods were landed at the Troon out of the wherry, which to me seems far-fetched for the Boat arrived there in the night and sailed off before day. This may or may not be true. As the event is doubtful on a Tryal, I cannot tell what to say. . . . Phil has wrote to one Hector Bryce near Ayr to claim the Boat in order to stand Tryal, but Bryce is a very unfit Person. I shall therefore require of you to direct herein in whatever manner you think best by claiming or by purchasing in a frugal way, for Phil would not like the wherry was lost. . . .'

The story of the landing of contraband at the Troon was not so far-fetched as he pretended. From a subsequent letter to one of those interested in the wherry's cargo it is clear that over three hundred gallons of brandy from Moore's cellars were put on shore, and that a portion valued at fifty pounds was afterwards captured by Revenue officers. The smugglers were dissatisfied with the apportionment of this loss, and Moore wrote plaintively to one of the malcontents, 'As my son has bore a sufficient share of loss in the wherry to accommodate that adventure, it is hoped neither you or any other concerned will grudge paying their respective share.'

Two months later Phil's wherry was released from custody, the authorities having failed to secure a conviction.

BALLAMOORE

Moore sought solace and relaxation from his business worries in the care and development of Ballamoore, his estate in Kirk Patrick, bought in 1750. The dwelling was small, consisting of a parlour, three closets with beds, and an upstairs room, and at first was used as a residence by his family for a few weeks in the summer, the rest of the year being spent at his house in Peel. He quickly set to work to build a new house and improve the farm. During the next seven years there are frequent indications of his keen interest in his new possession. He sent to Ireland for an expert in garden planning, 'for', he wrote, 'it is much wished my design of improvement be executed in a genteele taste, which perhaps would not prove more expensive than having my improvement in no taste or a bad one.'

He gratified his love of trees by laying out a large orchard of apples, pears and cherries, and planted many hundreds of ash and beech trees; at the same time trying to grow oaks, hornbeams, and chestnuts, from seed. His vessels brought bushels of acorns and pine cones from Scotland and New England, myrtles, hollies and spruce from Ireland, and grafted filberts from Holland, whilst his vinery was supplied with red and white grape vines from Southern France. Quick to snatch at commercial advantage, he introduced suitable varieties of sallows from Ireland so that he might have a plantation to supply barrel hoops, of which he often bought more than a hundred thousand in the year.

His first attempts at tree-planting were not very successful owing, he suggested, to the climate, and his newly planted apple-trees also failed to satisfy his too great expectations. Commiserating with his Irish brother-in-law John Onge he writes in July, 1752:

> 'I am not surprized with the misfortune your orchard mett with in your absence for I find nothing so well thrives about a farm as under the Master's eyes. I had but five apples growing last year and they were stole two months before they were ripe. Next year as I'm in hopes, as I shall have occasion, I intend setting fox-traps in my garden I hope will prove some security.'

Moore was equally energetic in the improvement of the farm. 'I'm fond of good fences and ditches,' he wrote, and the Lord of the Isle was asked to consent to a rectification of the boundary hedge, which was too tortuous in its course to please his orderly mind. The drains were cleaned and thousands of young quicks brought from Ireland for fencing. Red, white, and yellow clover was bought in London and Rotterdam for the pastures; and marl, found in two places on the estate, was used to enrich corn land. Later there is mention of an experiment in brickmaking from the same clay which ended prematurely when the Liverpool-born brickmaker deserted to his native town.

He improved the breed of his cattle by importations from Galloway, and an order was given to a Dublin craftsman for a new type of cart. In the end the peace of Ballamoore was disturbed by disputes with a neighbour, Captain Radcliffe, but before that occurred the French war broke out in 1756.

THE FRENCH WAR

The conflict seriously interfered with the merchant's business and increased the dangers to ocean-going trade. The seas swarmed with privateers, British and French, manned by desperate men, in many cases only to be distinguished from pirates by the letters of marque they carried from their respective Governments; and in home waters the naval authorities were engaged in a ruthless campaign to find seamen for the Fleet. 'On our coast there is such a warm Press for seamen and lookout for smuglers that our sales are greatly affected,' Moore wrote in 1757 to a French agent with whom he corresponded regularly, regardless of the existing state of war.

About that time the *Peggy* was seized in the West Indies by an enemy privateer, but within three days was retaken, together with her French captor, and brought to Barbados, whence she later returned to Peel with sixteen thousand gallons of rum. In the following year, 1758, a neutral vessel arrived in the bay from Rotterdam, and the master complained that off Dover he was boarded by armed Kentishmen who forcibly entered the hold and carried away the least weighty packages, including tea and gin. Moore was indignant at the seizure of goods he proposed to pass on to Scottish smugglers.

'It seems strange', he said, 'that notwithstanding so many repeated complaints against these Rovers the Government have not fallen on an effectual method to prevent such pilferings.'

A few months later the *Kingston*, in which he had a share, was taken by a French privateer, and then retaken. Scarcely had he received this report than news came of the beaching on the Cornish coast of a neutral vessel, the *Ceres*, carrying a cargo of Spanish brandy for Moore's account. Nearly all the casks were saved, and, wrote the obliging but pompous Customs officer at Falmouth, 'Notwithstanding the opposition of the country, which are generally very barberous on these occasions, they are all put into safe cellars and locked up with his majesty and my Keys.'

For some time before these last two mishaps Moore had been chafing at the restrictions the war placed on his trade with France, and in November, 1758, he wrote to his correspondent at Cette on the

Mediterranean pointing out that all vessels bound for the Isle of Man with French commodities on board would certainly be brought to port and condemned if visited on the passage by British warships or privateers, as all trade with France was entirely prohibited. Unless therefore he could discover some plan to evade the vigilance of the British Fleet he would have, for the time, to suspend his favourite design of obtaining brandy from France.

Whilst he was cudgelling his brains over the problem the safe arrival in the Island of three neutral ships to discharge cargo there filled him with envy, and still further whetted his desire for forbidden fruit. He was thus in a receptive mood when one of his associates, John Callin, approached him with a fantastic scheme involving the use of the snow *Peggy*. Callin, a man inferior to Moore in business qualities and balanced judgment, was part-owner of the snow which, at the time, was on her way home from America.

Together the two merchants made the following plan: Moore was to get a French pass through the good offices of his correspondent at Bordeaux. No difficulty was anticipated in this, as several similar passes had reached Ireland. Care was to be taken that Moore's interest in it should not be disclosed. Armed with this document the captain of the *Peggy* was to ship staves and hoops in America wherewith to make casks for rum to be bought in the French islands of Martinique or Guadaloupe. The pass would give protection, whether she sailed into a French port or was brought there by a French warship. After taking the spirits on board the captain was to apply to the British Admiral Court in the West Indies for a certificate stating that the *Peggy* was a lawful prize on her way to a British port. Such a document would save her from British cruisers and privateers; but how it was to be secured except by bribery, does not appear. Finally, insurances on ship and cargo were to be taken out in Holland.

Almost as soon as he had set his scheme in motion Moore was seized with misgivings—not from any doubts as to the correctness of his behaviour, but because he quickly realised the difficulties and dangers attending the plan at every stage. Apparently the advice he hastily sought from his friends and business agents did not allay his growing fears, and within a few days he had countermanded the application for a French pass, and abandoned the project.

He persisted, however, in his attempts to circumvent British law and the naval patrol, and some months later managed to convert the *Peggy* into a neutral vessel. A Danish captain was procured to make a fictitious purchase of the ship, after giving a bond for her value by which she might continue under the direction of her original proprietors. The Dane took passage on her to Bergen and entered her on the Danish register. Her cargo of tobacco unloaded and with Norwegian timber on board the *Peggy* returned for orders from her owners, who naturally desired that the change of flag should be concealed.

> 'To act with caution seems necessary,' Moore writes to his captain, 'for I would not by any means have it publicly known, for that may do harm and can do no good in case we should have occasion in the course of trade to make use of your old Register.'

The further adventures of the *Peggy* are, unfortunately, not recorded in the Letter Books.

Mishaps to his ventures at this time did not stand alone in their disturbing influence on his easily shaken nervous system. There was a number of long-drawn business disputes in which he was involved, arising out of the actions of his partners or trade connections. He comes well out of these controversies, for in his transactions he met his obligations promptly, and was always much more willing to submit a debatable point to arbitration than his opponents were. He asserted with truth that he was a man of peace and, like most of that profession, he sometimes suffered losses for the sake of it.

His participation in public life also brought its troubles. At first he had been on very good terms with the Governor, Basil Cochrane, but after his co-optation to the Keys in 1755 various questions arose— among them the construction of a bridge at Douglas and the grant of naturalisations to strange merchants—in which he found himself opposing the Administration. In 1758 he was elected Speaker of the Keys, and, until Cochrane's retirement from office in 1761, felt in ever increasing degree the weight of the Governor's animosity. To this he attributed Capt. Radcliffe's persistence in demanding quarry rights and a highway across the lawn at Ballamoore, and he accused Cochrane of an arbitrary exercise of his judicial functions which forced Moore to appeal to London for redress.

> 'My Profession' (he wrote in 1760) 'has from my youth up all along been that of a merchant untill of late, and for these two years past the most of my time has been taken up and imployd in Intricacies and disputes appertaining to Law than which nothing on Earth is more disagreeable to my Bent and Inclination, yet this takes me so much from the necessary Exercise of my Business that I may as well be a merchant in Japan as in Peeltown.'

On this note the first Letter Book ends.

THE REVESTMENT

When the second volume opens six years later the blow feared by Manx merchants for a generation has fallen.

By the Revesting Act of May, 1765, the British Crown acquired the regalities and customs of the Island from the Duke of Atholl. In the following month the so-called 'Mischief' Act with its inaccurate official description, 'for the prevention of smuggling into and from the Isle of Man,' came into immediate force.

It is strange that the English Government had not taken drastic measures sooner. From 1712 to 1765 Parliament passed a succession of enactments to that end, all more or less ineffective in operation. Moore's rum-laden *Peggy* sailed with other vessels into the security of the Irish Sea, under convoy of British warships. The Falmouth Customs officer carefully guarded his Spanish brandy, and when the *Ceres* was refloated allowed its reshipment for Peel. In Scotland, if his instructions to agents are to be taken seriously, the tolerant Law Courts helped him in the recovery of debts owing on his contraband liquor. And so he and his fellow merchants sat snugly in their offices and parlours, cutting respectable figures in social and public life, taking the waters at Bath, investing in the Funds, adding farm to farm, and leaving the risks of hazardous ventures to their ill-paid underlings. No doubt the smooth course of their trade was liable to interruption by storm, wreck and fire, inquisitive British cruisers or marauding privateers, but the profits were large, and the traders were always able to limit their liabilities by insuring ships and cargoes in London or abroad.

Then in June, 1765, British Customs Officers and preventive cutters armed with powers of search and seizure on land and water appeared at all the Manx ports, and the crazy edifice of the Island's prosperity came crashing to the ground. The golden age of Manx smuggling was at an end.

In the towns the results were catastrophic. The Duke's final negotiations for the surrender of his rights had been conducted secretly, and the merchants had little chance of hiding or disposing profitably of the spirits, tea and tobacco which filled their cellars. The sweeping prohibitions contained in the Act brought trade to a standstill, and the townspeople suffered great privations.

When news reached the Isle of Man that the 'Mischief' and Revesting Bills were before Parliament, the Keys sent a deputation of three—Thomas Moore, Hugh Cosnahan and John Christian—to plead with the Government for lenient treatment of the Island. They arrived too late to influence the final state of the 'Mischief' Bill, but Moore says they obtained the entry into Great Britain and Ireland, duty free, of goods which were the produce and manufacture of the Isle of Man. A second application was made in April, 1766, by George Moore and Thomas Moore, the Rev. James Wilks accompanying them to make researches. The only tangible result of the mission was that Wilks obtained a copy of the charter, 'until then forgot and unknown,' in which James the First confirmed the rights and privileges of the Manx people.

In November, 1766, the Keys returned to the attack for the third time and sent George Moore as their deputation. He went alone for reasons of economy and with some trepidation, because of fears for his health and the responsibility resting upon him. The second Letter Book gives a detailed account of his actions and experiences.

His first step was to have his case and requests arranged in proper form for presentation to the Lords of the Treasury. For this purpose the London agent of the Keys procured the services of a lawyer whom Moore found to be a tedious pedant. After weeks of maddening delay he produced a prolix document emphasising the prerogatives of the Lord rather than the rights of the people. Alterations had to be made and many weeks passed before it was ready for use.

'Patience', exclaimed the angry Deputy, using an image that must have appeared to him the most natural in the world, 'one should have bottled up, to be uncorked and refreshed with as Occasion offers!'

Meanwhile he had been interviewing personages likely to have some influence on the success of his mission. Of them all the one who was warmest in his sympathy was the Speaker of the House of Commons, Sir John Cust. He displayed great kindness and consideration, advised on the form and matter of the Memorial, and later received the thanks of the Keys.

A figure of ill omen in his negotiations appeared in the person of Lutwidge, a General Surveyor of Customs with headquarters at Whitehaven, who had been appointed Receiver-General of the Isle of Man at the Revestment. He had no great love for the Manx, but told Moore that although he had received many incivilities in the Island he would do all he could to obtain some Trade. As a Treasury official, however, his one object was to squeeze as much revenue out of the Island as possible and give nothing back, and the dislike which his autocratic conduct evoked was not confined to the Manx. After Wood was appointed the first Royal Governor, he had to dun the Home Office for his salary which Lutwidge was holding back, and in 1774 Governor Smith wrote, '. . . illegal and arbitrary every day I find the actions of the late Receiver General.' High in the favour of the Commissioners of Customs, he had in his pocket a plan for the annexation of Man to Cumberland, and tried its effect on Moore, who in January, 1767, wrote to John Taubman,

'Mr. Lutwidge asked me how we wd like being annexed to Cumberland by wch means we wd enjoy the Liberty of an extensive Trade. I told him that if it was with the Condition of being saddled with Taxes that I wd not at all like it, but supposing sayd he that it wd be without Taxes, That I said I wd be very glad of and wd be glad if he wd tell me of it with such Certainty, as that I might send an Express to the Island to acquaint the People of it and for their Opinion—that he said he had no Authority for, But he was sure there cd be no opposition. . . .'

Moore was often in conference with the Duke of Atholl, who promised his support and was obviously anxious that nothing should be done without his knowledge. Lord Clare, the First Lord of the Board of Trade, was suspicious of the proposals attached to the Memorial. Moore's description of the sufferings which had resulted from the stoppage of trade, the flight of the young people to other lands, the deserted dwellings and warehouses, failed to arouse the compassion of the noble Lord.

'The inhabitants of all the former trading towns, he said, were a Nest of Vermin collected from the Dregs of the neighbouring Countries. I told him that since the Trade was gone all or most of these Gentry were gone and had dissolved like snow, which as to myself I was not displeased with. . . .'

In this conversation as in others, when Moore was trying to overcome the prejudices which existed in official circles, he was embarrassed by the reports arriving in London of happenings at home—the attack by a Ramsey mob on a grain ship bound for Douglas, the pursuit of a Manx contraband-laden boat by a revenue cutter, and the rough handling a few months before of a squadron of cavalry sent to Peel to seize landed goods, when the people of the town, according to the official story, 'displayed a very abusive and seditious disposition,' bombarded the troops with stones and half-killed one of them. Some of the merchants, too, were evidently carrying on the forbidden traffic in a new way. Moore shyly hinted at it in a talk with the agent Wallis.

'I asked him' (he writes), 'supposing there were any merchants in the Isle of Man who privately were concerned in carrying on an illicit Trade on the Coast of Britain and Ireland with Boats that never appeared on or about the Isle of Man. Such a Circumstance he said wd greatly alter our Cause and destroy the Merits of our Application. I then asked him supposing that Mr. Lutwidge wd surmise a Trade of this Kind carrying on by Manx people. Mr. Wallis said it would ruin our Case and the Fact, cd it be proved, was certain Destruction. I told Mr. Wallis that I might say to him what I pleased, but it was necessary to be in Confidence; he shook his Head, and for me it remains to proceed in this very delicate affair as well as I can.'

The Memorial, which Moore finally handed in at the Treasury, argued very reasonably that the Manx people were not the chattels of the Lord of the Isle, but had inherent rights which had been recognised by the English Crown from ancient times. These rights could not be bartered away by the Duke of Atholl in any bargain he might make on his own account with the British Government. Among them was liberty of trade, including the import into and export from the Island of various commodities. If this trade, which was in accordance with Manx law, was vexatious because of the smuggling of goods from Man into Britain and Ireland, it was not because the Manx had refused to regulate it. In 1711 an Act of Tynwald strictly governed the export of goods and provided safeguards against their illegal importation into Great Britain. At the same time the hope was expressed that the consequent loss to Manx trade would induce the British Government to allow the entry of goods which were the growth, products, and manufacture of the Island, duty free. The Commissioners of Customs freely admitted the justice of the case advanced by a deputation which was sent to London, and gave hopes of sympathetic action. But after being kept in suspense for eight months the deputation had to return home without any satisfaction being given. The operation of the Act was therefore deferred by Tynwald from year to year, and Manx trade followed its old course.

Since the Duke of Atholl had received payment for the surrender of his sovereignty, the Manx people were similarly entitled to compensation for the curtailment of their trade. The concessions asked for were on the whole modest enough—the abolition of the herring custom; the free import of salt, barrel-staves and cordage; a bounty on imported English corn; permission to import a hundred sheep per year for the improvement of the flocks; and finally, the main object of the petition: liberty to trade, under safeguards, with America and Africa.

When at length in the course of its leisurely procedure the Board of the Treasury came to a consideration of the Memorial, it very soon appeared that the most important clause, asking for foreign trade, would not be granted. Lutwidge's plan for annexation to Cumberland, by which the Isle of Man whilst retaining her laws and constitution would pay English Taxes and Excise, was then read. On being questioned, Moore repeated what he had already told Lutwidge, that the Manx in existing circumstances could not pay the Taxes and that their imposition would reduce the Island to beggary. The Board did not dissent from this opinion, and the plan was not again heard of.

Moore was asked to appear before the Board at a future date to receive their answer to his application; and week after week he sat cooling his heels in the antechambers of the Treasury in a way

N

familiar to Manx delegations of that period, fobbed off with the excuse that Lord Chatham's absence from London had delayed business. When the great Earl reappeared in March, both the Duke of Atholl and Sir John Cust assured Moore that all hope of anything being done that session was gone, and he returned to Man. He had acted with discretion, shown great zeal and persistence in the prosecution of his task, and claimed to have thwarted Lutwidge's plot to make the Island part of an English county.

He received the grateful thanks of the Keys, but the conduct of his mission did not escape criticism in other quarters. The gist of his conversation with Lutwidge had leaked out and he was accused of betraying his country. The Isle of Man had not escaped the effects of the democratic ferment in Europe and the New World, which was soon to produce the revolt of the American Colonies; and a section of the Manx people was becoming highly critical of the Keys, the manner of their election, their exclusiveness, and their secret meetings. Moore's claim to represent the nation was contested by this body of opinion, which pointed out that his activities in London had been mainly for the benefit of one class of the community.

> 'Clouded complexions' (he wrote), 'Divisions and Oppositions every observer knows to be the Characteristick of our unhappy Island, in this way I found them on my Return from London, some pleased, some protesting against every step I took in the past present and future Tense.'

Later, following in the tradition of disillusioned public benefactors, he confesses:

> 'I am become quite tired about the general Good of the Community of this Island, and of thinking about it, for I find by Experience that it is alike thankless and useless. . . .'

THE TYNWALD OF 1770

One of the last Letter Book references to Manx public affairs relates to the first Tynwald held at St. John's after the Revestment. In the spring of 1770, Governor Wood suggested to the Speaker and his lieutenant John Taubman that the Keys should formally memorialise him to summon a meeting of Tynwald, according to ancient custom, and also to resume the sittings of the Common Law Courts and Courts of Gaol Delivery. The Keys complied with the Governor's wishes, and in July he reported to London that the Tynwald had been very successful and attended by a great and enthusiastic concourse of Islanders who were said to have numbered ten thousand.

Moore does not give a reason for the omission of the annual ceremony in the years immediately following the Revestment, nor does he say that the Keys had made any move before the Governor gave them the hint. This curious incident, coupled with the Speaker's expressed readiness to agree to annexation on terms, makes one wonder whether the Keys were so absorbed in trying to protect their material interests at all costs, that the preservation of some measure of Manx independence and of the symbolic Tynwald had ceased for the time to have any deep significance for them.

Moore cannot be accused of underrating the dignity and importance of the body over which he presided. He appears to have been the first Chairman of the Keys to insist on the title of Speaker, an innovation which was still questioned by officialdom long after his death. His fondness for the symbols and trappings of authority led him into further imitation of the customs of the House of Commons. He wore robes of office and he provided a silver mace for use at the sittings of the Keys.

RETIREMENT

At the end of 1779, George Moore decided to withdraw from public affairs.

> 'Every Day's Experience' (he wrote) 'increases the sensation of my declining State of Health. . . . This Debility it becomes me not to repine at, rather is it a Duty to be consoled with the Degree of Health wherewith the Almighty has been pleased to allow at my Time of Life and to be very thankful that at upwards of seventy his Goodness has hitherto upheld me.'

He had never felt the qualms which might have disturbed the conscience of a more sensitive man when he surveyed a long life spent largely in flooding South-West Scotland with contraband spirits. From the first he had taken it for granted that he was on the side of the angels, and, as a young man of twenty-five, did not hesitate to bargain for the most desirable seat in St. Peter's, Peel—the first on the south side of the altar—in return for a new church bell. This protective shield of conscious rectitude must have been strengthened by the way in which the news of his retirement was received: not only by the praise of the Keys, but by the sympathetic attitude of the representatives of the Crown.

Richard Dawson, the Lieut. Governor, writing with warm expressions of friendship and esteem, said, 'Your resignation goes to my heart; it gives me inconceivable sorrow to lose you as Speaker. . . .' John Taubman, who succeeded to the Chair of the Keys, voiced their appreciation in sonorous phrases. 'We behold with pleasure', he wrote, 'the steady able and upright Patriot and exceedingly regret his Departure as a real and public Loss,' and he expressed the hope that the merited applause of his fellow citizens might throw a lustre about his setting sun and crown the remainder of his days.

In a farewell letter to the Governor, Col. Smith, Moore incidentally revealed his own and the Governor's keen interest in the Peel Mathematical School, where Smith paid for the education of two scholars. Two years before he had reminded the Governor of a suggestion that he should be granted a knighthood and be made a Privy Councillor of the Isle.

> 'In the Island' (he said) 'the traces of honorary distinctions are yet distinguishable, the Notion of Titles and the names of Barons. ... If my wishes are attainable they aim at the Honor of being a Manx Baron, and for this Purpose that the King may be pleased to order Letters Patent to be passed under the Seal of this Island containing His Majesty's Grant of the Dignity of a Barronet to me and my heirs.'

In 1781 Moore was for a time in better health and with John Cosnahan appeared at the Bar of the House of Lords in successful opposition to a Bill promoted by the Duke of Atholl. It was during this visit to London that the old man received the long-wished-for accolade of knighthood and so came to a partial fulfilment of his dreams. He lived six years longer and lies buried in the churchyard of Kirk Patrick with other members of his family.

The estate over which he had exercised so intelligent a direction passed from the hands of his descendants long ago, and the house in which his son Philip entertained the Duke of Atholl on the eve of Tynwald in 1793 has vanished, but several relics remain as examples of the taste of his period. The first is the hollow in the old garden once used for cock-fighting. Of the others he wrote in August, 1758:

> 'When I was this summer in Bath I took a walk with my son to see Mr. Allans Garden, in our way there we called in at a stone cutters. To look at and cheapen some stone vases was my Business and I bought and paid him for two Eagles and two Pomegranates which with their Pedestals he promised ... to be ship'd at Bristole.'

The eagles and pineapples—not pomegranates as he mistakenly thought—have survived the vicissitudes of two centuries and now adorn the approach to the present unpretentious house. These silent witnesses to the mutability of human fortune recall words once written by Moore when he had met with one of the great disappointments of his life. 'How uncertain are our Wishes!' he cried. 'How uncertain are our Wishes, how uncertain our Hopes!'

XIV

THE POTATO RIOTS, 1825

Of the various kinds of taxation the direct form is notoriously the most unpopular, and the annual levy made by the Church has always been attended by bitterness and strife.

Certainly the numerous exactions to which the Manx had to submit must have been a great strain on their patience, and they were prepared not only to avoid payment of old impositions whenever possible, but also to resist stubbornly any new demand of the Church. The ecclesiastical records contain many revealing stories of the attitude of the parishioners and of the trouble which arose when the impoverished clergy set out to obtain their lawful dues from a sullen and equally impoverished countryside.

John Cubbon of Kirk Arbory said indiscreetly of the collectors of 1666, 'They are a kind of witch that carry off the tithes,' and did penance for so insulting a description.

John Callister of Kirk Andreas cried, *Mollaght Jee ort!* 'The curse of God on you!' continuously in a loud voice as long as the proctors were in his fields; and Thomas Clucas of Kirk Marown gave vent to his irritation by pounding the Vicar's horses—'contrary to all law and Justice'—for eating his grass whilst the Vicar's servants were loading the Tithe corn.

Even clerics highly esteemed in their cures did not escape the odium attached to the collection. John Crellin, the popular seventeenth century Vicar of Kirk Arbory wrote to the Bishop describing his difficulties in the matter. When with his servant and horses he was drawing the Tithe corn on Ballamaddrell, he was met by the owner, who flourished a club and threatened

> 'if hee came that way againe there should but one returne alive, and so', says the Vicar, 'your poor dejected oratour turned home with his man and horses and presently made his redresse to Castletowne and findeing not Yr Lship there went to the Deputy Governor who gave yor petitioner his worships token with this provisoe that he should take the Deemsters advice along with him, but before that your Lships dejected oratour should reach the Deemsters House hee mett with the Maddrells father and sonne comeing furiously rideing towards him like wood *carnes* with the white of

their eyes upward and their switches in their hands threatening to strike but did not, but rather worse, for they upbraided your Lships poore petitioner with most grosse opprobious abusing termes unbeseeming them to doe to one of his cloth, and called him a beggar and the Issue or Generation of Slewe Whillian.'

In the eighteenth century the increasing cultivation of the potato and, at a later time, of the turnip, began to disquieten the clergy, since no precedent existed for a Tithe on these new crops, and there was no compensation for the loss resulting from the smaller acreage subject to Tithe.

As early as 1712, Bishop Wilson and his officials ordered payment on potatoes; but whatever immediate effect the Bishop's decree may have had, it is clear that in the latter half of the century Tithes on potatoes had lapsed. During the same period the Fish Tithe—so often the subject of bitter dispute—was abandoned. The fishermen, with the alleged connivance of the civil authorities, refused to obey Orders in Council in 1769 which recognised the legality of the Tithe, and after that time its collection fell into abeyance.

The loss of the Fish Tithe and the consequent reduction in the clergymen's meagre incomes made them all the more anxious to establish their right to a tenth of the value of the green crop (potatoes, turnips, etc.).

In 1817 the Bishop, George Murray, a nephew of the Governor-in-Chief, the Duke of Atholl, determined to clear up the legal position once and for all. In May of that year he filed a Bill in the Insular Court of Exchequer against Robert Farrant, of Ballamoar, Jurby, to subject his farm to the payment of Tithe of Potatoes. Two years later the Bill was heard and decided in favour of the Bishop. Similar action was taken in the case of another farmer, Caesar Tobin, of Balla-middle, and once again the Bishop won his suit.

After this result, which was announced in 1821, the two defendants appealed to the Privy Council. Tobin claimed that no Tithes had ever been levied on potatoes, turnips, and other root crops. William Farrant, who had succeeded to his father's estate, took a similar stand. In addition, he said that in place and in full satisfaction of all the small Tithes which comprised potatoes and turnips he was accustomed to pay the Vicar of Jurby *Buinn faillee dy voain*—literally, a rent digging of turf—that is to say, as much turf as could be raised in a certain turbary in Ballamoar by an ordinary man in an ordinary day's work.

The Privy Council, under the presidency of Lord Mansfield, outdid the Insular Court in the snail-like speed of its operations, but at length on June 1st, 1825, it rejected the appeals and affirmed the two judgments of the Manx Court.

The Bishop announced his victory in the following month—a delay in publication which his opponents ascribed to his desire to spring a surprise on an unprepared diocese. His declared intention to proceed in November with the drawing of the new Tithes was received with little interest in the four towns, but there was an immediate stir in the country districts.

For some years there had been growing irritation with the methods of Tithe collection. Up to the time of Bishop Richmond (1773–1780), Tithes were let to the clergy of the respective parishes. During his episcopate the Tithes were put up to public auction and let to the highest bidder, who in turn relet them, often at prices above their value.

Until the period of agricultural prosperity ended with the defeat of Napoleon, the defects of this system did not press too hardly upon Tithe payers. But after 1816 came the usual post-war fall in prices and there was much distress among those who occupied small farms and crofts. In addition the rents demanded by the Duke and Bishop had been advanced, and their proctors occupied the time of the Vicar General's Court with an unprecedented number of suits for recovery of dues, many of the defendants being committed to gaol.

The poorer tenants—crofters and landless men—had hitherto been indifferent on the whole to the warring political parties. Indeed they leaned as often to the Duke's side as to that of the well-to-do Manx landowners and merchants, who appeared to be no more alive to the problems and distresses of the poor than the corresponding class in England. But the news that the Bishop proposed to act on the Privy Council findings immediately united all sections in a determination to oppose the new levy.

The first public protest was made in Jurby, where church joined with chapel; and Humphrey Stephen of Ballavarran, a noted local preacher, and Juan Lewin, the eccentric church Sumner and Carval writer, were active supporters of the Captain of the Parish, William Farrant. He addressed a meeting in Manx and English and then produced a bond which was signed by those present. Its terms were as follows:

> 'That if any Proprietor of Land should either take his own Tithes of any kind whatever, or Tithes of any other Farmer, or give aid assistance or countenance to any Proctor or Agent of the Clergy or refuse to join in the said Bond such Proprietor should be debarred of all society or intercourse with his neighbours and if guilty of breaking the terms of the Bond should be fined £20 to go to mending the Highways; that all Tenants refusing to join in the same should be driven from their Lands and that all Labourers should be refused work or any relief or assistance from the Parishes.'

The example set by Jurby soon spread, and similar documents were signed in Ballaugh and Kirk Michael with the active encouragement of the Parish Captains, while Kinly the advocate partner of John Llewellyn, High Bailiff of Peel, prepared Bonds for Kirk Patrick and Kirk German.

Such agreements, or Combinations as they were called, had been banned in England by the Pitt administration; and this bold Manx anticipation of the Irish boycott campaign of 1880 was not entered upon without some misgivings among the leaders, who showed signs of an uneasy realisation that they were walking on dangerous ground.

Naturally enough the Bishop was loud in his protests to Government, and especially directed his complaints against the Captains, who, he erroneously believed, were chief magistrates of their Parishes, but had in fact been shorn of much of their powers after the Revestment.

The Lieutenant-Governor, Cornelius Smelt, had no reason to be partial to the Murrays, who had worked on various occasions for his supersession; and his sympathies lay with the Manx people. Having held an enquiry into the Parish meetings, he mildly declared that

> 'William Farrant, John Hughes, and John Caine, Captains of Jurby, Ballaugh, and Kirk Michael, respectively, have conducted themselves with great impropriety, but are hereby only reprimanded in the hope that they may have acted from error rather than wilful intention, by lending their names and influence to such improper and unlawful measures.'

If Colonel Smelt had foreseen the course of events during the following months, he would probably have expressed his disapproval in much stronger terms.

The Duke and his nephew were men of good intentions, but often displayed a capricious and autocratic temper which was perhaps more easily tolerated by their Perthshire clansmen than by the touchy and independent Manx. Both were extremely tenacious in the pursuit of any desired object, and the Duke's claims to various rights in Man were pressed with unwearying and relentless persistence upon greatly irritated British governments for half a century. In a letter of 1787 the Duke frankly revealed his aims.

> 'I am on my way to the Island', he said, 'to see by what mode it may be made more advantageous to the Public and to my family.'

If the Bishop had in view the increase of his own stipend he was also sincerely anxious to improve conditions in his diocese, and saw in the new Tithe imposition one way of aiding the clergy, of whom only four at that time had more than a hundred pounds a year.

But he was singularly unhappy in the choice of his advisers, the chief being William Roper and James McCrone. In 1824 he had appointed the picturesque Roper as one of his Vicars-General, thus setting at defiance a tradition that the vacancy should be filled by a clergyman distinguished for piety and learning.

Roper was an Irish attorney who had come to the Island in dubious circumstances. He was said to have fled there to escape a debtor's prison, and in the course of his eventful career had kept a milkhouse in Liverpool, and had been twice bankrupt. In 1822 he was admitted by the Duke to a hostile Manx Bar, whose attitude to him is sufficiently indicated by the opinions of two wrathful brethren of the law, expressed in the full-blooded diction of the period. Thomas Bluett said of him, 'He is the greatest sycophant that ever disgraced mankind.' Deemster Christian wrote, 'He is the most perjured villian almost in existence.'

Roper had his point of view, too, and boasted in a moment of self-revelation,

> 'If in combatting the exertions made by a combination of the entire profession, Bar and Bench, against me I have used strong expressions, the fearfulness of my heart never has protected the insolence of my tongue. . . .'

He had ability and proved a very useful servant to Duke and Bishop at a time when no native lawyer was prepared to offend the Anti-Atholl party, with its powerful family connections in the Keys and on the Bench. His advocacy of the Murray causes made him therefore an unwelcome pleader in the Courts, which, although they had fallen to a low level in dignity, found his truculent and abusive approach more than even they could stomach. In 1825 he was disbarred by Governor Smelt at the instance of Deemster Christian, who accused him of contemptuous and threatening behaviour.

His two patrons were highly indignant at the loss of one they considered indispensable to the transaction of their business in the Courts, and brought backstairs pressure to bear in Whitehall for Roper's reinstatement. This having been obtained a year later, the astute and unscrupulous lawyer lost no time in seeking revenge. Seizing upon a foolish indiscretion of the Deemster, he sued him for libel and subjected him to the humiliation of being a defendant in his own Court— a result not altogether displeasing to the Duke and his adherents.

James McCrone, a hard and unsympathetic Scot and the Duke's confidential agent, had been arrested some years before and held in prison for alleged perjury relating to the Tithes on Castleward. An acquittal did nothing to dull the edge of his resentment, and although Deemster Gawne's grant of the arrest warrant was legally correct, both Duke and agent regarded it as a malicious blow from their political opponents.

In his position as Chief Tithe Agent or Proctor for the Duke and his nephew he appears to have stimulated their already keen desire for drastic action in enforcing the ruling of the Privy Council. They in truth needed no urging, and in 1818 had asked the Secretary of State, Lord Sidmouth, for military help from England to secure the payment of the lapsed Fish Tithe. But Sidmouth, confronted with grave social unrest in every part of the kingdom, did not welcome a request involving such dangerous possibilities.

> 'I am concerned to learn', he wrote to the Bishop, 'that any part of H.M. Dominions should be in such a state of Insubordination that a class of H.M. subjects should be deterred through the Fear of Violence from asserting and enforcing their legal Rights; but', he blandly continued, 'your Lordship must be aware that the re-mote Provinces of all states are exposed to this Inconvenience and that in many it is felt to a far greater degree than in the Isle of Man.'

The intentions of Bishop Murray were announced at the Parish Churches, where the public were informed that a Tithe of twelve shillings per acre would be levied on potatoes. Even in normal times this rate would have been considered excessive since the common price in Ireland was three shillings and in the North of England half-a-crown. The Lieutenant-Governor was of opinion that if the English rate had been proposed the offer would have been thankfully accepted and the Tithe commutation paid without a murmur. But potatoes and herrings were the main subsistence of the poor, and the new levy appeared neither wise nor humane, for the crop this year was bad, and the herring fishing had been a total failure.

The first attempt to draw the Tithe was made in the parishes of Kirk Arbory and Kirk Christ Rushen, and the way in which it was conducted is illustrative of the disregard of public feeling which McCrone displayed. He had appointed two deputies of notoriously bad character—a tide-waiter and a discredited coroner—who were sent to their task with three assistants and three carts on the evening of a Fair-day, Friday, October 28th, 1825, when the farmers for the most part were absent from their farms.

At first the proctors drew some of the Tithes without incident. But their provocative manner enraged a number of labourers who had collected in Kentraugh, and high words ended in the Tithe gatherers being knocked down and beaten. When they appealed for protection to the owner, Edward Gawne, he answered evasively that he would speak to his people in the morning. The proctors thereupon fled into

Port St. Mary. The houses where they took cover were surrounded, windows were broken, and the attackers threatened to make an end of the two proctors if they could lay their hands upon them. The Tithe carts were overturned and broken, and the horses driven into the sea.

When the news reached Castletown the next morning, the High Bailiff went to the scene of the disorders with constables, and three offenders were taken into custody. On October 31st another attempt to arrest ringleaders was made, the Captain of the Parish having said that the magistrate and he would be able to execute the warrants without resistance. His optimism was not justified; a prisoner was rescued by the demonstrators and the constables were forced to retreat.

On November 1st the officers returned once more, and McCrone added a touch of comedy to the proceedings by sending with them Cobb, the Bishop's gardener, armed with a horse pistol. The men of Rushen were not to be intimidated by gardener or pistol. Cobb was set upon and beaten, and the constables accompanying him were stoned and hunted out of the parish. McCrone professed to be delighted with the disorders, since it afforded an excuse for sterner measures, '. . . so that', wrote Deemster Christian, 'poor deluded and half-starved wretches should be put down by the military rather then the milder coercion of the civil power.'

The handful of veteran troops in Castletown had already been joined by a detachment quartered in Douglas, and for the next two days the High Bailiff used them in his search for the law-breakers.

They had gone to earth, however, and were not to be found, whilst the presence of soldiers and constables did little to allay the excitement and spirit of revolt against the new imposts.

On Thursday morning, November 3rd, a crowd assembled at the Smelt Mill near Port St. Mary, under the impression that the building contained Tithe potatoes. Hoisting a red flag, the countrymen then marched on Castletown.

The Council was sitting at Castle Rushen, and in upon its deliberations burst the agitated High Bailiff with news that a large body of men, estimated to be at least one thousand, were approaching the town and were prepared to make proposals. The Coroner of Rushen, the famous Archibald Cregeen, was at once sent to ask what they wanted.

As the Coroner did not return, the Bishop drove off to Douglas, and later Deemster Christian and the Coroner followed him there. Cregeen then presented a statement on behalf of his parish, to the following effect:

'The inhabitants of the Parish of Kk Christ Rushen beg leave to acquaint your Ldship that it is unreasonable to expect to be able to get the Potato Tythe paid this year when there is not half a crop in the Isle but we are ready to deliver all other Tythes and dues or pay a fair value for them. By so doing and passing a free pardon to those confined and a general indemnity for what is past you will restore peace and comfort to us and confer a Blessing on your Ldship. The above is the wish and desire of the whole Parish; and the Parish is also willing to make good all damage and delapidations that have been committed respecting the same in the said Parish.

'I do believe the within to be the sentiments of the People.
(Signed) A. CREGEEN.'

The Deemster and Coroner asked the Bishop to remit the Tithe. The Coroner described the distressed state of the Sheading and the limited diet of the poor, whose only food was potatoes and salt. The Bishop, who seemed to be unaware of the extent of their poverty, was shocked by Cregeen's revelations and expressed himself very feelingly. 'He offered me his hand', wrote Deemster Christian, 'for the first time since the great offence of Mr. Roper's dismissal from the Bar.'

Whatever sympathy the Bishop may have had for the deplorable economic condition of Rushen appears to have been soon swallowed up by his indignation with what he considered were the unreasonable opposition and illegal actions of the countrymen. His own later account of the interview conveys no hint of humanitarian motives having changed his intentions. On the contrary he declares that the decision he came to was the result of the solemn assurances of the two envoys that the threats and denunciations against his Lordship and family were dreadful, and that their safety was only to be secured by satisfying the people.

The Bishop returned to Castletown the next morning, November 4th, carrying with him a document in which he promised to forgo his right to the Potato Tithe for that year. Church bells were being rung, and horns blown all over the countryside; and not long after his arrival the exclusive inhabitants of the Parade were gazing once more with distaste upon the red flag and a great concourse of men in homespun, who had come for the Bishop's answer.

The Castle gates had already been shut and the walls manned by the Veteran Corps. The Bishop called for Martial Law, but the Lieutenant-Governor parried this request by pointing out that the total regular troops in the Island numbered not more than seventy men and were only sufficient for the defence of the Castle. The old man, who was a popular figure, went out into the crowd and ordered them to disperse. They received him with respect and many began to make their way out of the town, but they were met by Gawne of Kentraugh, who asked them where the Devil they were going. They replied in Manx that they were going home, for the Governor had given them a slap in the face. Some then turned back to the Market-place.

Meanwhile a deputation had been taken into the Castle, where the Bishop reluctantly gave them his written renunciation of the new Tithes for that year. Afterwards he attributed the success of the Rushen agitation to the irresolution of the Lieutenant-Governor, who, he considered, was too old for the quick decisions and prompt action needed to crush the subversive spirit of the protestors.

The extent of the disorders, which after all did not result in death or even serious injury to any victims, was greatly exaggerated by the Atholl party. Although the red flag of the Smelt Mill had no political significance whatever in the minds of those who followed it to Castletown Parade, the Bishop's supporters called it 'the bloody flag of revolution', and drew a fantastic picture of an Island almost in rebellion.

Colonel Smelt did not subscribe to this view of the situation.

> 'The people', he said, 'are loyal and attached to their King and very submissive to their Superiors and very respectful to the Military; but they have been ill-treated throughout by the Head Proctor and his Deputies. . . .'

and he went on to describe the deference with which the crowd received him when he spoke to them, and their offer to draw the Bishop's carriage when he left Castletown after his statement relating to the Tithe.

> 'The people having expressed themselves satisfied and thankful returned peaceably to their homes.'

The inhabitants of the two parishes involved showed their good sense and good citizenship later by paying for the damage inflicted in the disturbances.

In Kirk Patrick, the other focus of active resistance, events took a more serious turn. The first meeting of the farmers was at Glen Maye Bank, and then and later the anti-Tithe protest appears to have been more or less actively supported by the occupiers of nearly every shore farm in the parish—from Knockaloe to the Creggan Mooar—though when the agitation acquired momentum the chief owners and tenants were satisfied to let the crofters, labourers, and hangers-on from other districts bear the responsibility and consequences of their irregular behaviour.

From the first there was much drinking at various public-houses and farms where the sympathetic, or, as was sometimes alleged, terrorised occupants provided liquor for the mob. Church bells were rung and horns blown, and for several days the demonstrators, hundreds in number, moved aimlessly from one alehouse to another.

On the 4th of November the mob was told that Tithe potatoes had been stored at the house of Vicar Cottier. They marched there, and stripping the roof from the storehouse burnt it with the Tithe cart. After they had had more drink at inns, the idea of marching on Bishopscourt to destroy it began to take shape. Then someone cried out that they should go to Knockaloe, farmed by a man named Kennedy, whose son had made himself very unpopular as a deputy proctor for the Bishop.

Here were witnessed the gravest excesses of the week. The crowd, which had dwindled to a hundred men, came about the house and called for the surrender of Tithe potatoes which had been collected. After some hesitation they then attacked the dwelling-house, smashing windows, doors and furniture. Glowing turf from the kitchen fire was carried out on a spade, and soon all the stacks in the haggard were ablaze—fourteen of corn, two of hay, and one of peas. Old Kennedy said, 'Boys, there is no occasion for fire. There is no leavings to that,' and was struck on the head. But the spectacle of seventeen stacks going up wastefully in smoke and flame sobered the rioters. Arson was an unheard-of crime in the Island, and its commission struck hard at the deeply-rooted habits of farm thrift common to Manx countrymen.

So although next morning the unfortunate Kennedys—man and wife—were dragged some distance along the road to Kirk Michael that they might witness the firing of the Bishop's palace, the wilder spirits in the mob had lost their appetite for destruction. The High Bailiff of Peel intercepted what he described as an immense concourse of people from Kirk Patrick armed with sticks, but he had no difficulty in prevailing upon them to disperse, on a promise that he would write to the Bishop for the same concession as had been made to Rushen.

Before he had received the High Bailiff's letter, the Bishop, who had grown increasingly apprehensive for the safety of Bishopscourt and his family, wrote by express to the Home Office. He accused landowners and some of the Keys of exciting a malignant spirit in the people, and ended dramatically, 'I am interrupted by the approach of a Mob and have only time to repeat my earnest request for assistance and Protection. . . .'

Men from several of the northern parishes were at the time assembling within a mile of Bishopscourt, but they returned home before nightfall, and this day, November 5th, marks the end of the mobs and their demands. On the same day the Castletown garrison, twenty-three in number, was despatched to the Palace in post-carriages and later escorted the Bishop's family to Castle Mona, whilst Colonel Smelt, acting under pressure, applied to Liverpool for two companies of infantry, though, as he was careful to explain, tranquillity was already restored. For this he gave credit to the Bishop, who on November 7th issued formal notice of his intention to give up the Tithe of Potatoes throughout the Island.

It was in a bitter mood that he admitted surrender. 'An open and undisguised robbery has been made upon me and the Church,' he declared; and well-informed observers believed that nothing was further from his purpose than the final relinquishment of the Tithe. Indeed, not many days had passed before some of his friends and his subsidised newspaper, the *Advertiser*, were hinting at a renewal of the campaign.

The Bishop was, however, shocked and discouraged by the strength of the resistance which had met his collection. The Duke's abdication from the Governorship-in-Chief and departure from the Island could not long be delayed, and he himself had as his objective a diocese which would be more amenable to his benevolent but autocratic direction. In less than a year he had left the Isle of Man for ever.

The British Government criticised Colonel Smelt's handling of the disorders. It was suggested that he had not taken a grave enough view of illegal actions committed, and that the three Parish Captains should have been removed; that the Rushen deputation should not have been admitted within the Castle walls; and that in publicly praising the Bishop's surrender he should have expressed regret that the restoration of peace had taken place in consequence of a forced abandonment of legal rights.

The Insular authorities felt the cold wind blowing from Whitehall, and made an impressive demonstration of their zeal in bringing the wrongdoers to justice. On November 21st, in the dead of night, the High Bailiffs of Castletown, Douglas and Peel, supported by strong military forces and a large posse of constables, made a descent on Glenfaba and arrested eight men. Of these only two were brought to trial, and the account of their appearance before the Deemster in December, 1825, provides an example of the reactions of Manx juries and their detestation of the death sentence.

The accused were charged under the Act of 1817, by which the malicious burning of stacks, any such stacks being adjoining to any house, outhouse, etc., in which there was any person, was to be Felony and Arson and punishable by death. The important word was 'adjoining'. If the burnt stack was not adjoining to the house the maximum punishment was transportation for life. The Bishop was said to favour the extreme penalty for convicted rioters, and the British Government was equally desirous of exemplary punishment.

But when the indictment was read out, the jurors refused to sign that part relating to the Capital charge. They declared that though the nearest stack was only two yards from the Kennedys' house it did not actually touch the building and consequently did not adjoin it. Deemster Christian's comment on the jury's attitude recalls the jibe of the *Stanlagh Mooar*: 'There are no lawyers in Man, for they are all lawyers.'

Writing apologetically to London, the Deemster said: 'They positively refused to sign the Capital part . . . from an obstinate persuasion, which I could not beat out of them, that they were the judges of the law as well as of the evidence. After fruitless discussions the Acting Attorney-General was obliged, with my concurrence, to omit the Capital charges.'

The two scapegoats were thus saved from the gallows, but were transported for life to Botany Bay. It is only fair to add that the Home Office expressed sympathy with the stand made by the jury.

A year later there was an echo of the Tithe troubles when the stack of a deputy proctor in Lezayre was fired. A man of bad character was charged with the crime, and was probably guilty. But the jury, led by McWhannell, a banker of Ramsey, refused, on evidence they regarded as inconclusive, to be browbeaten into a verdict pleasing to Authority.

After the riots, among measures designed to meet similar situations came the first creation of Justices of the Peace—a step not welcomed by the Manx Bar. Bishop Murray, who had been translated to Rochester but still nursed his grievances, was quick to draw the attention of the British Government to various names on the list, and managed to secure cancellation of the commission of John Hughes of Ballamona Mooar, who had led the Tithe agitation in Ballaugh.

The fears which the outbreak had aroused in official circles long persisted, and a decade afterwards the appointment of a Justice in Kirk Michael was considered a happy one since he could easily reach Bishopscourt in time of need.

The Church suffered greatly as a result of the clash between Bishop and flock. Colonel Wilks writing in 1826 said, 'A spirit has recently been generated quite foreign to the former character of the people and greatly injurious to the Established Church,' and two years later the Attorney-General deplored the state of the Manx Church and said that it required great renovation.

DOUGLAS, 1795

The Fort is in the centre. Behind St. George's Church is the " Hills " house

Schemes for Commutation of all Tithes which had been introduced by the Atholls were revived when the new Bishop, William Ward, arrived in 1828. He wrote, 'The great mass of the lower classes have been driven to the Methodist meeting houses by Tithes,' and adds, too optimistically as events showed, 'Almost all would return if the Tithes were settled. . . . Peace on the subject of Tithes will be the commencement of the prosperity of this interesting little Island where there has been nothing but war, as long and as bitter as the siege of Troy.'

Ten more years had to pass before a Commutation plan was discovered which was acceptable to all parties, and even then final agreement was only brought about under pressure of the British Government. In 1836 an Act was passed at Westminster by which the See of Sodor and Man was to be suppressed on the death or translation of Bishop Ward. The chief arguments in favour of so doing were the small size of the See and the need for augmenting the stipends of the parish clergy from its revenues.

The Bishop, who loved the Island and had worked hard for the improvement of his diocese, led a belated but successful protest against its absorption in the diocese of Carlisle. In 1838 the bishopric was restored by special Act of Parliament after a bargain had been struck with the Manx Legislature. An official communication from London written in that year ran,

> 'I am directed by Lord John Russell to acquaint you that supposing the Legislature of the Isle of Man should pass a Law carrying into effect the scheme in regard to tithes . . . the advisers of the Crown would be disposed to entertain favourably the proposition to retain the Bishopric of Sodor and Man upon the scale proposed. . . .'

Thus the passing into law of the Bill for the Commutation of Tithes in 1839 saved the Bishopric, and brought to an end controversies which had embittered Island life and disturbed the unhurried days of Home Office officials for a quarter of a century.

o

XV

BALLAUGH

When T. E. Brown walked through Jurby, one day near the end of his life, he declared that it was the last squeak of expiring civilisation—the civilisation he meant of the thatched roof and the open hearth, the griddle and the barley cake. What he would say of poor Jurby now if he revisited the glimpses of the moon is perhaps beside the point.

But I think that he would agree that Jurby's neighbour, Ballaugh remains, with some small unnoticed differences, the same in appearance as when he came down upon it from blackberrying in Glen Shoggil, over fifty years ago, and that it is indeed one of the least spoilt of Manx parishes.

One returns to it from districts afflicted by ribbon development and the unrestful inventions of modern architecture with great content—a content which, upon reflection, is tempered by the fear that sooner or later the blight of tasteless houses may descend here also; and that one may see the realisation of the disturbing vision of an Islander, who some years ago looked forward to the time when the road from Ramsey to Kirk Michael, now perhaps the most enchanting highway in the Island, would be lined on each side with 'desirable' residences.

THE BALLAUGH SHORE

The Ballaugh shore, like the rest of the lovely stretch of sand and gravel that extends to the Point of Ayre, has miraculously escaped commercial exploitation, but its continual wasting by the sea is an example of the apathy shown at various times by the responsible authorities with regard to the protection and preservation of the Island beaches.

In the nineteenth century Welsh schooners were permitted to land on the Ballaugh and Jurby shore, and carry off to Liverpool large quantities of the stones which had terraced the base of the brows and offered resistance to the attack of the sea. Since that time requests for groins or similar works to save from destruction the excellent farming land which runs northward along the coast to the Carlane and beyond, have met with little response from the Insular Government.

One interesting point is cleared up by a document of 1703 relating to coast erosion, in which the owner of Ballakinnag complains that persons have raised and carried away limestones from under his estate at Hanmer Hould, whereby the sea has encroached on his land and washed it away.

It is evident from this reference that the fort of Hanmer Hould stood at the Ballaugh Cass ny Howin or river mouth, and not at the Lhen as has been conjectured. It was built by John Hanmer, Captain of Man in 1575, in anticipation of attacks from Galloway and the Hebrides, and has long ago melted into the waves with many more acres of the parish.

Here, near the Cass ny Howin, from time immemorial the Militia kept Watch and Ward by day and night. In 1627 'Whetstone Hill' is given as the post for both watches, but all memory of this name has been lost. It was probably a boulder-crowned tumulus on the brows of Ballakeoig, and its site, like that of the Fort, now lies below the tide mark.

The Dubbyr Mooar, the Great Dub or Pool, formed by the river at its mouth, has also vanished in recent years, swept away by fierce gales from the south-west.

At the beginning of the nineteenth century and in preceding times, it was a scene of great activity, for the river creek gave shelter to from ten to twenty fishing boats. Nearly half of them were of the kind called 'Scouts', manned by eight men apiece, and went to Kinsale for herring. The light boats found plentiful supplies of fish on the Ballaugh Bank, until later times, when, according to local report, poaching trawlers scraped the ground clean of spawn and fish.

But the Dubbyr Mooar was greatly interesting for another reason. It was in this pool and afterwards on the Bank that young Edward Forbes made his first explorations in marine biology, and laid the foundations of his reputation as one of the most brilliant of Victorian scientists.

These places will always be associated, in the words of Professor Herdman, 'with the immortal memory of the great Manx naturalist who first made known the abundant treasures of our seas.'

Not far away is Ballabeg, the home of his mother's people, where he spent his boyhood vacations. Now it is roofless and desolate, like so many other old Manx country houses of its type—its voices stilled and the fire on its hearthstone long cold.

THE BOLLAGH JIARGEY

At the cross-roads near the church stands the old smithy, the only one left in the parish, and close by, the river is spanned by a stone bridge giving access to one of the oldest trackways in the Island, the Bollagh Jiargey (Old Red Road). It is a continuation of the coast road from Kirk Bride, negotiable all the year in ancient times, and the life of the northern parishes has moved over it for untold centuries. Along it came Neolithic man to his extensive settlements on the Broughjiarg. Along it, according to one tradition now sometimes disputed, came the men of the South to fight against the North at Santwat, near Kirk Patrick of Jurby; and along it from the barony in that parish came the Bishop's tenants with creels and sleds, bringing reluctantly to his palace at Ballacurry their customary rents of turf, grain, sheep, geese and hens—not always the choicest of their stores, to judge from the protests which were sometimes made by the indignant prelate.

This nineteenth century bridge was preceded by a wooden structure which was kept in repair by erring sons of the Church. In 1672, for example, the Rector, Robert Parr, in a communication which incidentally reveals the tender consciences possessed by Ballaugh men, reported to the following effect:

> 'The offender hath made his penance in penetentiall habit in tyme of Devine Service on good fryday and to my knowledge he was sorrowful and ashamed of his offence, insomuch that I went to his house severall tymes to give him godly counsel to keep him from despaire. . . . The fault was forgiven him—only hee to repaire the bridge.'

There are similar records relating to the Carlane Bridge and the High Bridge of Ballaugh on the Ramsey-Kirk Michael road.

The penance was not as costly as it sounds, even when allowance is made for the great scarcity of money at the time and its high purchasing power. In 1668 the Captain of Jurby, who had transgressed, duly appeared before the congregation in the customary white sheet and was then given the choice of making up the Lhen Mooar bridge or paying a fine of ten shillings. He wisely decided to build the bridge. He bought the wood of the old structure for five shillings, spent half-a-crown on new wood and labour, and so completed his penance for the not unreasonable sum of seven shillings and sixpence.

Of two tumuli on Ballabeg and close to the Bollagh Jiargey the Cronk Coar (Smooth or Pleasant Hill) has been levelled after suffering severely at times from the attentions of enthusiastic but unsystematic amateurs. The other in the Magher ny Shen Rullick (old churchyard field) is in a fair state of preservation, with nine encircling boulders still in position.

At the beginning of the Bollagh Jiargey is the by-road to the farm of Ballakeoig. It was probably the original homestead of the Ballaugh Corletts. The position of this coast farm made it inevitable that the owner should be an officer of the Watch, and the post was held by one member or another of the family for hundreds of years.

Thomas Corlett was the most famous of the clan. He was made Sumner-General by Bishop Wilson and was one of his most faithful followers.

Governor Horn imprisoned the Bishop and his Vicars-General in 1722, on their refusal to pay a heavy fine. After two months confinement in Castle Rushen the Bishop wrote to Horn offering to pay, without prejudice to their right of appeal, and Thomas Corlett carried the letter to the Governor, who whatever virtues he had, was certainly a man of violent temper.

In an affidavit describing his reception the Sumner-General says:

'I, Thomas Corlett, one of the 24 Keyes of this Isle, Do Certifie and will Depose that upon my Delivering the within writing to Governor Horn he called me Villain and Rogue repeatedly, and said I deserved to be put in the Dungeon; and upon my asking him what answer I was to return my Lord Bishop he said, "you may tell him that I called you a Villain."

Aug., 1722

(Signed) THO. CORLETT.'

THE OLD CHURCH

The old Church of Ballaugh occupies an elevated position close to a sheltered creek of the sea, and at the junction of coast and landward tracks—a site which must have been important in prehistoric times. A hundred yards east of the churchyard at one period stood a tumulus at a spot still marked by the swell of the ground, and there are two holy wells not far away.

As in the case of the other Manx parish churches, old St. Mary's contains in its walls materials from previous works, and is probably an epitome in stone of all the sacred buildings and monuments which have occupied the church enclosure since Neolithic man came to the Island. One finds another example of the thrifty use of ancient stones in the old Methodist Chapel, now the Village Hall; for it is partly constructed of the remains of an early keeill which a hundred years ago stood nearby in a field of Ballamoar.

The church was enlarged by Bishop Wilson and Dr. Walker in 1717, a date commemorated on the weathercock which surmounts the characteristic and attractive bell turret of the period. Upon a petition from the parishioners a gallery was added in the second half of the eighteenth century. The approach was by an external double staircase over the main entrance.

After the building of the new church in 1833 old St. Mary's became ruinous but received a new lease of life in 1849, when the building was shortened and the gallery and stairs removed. This was during the Rectorate of Thomas Howard, the memory of whose mild and benignant personality lingered long with old people in the parish.

In 1877 the church was once again rescued from decay by Rector Kermode, and has ever since been kept in a good state of repair.

The most important object inside is the Runic Cross of the eleventh century—the only one known in the parish, though others may lie hidden in the churchyard or in the walls of the church. It displays features characteristic of the work of the famous sculptor Gaut, of Cooley, and his school. On one side the shaft is decorated with the tendril pattern, a ring chain design on the right, headed by a small Celtic cross, the space on the left filled with the pattern known as key-fret. On the other side the ornament of the head terminates in the arms with the looped buckle and ring design discovered by Gaut, whilst the space to the right is occupied by plait of four. On the left the Runic inscription runs up into the head:

Oulaibr Liutulbsunr raisti krs thana aiftir Ulb sun sin;

'Olaf Liotulfson erected this cross to the memory of Ulf his son.'

From Olaf or Oulaibr comes the surname MacAuley or Cowley; Liot is found in Macthorliot or Corlett. Whether these two names are directly connected with the persons commemorated on the cross will never be known, but both are found in the earliest records relating to the parish and MacAuleys and MacCorleots owned land adjacent to the church in 1500. The Corvalley is still in the possession of descendants of the Corletts of that time.

The font is of unknown antiquity. It is made out of a red sandstone block built into a window seat. It is decorated with a cross, once painted in blue and red; and an inscription in Manx reads:

Ta un Chiarn, un Credjue, un Vashtey,
Un Jee as Ayr jeh ooilley—

'There is one Lord, one Faith, one Baptism,
One God and Father of all.'

The lid is modern. Two chairs in the Chancel were given to the Church by Bishop Wilson in 1717.

THE CHURCHYARD

Of the external features of the church perhaps the leaning gateposts have, naturally enough, excited most comment. It has been seriously suggested that they symbolise a primitive religious cult. The simplest explanation, that the foundations have slipped, is probably the correct one, for one cannot imagine any Manx mason deliberately building such an eccentric gateway, and exposing himself to the barbed witticisms which would pursue him relentlessly for the rest of his life.

Among the interesting gravestones is one near the church door to the memory of Thomas Corlett, of Ballacrye, who died in Jamaica in 1757. His father left his adventurous son five shillings if he would come for it. Thomas's ironic commentary upon his parent's will was to bequeath £300 to the poor of the parish, in addition to legacies for his family.

There seems always to have been a considerable amount of emigration, in spite of impediments made by the Insular Government to prevent loss of population. A Manx cloth merchant named Christian lived in London in Elizabethan times, and long before the famous Philip; there was a little colony of Manxmen (including a Stevenson of Balladoole) in Barbados, in 1650; a Castletown man died in Arabia in 1707; a son of Archdeacon William Mylrea, of Ballaugh, was one of the crew of a Guinea slaver in 1788; a Craine of Squeen was a merchant in the West Indies at the end of the eighteenth century; and so one could go on indefinitely; for the Manx have lived and died on all the shores of the world.

WRECK

According to tradition a Mylrea tomb close to the church gate was once used for the concealment of goods obtained from wrecked vessels.

The Ballaugh men were seldom exposed to the temptation to plunder wrecks. They were not more virtuous in the matter than those living on the rockbound coasts of the east and south, but the opportunities were fewer. When, however, on rare occasions, an apparently considerate providence cast a vessel ashore under the Broughjiarg, they were not slow to avail themselves of the chance given them.

One long remembered wreck occurred in 1697. Eighty years later the Rector, James Wilks, noted it as a remarkable happening, and said the ship carried the first cargo of brandy ever known in the Island. The advent of a new type of alcoholic stimulant may have given rise to legends of joyous carousals in the parish, and prolonged its memory, but no doubt what added piquancy to the event in the eyes of the sinful Ballaugh men was the fact that the Curate in charge of Ballaugh, who had so often assisted them on the penitential way, was himself accused before a jury of buying a saddle, rich cloths and other articles from wreck.

The fate of the brandy is indicated in the artless petition of one found guilty of carrying off some of the liquor:

'1699: To the Hon. Nich. Sankey, Governor of this Isle.
   The humble petition of Dan Cowell, of Ballaugh
   Sheweth

'That your petitioner chanced to carry a small quantity of brandy off the strand when the late ship was wracked, which he sold afterwards to one James Radcliffe and which occasioned a suspicion in a simple Jury that your Petitioner procured the said brandy otherwise, and therefore returned him in fine.

'Therefore he humbly begs your Honour to consider how fallible such suspicion may be since but few persons that were on the strand that day could free themselves of that wrack;

   'and your Petitioner not doubting but some of that said wrack may afford intertainment by some as yet.

   'From which he humbly implores your Honour to mittigate his said fine and he as in duty bound shall pray. . . .'

SIR ROBERT PARR

Besides the Archdeaconry and the Rectory of Andreas which was generally attached to it, the benefices of Ballaugh and Bride were the two modest promotions for which the Island clergy might reasonably hope, and, as a result, the lists of Rectors, of Ballaugh in particular, include most of those clerics who are famous in Manx church history. Among them in the earlier period are Sir Robert Parr, Sir Charles his son, William Walker, Matthias Curghey and Matthias his son, and James Wilkes. All of these were Vicars-General, selected for their eminence in sanctity and learning—a tradition which was broken in 1824 by the appointment of a layman with dubious antecedents.

The most notable of the seventeenth century Rectors of Ballaugh was Sir Robert Parr (the title 'Sir' by the way was used at that time in the case of a clergyman who had not graduated at a university). He was not, as his biographers have suggested, a son of the Bishop of the same name. His father was Robert Parr, Parish Clerk of Kirk Arbory, who owned the property now known as Parville, and was probably descended from William Parr, Comptroller of the Island in 1497. Thomas, another son of the Clerk, was fifty-four years Vicar of Malew, and has revealed his quaint and amusing personality, with humourless candour, in the Malew Register and various other documents.

Robert appears to have been a man of ability and came to Ballaugh in 1640. It was alleged with a great show of truth that he was in the counsels of the Illiam Dhone party and knew their plans, but he escaped the penalties visited on the insurgents and retained the favour of both sides.

He was probably not quite as Vicar-of-Brayish in his ability to steer a middle course, and catch the wind from whatever quarter it blew, as commentators have made out. He did not, for example, shrink from a quarrel with Bishop Rutter, the favoured protégé of the Stanleys, and used such downright expressions of disagreement that the Bishop accused him of abusing and belying him, and he was promptly consigned to St. German's prison.

Bishop Barrow, a shrewd judge of men, re-appointed him Vicar-General, and there are various indications that he performed his Rectorial duties and supervised his parish officials with efficiency. In 1665, for instance, Barrow, who had begun to discipline the demoralised diocese, demanded returns from the parishes. When they were not forthcoming every churchwarden in the Island was gaoled, except those of Ballaugh and Kirk Bride—a notable and probably unique prison assembly of over sixty church wardens which excites the imagination.

But what they said in sorrow or anger in the time of their adversity, what pious resolutions they made, are unfortunately lost to us. The Ballaugh men, no doubt, appreciated the good counsels which had saved them from the inhospitable dungeon of the Peel. In their reply to the Bishop's questions they said, 'The minister is a constant preacher, and that verie much to edificacon in our own tongue, a man of sober liffe and meeke condicon.' Asked concerning his dress, they said, 'For his habit we think it decent.'

The most famous of the Manx Parrs was the Vicar-General's son John, born at Ballaugh in 1651. He became Deemster, and it was said of him, with regard to his ability and integrity, that no better judge had ever occupied the Deemsters' bench.

'That great and learned man', wrote an English judge in 1817, 'that great and learned man Deemster Parr, of whom we have spoken with that praise which so justly belongs to him.'

His virtues brought him little pecuniary reward. He died in 1713 and was buried with his ancestors in the chancel of Kirk Arbory.

CHURCH RECORDS

The Ballaugh Parish registers are the oldest in the Island, the earliest date being 1598. They suffered severely owing to the negligence of the incumbents at various times, particularly in the Restoration period, and because of the inadequate protection they received.

In 1675, for example, the churchwardens were presented for not repairing the church door, the church chest, and church lock, whereby, says the chapter quest, 'the bookes and surplice are much abused and cutt with mice.' Through similar neglect and the damp chambers where they were stored, the early Diocesan records suffered greatly.

Sir Nicholas Thompson, Rector of Ballaugh and Episcopal Register, wrote in 1621 that of the Diocesan record books before 1572 most of them were perished before he had them, 'yett God willing,' he says, 'I shall doe my best to preserve what is left.' After his time there was more destruction, and the earliest will I have found on record does not go further back than 1598.

The wills were not infrequently written by the parish minister when the testator was *in extremis,* and describe his last minute arrangements for the disposal of his earthly possessions. In the result such documents exhibit an unusual quality of drama. Here is part of a Ballaugh will of 1678, written apparently by the Rector, Sir Charles Parr, who inserts the word 'loud' in two places, like directions in a play. (The husband, as was usual, left half the team of oxen and half the crop to his son, the other half being, by law, reserved for the widow.)

'To his eldest son Thomas Corlett,' says the will, 'his parte of the croppe of corne and teame of oxen, and desired his wife to give her consent that the said Thos. should have her parte of the cropp of corne and team of oxen but she replied, alas will I have for my parte of them but three pounds that were little enough for the nursing of the child if I be with child, and upon this he said againe (loud) you have your owne still. After which discourse both the testator and his wife held their tongs for a prettie space, and then againe he said what say you (loud) will you give your consent to halfe the teame of oxen and she replied I wille.'

And here is another seventeenth century will which strikes a note of victory, and demonstrates the truth of the Manx adage that the grey mare is often the better horse. The testatrix had been deserted by her husband, a Ballaugh man, and begins by cutting him off with sixpence. In addition, to make doubly sure that he should not be able to claim a widower's right in her property, she described how she had come by it.

He ran away, she said, leaving her with but half a cow worth ten shillings, and a small house also valued at ten shillings; but this was reserved with much ado for the satisfying of her son William to whom twenty shillings were owed by his father. She sold her only asset, the half cow, and, with the price and borrowed money, bought another cow which, she says in Biblical phraseology, by God's blessing increased to fourteen beasts, and of the same increase and breed were every one of the beasts she now possessed. She therefore left all to the son.

Occasionally one comes across a footnote to history as in a will of 1655. 'Robert Christian of Ballaugh', runs the simple statement, 'went to England, a souldier with the Earle of Derbie and did not returne.'

He was one of ten men recruited from Ballaugh, as from each of the Island parishes, and taken by the Earl in his ill-judged expedition to Lancashire in 1651. There they were cut to pieces in the battle of Wigan Lane, those who did not fall in the fight being hunted to their death through the countryside.

With the wills are often found marriage contracts arranged by the parents of the betrothed young people; and these documents became fruitful ground for disputes on the death of one or other of the signatories many years later.

The bride's portion was an important part of the agreement. When a Kirk Bride girl married the *eira* (eldest son) of a Ballaugh quarter-land farmer in 1649 she brought, as her dowry, two oxen, three kine, twenty sheep, six blankets and one mare and foal. In addition her parents provided a wedding dinner of thirty messes.

A normal feature of Ballaugh wills was a bequest to the Rector, generally a mutton, and to the poor of the parish varying quantities of corn, meal, and malt—as a rule a firlot, a measure equal to two bushels of wheat and to three of barley or oats.

In 1664 an enquiry by Bishop Barrow and his Vicars-General showed that the executors and the supervisors appointed to watch the executors did not carry out the testators' wishes in this respect, but with their friends made use of the best of the gifts to the poor by eating and drinking them at the funerals. This revelation had an immediate result, and two years later it was stated that few gifts were then left to the poor, but what was left was still spent at the funerals.

The custom did not, however, die out. In 1678 a John Corlett, of Ballaugh, left a firlot of barley to be given to the poor at the Cross of Douglas, and there are many similar cases in the eighteenth century

An important part of the funeral ritual was the feast of 'the corpse lodging', apparently the night preceding the burial, though drinking also took place before and after the funeral ceremony. At the funeral feast in 1692 of Susannah Murrey, a Castletown merchant's daughter, the following were consumed: ten bottles of brandy, twelve bottles of wine, ten dozen cakes, one and a half barrels of beer, and quantities of meat equal in value to an ox, with sugar and spices.

Manx country people could rarely indulge in such a generous expenditure and the Ballaugh records are therefore modest. In 1663, for example, a woman left 'four shillings worth of beere to be dranke by her friends and company the time of her lodging'. In 1721 William Craine, the Glaick, left two sheep for the feast.

One curious mention of the corpse lodging may be quoted from the neighbouring parish of Jurby, in 1725, when Thomas Teare, of Lough Croute ordered and desired an undutiful daughter to restore a certain pewter dish the same night he should be lodged in his own house; for, as he no doubt shrewdly calculated, she would not dare to disobey at such a fateful hour.

In the seventeenth century burial often took place within the church beneath the family seat of the deceased. The floor of St. Mary's was unpaved at that time, and the church wardens excused its condition by referring to the constant disturbance caused by the interments.

Poor people were buried coffinless, their bodies wrapped in a blanket and fastened to the bier with bands made of split osiers or briers. Sometimes a wattle coffin woven with similar material was used. The leaves of the magic trammon were strewn in the grave as a specific against evil influences and occasionally carved on the gravestone.

THE OLD RECTORY

The old Rectory adjoining the churchyard was built by William Walker, who was born in 1680, and was probably the most learned and respected Manx divine of his period.

The romantic story of his rise from farm boy to Rector of Ballaugh, Vicar-General, and intimate friend of Bishop Wilson, is well known. With his fellow Vicar-General he shared the imprisonment of the Bishop in Castle Rushen. In this dispute between the temporal and ecclesiastical powers, Ballaugh provided two of the chief figures in each of the opposing parties—William Walker and Thomas Corlett, the Sumner-General, supporters of the Bishop, and the two Mylreas, Deemster and Attorney-General, on the side of Lord Derby.

Nothing confirmed William Walker's popularity in Ballaugh more than the modesty of his behaviour on the occasion of his return to the Island with the honour of the Doctorate of Letters fresh upon him. His mother was among those assembled to welcome him, and he knelt before her to receive her blessing, in accordance with a charming Manx custom which did not long survive the eighteenth century.

It was usual for children to greet their parents at the beginning of the day by asking for a blessing.

'*Dy der Jee dou e vannaght!*' they said, bending the knee: 'God give me His blessing!' and received the answer '*Dy bannee Jee oo!*' —'God bless thee!'

'When didst thou last ask thy mother's blessing?' enquired the ecclesiastical judge in 1716, in a case where mother and son were at variance.

'I have not asked it these seven years,' replied the son, and shocked the court by such evidence of filial depravity.

In the old Rectory, one fine June morning in 1781, Rector Daniel Gelling entertained John Wesley to breakfast—'very agreeably,' says the famous Journal.

Daniel Gelling and Henry Corlett, a Ballaugh man, appear to have been the only two Manx clergymen who refused to be intimidated by the Episcopal ban upon any commerce with the Methodist movement.

On the other hand their clerical brethren generally were no doubt in sympathy with another Ballaugh man, Archdeacon William Mylrea, who was greatly exasperated by some of the phenomena of the new religious revival which had delivered such a shock to the complacency of eighteenth century churchmen, secure in the belief that they lived in the best possible of worlds.

It is true that he complained with some reason when a woman who was guilty of some of the extravagances which accompany new and vigorous movements, 'broke out', he says, 'with wild enthusiastic effusions fraught with insinuations of breach of Duty in the Rectorship with many expressions indecent and unseemly. . . .' When quite exhausted with her enthusiastic harangue she advised her audience to accompany her to a Love Feast when many of those tinctured with Methodism, some on foot and some on horseback, immediately hurried along with her—'as if hurrying to a fair!' says the horrified Rector—'to a meeting holden at Ballaugh on the same day.'

In 1787 the Church Courts were still able to deal drastically with obscure rebels against ecclesiastical authority, and the Enthusiast, a significant eighteenth century synonym for 'fanatic', was fined and committed to prison until she found bonds for her good behaviour.

THE OLD SCHOOL

Dr. Walker died in 1729. In his will, which contains a glowing tribute to the Stevensons of Balladoole who had befriended him in his impoverished boyhood, he left funds for the erection of a parochial school which had, so far, been held in the church.

This building stands on the highroad a quarter of a mile from the church. In the nineteenth century it was known as the Old School or the School at the Low End, and is now a dwelling-house.

In the seventeenth and eighteenth centuries Ballaugh was more favourably situated in the matter of education than many of the other country parishes.

A report of 1670 proudly stated, 'School was kept all year though not only for our own parish children, butt for such as come from Kirk Michael and Lezayre.'

But apart from study of the catechism and preparation for Confirmation the children's schooling does not appear to have been of much account, and if one is to judge from signed petitions and other documents a large proportion of the country people were illiterate until the nineteenth century.

Indeed nothing more could be expected. There was an almost entire lack of school books, and no certainty of continuous instruction. This was owing to the wretched pay of the licensed schoolmasters, who eked out their scanty wages with other occupations, and had little to lose if suspended for negligence. The case of the parochial master of Kirk Conchan, who was presented in 1810 for keeping a cow in the schoolhouse, was not likely to surprise the people of that time.

On the other hand there is ample evidence of the anxiety of parents to obtain what education they could for their children. In Ballaugh in 1680, when the Church authorities failed to provide a school, twenty of the parishioners maintained one at their own expense. Indeed, one of the things which force themselves upon one's notice in going through the church records of the seventeenth and eighteenth centuries, is the constant prayer of the patient Manx laymen for regular church services, preferably in Manx, with instructional sermons, and religious and secular teaching for their children.

THE DOLLAGH

The Dolly is a little group of houses built round a triangular green which until the middle of last century was the scene of the patronal fair. This was held on August 26th, the Assumption of the Virgin Mary, called in Manx *Laa'l Moirrey Toshee*, 'Mary's chief feast day'. 'Dolly' is a worn down form of 'Dollagh', the name of two quarterlands, and derived from the ancient Dhoolough (black lake), still existent but reduced in size.

Ballaugh has always in spirit been one of the most independent and democratic of the Manx parishes. Perhaps it owes this to the fact that, unlike some other parts of the Island, it has never produced a family capable of dominating its neighbours. It is true however that the Mylreas of the Dollagh Mooar quarterland were prominent in Church and State for over a hundred years.

The first was William Mylrea, who was out with the Ballaugh company in the Illiam Dhone rising, but went to some pains to convince the Restoration authorities of his loyalty to the house of Stanley. He was successful in this and was eventually made Captain of Ballaugh. Illiterate and of somewhat truculent temper, he came into collision, in 1671, with the Rector, whom he affronted by using the familiar 'thee' and 'thou' instead of the polite 'you'.

He demanded who had written verses about Mylecharane and himself, and evidently suspected Sir Robert Parr. One would like to think that here is an early reference to the Mylecharane ballad. Apparently, however, some country poet had been exercising his satirical wit upon the military record of Mylrea and William Mylechraine, of Lezayre, neither of whom had cut a very heroic figure in the events of 1651.

His son, Daniel I, filled various posts, including that of the Coronership, which was still sufficiently important to provide, as in his case, a step to the Deemster's bench. He was also Deputy Governor. He strengthened his claim on the benevolence of the Lord by a whole-hearted support of the Governor's party opposed to Bishop Wilson, and the Deemster's son, Daniel II, was made Attorney-General, and later, Deemster.

The Attorney-General's heir, Daniel III, in his turn, received the Deemstership, and the second son, William, through the influence of his father with the Duke of Atholl, became Archdeacon. The death, in 1832, of William's son, Daniel IV, who also was Archdeacon, completes the tale of four generations of the Dollagh Mooar which in that time had produced three Deemsters and two Archdeacons.

But although the Mylreas had such a remarkable succession of public posts, their reign was too short to create a tradition of superiority in the parish, and their land-holdings, disposed of in 1777, were not sufficiently important to give them the prestige which at that time arose from the possession of large estates.

It has often been asserted that in Hall Caine's 'Deemster' the unattractive character from whom the book takes its name was the portrait of one of the Mylreas. But the novelist denied the identity of his characters in that book with any particular figures in real life, and claimed the right of every creative artist to the paternity of the child of his imagination.

The popular Manx Christian name Daniel, which figures so prominently in the Mylrea pedigree, was, of course, a corruption of Donald or Danold. In the eighteenth century it was confused with the Biblical name, and under the influence of the religious revival of the time supplanted the native Donald. Patrick, another popular Ballaugh name, passed into eclipse about the same time and for much the same reason.

THE NEW CHURCH

The new St. Mary's was built in 1833 to the plans of John Welsh. His work has been adversely criticised, and his church at Ballaugh received the equivocal compliment of being classed the best of the bad designs for which he was responsible.

An interesting possession of the Church is a silver Communion Service, presented by Lady Buchan, daughter of Col. Wilks, and granddaughter of Vicar-General Wilks, who was Rector of Ballaugh and died there in 1777. The Buchan School at Castletown was named after her, and in extreme old age she still retained vestiges of that unusual beauty which captivated Napoleon's entourage during her father's governorship of St. Helena.

THE VILLAGE

The village of Ballaugh came into existence at the end of the eighteenth century, with the improvement of roads and transport.

The population of the parish steadily increased to its maximum in about 1840, when it was 1,500—three times its present size.

A list of its activities makes melancholy reading for those who deplore the decay of the countryside. In addition to over a hundred men who went to the seasonal fishing from the Cass ny Howin, there was a considerable number of skilled craftsmen in varied occupations. There were at least three smithies at work, and two nailmakers' forges; hat factories of modest size, where beaver and straw hats were made, the straw being plaited in various homes; a tannery; a walk mill; weavers and bleachers; lime burners; glove-makers who produced strong leather gloves; and of course, shoemakers, tailors, carpenters, masons and millers. Finally there were three breweries.

In times before coffee, tea and cocoa came into common use, beer was regarded as an important and indeed essential article of diet.

It is interesting to note the attitude of a Church Court before which a Kirk Arbory man appeared in 1720 for drunkenness. He was punished not only because he was intoxicated, but also because he had wantonly spilt good ale on the road as he carried it homeward.

In the fifteenth and sixteenth centuries Ballaugh had its two parish ale-tasters who kept a watchful eye on the quality of the drink and saw that it was sold in sealed measures at the price fixed by law.

The Stanley régime encouraged home brewing by letting out brewing pans at a yearly rent, and as late as 1715 there were twelve of these circulating in Ballaugh alone.

The eighteenth century witnessed a change for the worse in the drinking habits of the people, due to the growing contraband traffic and the cheap spirits which flooded the country. Prior to the Revestment the duty on these was only 1d. a gallon, and as late as 1830 Bishop Ward declared that cheap liquor was the curse of the Island, and that a man could make a beast of himself for sixpence.

The social deterioration displays itself in unexpected ways. In Ballaugh not only did prosecutions for drunkenness increase as the

RAMSEY BAY FROM BALLURE GLEN, 1795

With the old Douglas Road in the foreground

eighteenth century moved on, but presentments for using bad language reveal that even the curses, which had on occasion shown some traces of poetic quality or an unexpected turn of expression, had degenerated into the coarse and monotonous profanities of the pot house.

In 1820 the House of Keys made sound, if belated, suggestions to restrict the sale of intoxicants, but ten years later Ballaugh, although not so plentifully equipped as other districts, still possessed one hotel and seventeen public houses. Out of the violent and inevitable reactions to this state of affairs sprang the temperance movement, which swept the Island, and other countries suffering from the same evils, with a crusading fervour which did not lose its intensity until the end of the century.

PARISH BOUNDARIES

More than a mile north of the village on the Ramsey road is still to be seen one of the white boulders which Bishop Wilson, in 1715, accepted as a Ballaugh-Lezayre boundary mark. From there the line runs through the Curragh and finally follows the course of the Carlane Water to the sea.

The upper part of this stream flows through the Lag ny Foillan (the hollow or cove of the sea gulls) below Ballavolley. According to a legend once current in the parish, sea raiders coming in at the Lhen in ancient days were able to penetrate the undrained Curragh to this point in their flat-bottomed boats, and then landed to plunder and burn.

In 1677 the Ballaugh-Kirk Michael boundary was in dispute. Ballaugh witnesses declared that it came down the Bishop's Glen, through the Chapel and so by a devious route to the Purt Noa on the sea at Balnahowin.

The witnesses also asserted 'that in ancient days the respective Parsons and Vicars did severally officiate divine service, the one at the one side or end of the said Chappell and the other at the other side or end . . . alternately upon the . . . dayes of perambulation'.

In 1741 Bishop Wilson drew the attention of his clergy to their failure in not maintaining the traditional practice of walking the parish boundaries annually on Holy Thursday, and called upon them to resume so laudable a custom. His orders were carried out for a time, but later only at long and irregular intervals. There was a Ballaugh-Kirk Michael perambulation in 1860, and one on the Jurby boundary in 1877. The last recorded in the 'Parochialia'—the admirable parish record instituted by Rector Kermode—was between Ballaugh and Kirk Michael on May 23rd, 1882.

The Rector and Vicar took part in religious exercises at the Purt Noa, on the coast, and continued the service in Bishopscourt Chapel,

P

taking up their traditional positions in that building. The boundary walk was then resumed to Druidale and the Sulby river.

THE GLEN

At the entrance to the Glion Dhoo—the Glen of Ballaugh—were two circular earthworks occupying dominating positions on the flanking hills. The western one on Slieau Curn was destroyed early in the nineteenth century. The other, the Castal Lajer (strong castle) still stands high up on Slieau Vollee.

There is no record of its ever having been systematically examined, and its original purpose is not known. There is a tradition of an underground chamber, but whatever entrance it had is now hidden. The earthwork approaches sixty yards in diameter and on the lower side of the slope the embankment is still twelve to fifteen feet high.

The Glen has many euphonious names to match its natural beauty —the treen names Carnedal, Scrondal and Glion Dhoo; field names like Breckan y Kayl and Magher ny Castal; the hill slopes of Brough ny Vannag and Ard ny Crongan; and the subsidiary gills of Glion Voirrey, Glion Shoggyl, Glion Shellagh, and Glion na Phaalana.

At the Carmodil Glen foot, where its stream joins the Ballaugh river, is an interesting little group of houses, one of them with outside steps, and nearby is the site of Keeill Voirrey, the Chapel of the Virgin Mary. A boundary hedge crowns the chapel hill, which on the far side has been completely dug away. There is no visible evidence of the building which once stood there. From time immemorial the Mollavorras—the devotees of the Virgin Mary, and perhaps the original guardians of the keeill—have clung to the slopes of the glen, and the Anglicised form of the name, Morrison, is still to be found in the neighbourhood.

The oldest Ballaugh mill was that of Scrondal, and the only one mentioned in the Manorial Roll of 1513. Another corn mill was established at Squeen in later times. To this the crofters were compelled to take their grain, whilst Scrondal was reserved for the use of the quarterlands. This ancient mill, like fourteen others in the Island, had the doubtful privilege of paying an annual Tithe pig, which would be expected to be of high quality because of the abundant provender under the miller's control. In the eighteenth century, the tithe in kind was commuted for a sum of money.

THE COMMONS

On the eastern side of Glen Shoggil, above Ballathoar, are some remains of the ancient earthen fell dyke which marked the limit of the

Common Lands, and is often mentioned in the early laws. After 1866, it was replaced by drystone walls, excellently built by Scottish dykers.

At the beginning of the eighteenth century, various encroachments were made by the Lord upon the mountain lands. In some cases, Government officers acquired portions, and in others stretches of land were granted to lessees—in particular, one McGuire, of Dublin.

In July, 1724, bitter resentment was aroused in Ballaugh when it was reported that the commoners' rights were threatened, and that the Governor's officers and McGuire were making a survey in the hills. A body of men assembled at Cronk Ould, and made an attack upon a cart conveying provisions and liquors for the survey party. The rope harness was cut and, according to the indictment, the Ballaugh men 'behaved in a most raging manner'.

When the soldiers who had been prudently brought by the officers appeared on the scene, Robert Corlett, of Ballakeoig, boasted that he could beat any two of them, for he did not feel them in his hand; and the Coroner of Michael said he heard another cry, 'Maugher!' 'which in English', he said, 'I take to be "Battle!" '

Bloodshed, however, was averted, and the ringleaders punished. Adam Cain, who had taken the lead, was heavily fined and put into the stocks of the four towns for two hours in turn, with a paper on his breast, naming the crime. Ten others, who included representatives from seven of the Corlett quarterlands of the parish, were given similar punishment, but of less severity.

THE PORT

From Scrondal upwards, the glen was full of legend, now only vaguely remembered by a few of the oldest people, and most of it forgotten in the last generation—of fairies and bugganes, of small snow-white goats dancing in the moonlight and making thunder as their dainty hooves struck the responsive ground; and of powerful witches, one of whom was recalled when cloud or mist wreathed the head of Slieau Dhoo, for then they said that the mountain was wearing the cap of Nan-y-Caillagh.

The Port had its stories of robbers hiding in the ravines, of eagles carrying off lambs, and the dismal end of travellers who met bad weather on the hillpath from Injebreck and were found dying or dead, disfigured by the beaks of carrion birds of prey.

There is, as a contrast, the adventure of one coming from Douglas on a Saturday night in 1715, who was so drunk that he fell off his horse on the mountains and did not find the animal till the next day. His descent into Ballaugh was observed, and he was presented for Sabbath-breaking.

His excuses were, however, accepted by a sympathetic Court which found in happily-chosen phrases that he was indisposed by an ague—a complaint common in the Curragh before it was drained—and was, therefore, intoxicated unawares!

On a summer's day, the Port is a delightful spot, joyous with birds and the music of the swift bright river. But when the westering sun deserts this strange and beautiful amphitheatre among the hills, and the shadow of Slieau Curn creeps across the green flats, people sensitive to environment find that the place acquires a subtle and disturbing quality in the evening light.

The harsh, impatient croak of the ravens still quartering the sky takes on a more sinister note; and a solitary *cor-ny-hastan* (heron) looms up gigantic and threatening through the growing dusk, as he flies with heavy wing towards the ridge above the Glen Dhoo.

It is not to be wondered at that the imaginations of the little community which once existed here responded to the atmosphere and that they saw and heard unusual things. The Port is now deserted, the river flats are no longer tilled, and the tuckmill is a roofless ruin.

Above the Port, a gully, called the *Glion-na-Phaalana* (Glen of the Fold), comes down Slieau Curn into the narrowing Glion Dhoo. Half-way up this little ravine are the remains of two earthworks. The one more strongly defined is a pentagonal enclosure, each side about fifty feet in length, standing on the south bank of the rivulet which divides the gulley. They are believed to have been made in 1779 when the Parish Captains were ordered to establish places of refuge in the hills, in case of invasion.

ARDRENK

The parish of Ballaugh climbs over Slieau Vollee and Slieau Dhoo down to its last outposts in the valley of the Awin Mooar (Great River), as the Sulby was once called. There, under Druidale, Ballaugh makes rendezvous with three other parishes—Kirk Braddan, Kirk Michael and Lezayre—at a point to which some significance, religious or territorial, must have been attached in far-off times. It is the site of urn burials, and the remains of a chapel, Keeill Vael, and a holy well are to be found there.

The wedge of Ballaugh which comes down to the Great River, between Kirk Michael and Lezayre, forms the isolated treen of Ardrenk—the Height of the Dancing—and constituted the Forester's Lodge. In ancient days, it was the perquisite of the Lord's Forester, who guarded his master's rights and prerogatives in the Forest. Out of this land he paid customs of oats from ground now gone out of cultivation.

It was from here that he set out annually on St. Columba's Eve, June 8th, to sound his horn thrice on the summit of Snaefell. Two days after this symbolic ceremonial, and carefully watched by the justly suspicious sheepowners, he ranged the hills in search of unshorn sheep whose fleece became his lawful due.

The Lodge has been in ruins for more than a century, and its land is now merged in the Commons.

KIRK PATRICK OF JURBY

In former days the newly arrived stranger in Jurby at first found little except the distant prospects to excite his admiration; and he would, alas, discover still less at the present time.

The salt winds which sweep in from the south-west and the Atlantic gales roaring down the North Channel in their attack on the crumbling brows of Knock Shavell and Sartfell have been fatal to the growth of trees, except in more sheltered inland places like the strip of country which lies between Ballacaine and Ballahasna and includes the fine plantations of Ballamoar. But the monotony of the treeless hedges is soon forgotten in the exhilaration of wide untrammelled space and light. Like Kirk Andreas and Kirk Bride, Jurby probably includes within its boundaries the sunniest and driest part of the Isle of Man, and there is a translucent quality in its bright skies, born of the light-reflecting sea, which one finds over shores that look towards the setting sun.

Facing Ulster and Galloway and the gateway to the Hebrides it has shared in the vicissitudes and the legends of the most romantic coast of Man. Once the Isle of St. Patrick, when the waters of the Lhen and Carlane completely encircled it, its people cherished traditions of the landing of the great apostle of the Irish Gaels; and the descendants of his converts saw the longships of Orry swinging in upon the Lhen shore, to found the Kingdom of Man and the Isles.

The third great event of far-off times in which Jurby claimed to have been the scene was the battle of Santwat in 1098, when North met South at some place within St. Patrick's Isle, and, according to legend, won only by the intervention of their heroic women. But it will never be known with certainty whether Sandygate or the ford in Glenfaba was the scene of the fight; whether, indeed, the creek at Jurby Head, once known locally as St. Patrick's landing place and now under the waves, saw only the arrival of one of the Saint's disciples; and whether it was not royal Orry but a Viking of lesser breed who beached his war galleys below Keeill Colum on a cloudless night of stars.

MYLECHARAINE; THE CARRASDOO MEN

Of other Jurby legends two have been set down in verse—'Myle-charaine' and the 'Carrasdoo Men'. All the known variants of the traditional ballad 'Mylecharaine' give Jurby as the location of the story, and for centuries the surname in various forms, some of them abbreviated like Charran and Charane, figures in the parish records.

At the end of the seventeenth and in the first quarter of the eighteenth century some ill-feeling arising out of drainage and boundary disputes existed among various holders of land drained by the Carlane river. In 1720 William Mylecharaine was in conflict with Christian of Ballamoar over a Curragh boundary at Lough-ny-Creeagh, through which the stream made its way. In a petition complaining of the arbitrary conduct of the Administration the Keys accused Governor Horne of a brutal assault on Mylecharaine, who had displayed an exasperating stubbornness in pursuing the family claim. He was finally committed to Castle Rushen for refusing to obey the order of the Court. He did not long survive his experiences in what the Governor's Council were pleased to call the 'dry and wholesome' dungeons of the Castle.

In 1723 the Mylecharaines were presented for not cleaning the watercourse from Lough-ne-Caran (i.e. Lough Mylecharaine) downward to Lough-ny-Creeagh. These two names are now forgotten and the loughs drained, but Lough-ny-Creeagh was on the Ballaugh-Jurby boundary and partly in the Ballamoar curragh land. It is interesting to note that a couplet in what is probably an eighteenth century version of the ballad, found by Mr. C. J. Paton, runs:

> *Osnageyn trome va thie Mylecharane*
> *Tra hie'n sthock as yn stoyr sheese dys y Charlane:*

> Deep groaning there was at Mylecharane's house
> When the stock and store went down the Carlane.

It may be reasonably assumed that the Mylecharaine of Mr. Paton's version lived, like William's kindred, close to the Ballamoar boundary and the Carlane river, a few hundred yards after its entry into Jurby.

Another literary allusion to Jurby is found in *The Carrasdoo Men*, the best known poem of the gifted but ill-fated Esther Nelson who was born in Jurby in 1805 when her father, John Nelson, was vicar of the parish. The outlaws of Carrasdoo are said to have their rendezvous in Jurby Curraghs.

> 'O I rede ye beware of the Carrasdoo men
> As ye come up the wold!

I rede ye beware of the haunted glen,
Be ye ever so brave and bold.'

The origin of the story and its location has sometimes been debated, but it is evident that the poet embellished, in the romantic style popularised by Sir Walter Scott, an eighteenth century murder long remembered in Jurby. The crime was said to have been committed in a cottage a short distance over the Jurby boundary on the edge of the Curraghs and by the road to the Craige. A pedlar taking refuge there for the night was killed for the sake of a bag of gold pieces which he carried and imprudently displayed. The cottage was still standing forty years ago but no trace of it now exists.

THE CRONKS

On the windy heights by the Jurby shore and on elevations inland the Viking settlers raised their great funeral mounds, of which only three have survived more or less intact—Cronk-ny-Arrey-Lhaa (Hill of the Day Watch), one of the twin tumuli of Knock-y-Dowan on Ballachrink Clucas and Cronk-y-Vargee (Market Hill) on the Glebe.

Cronk Elliot disappeared some years ago in the fall of the shore brow upon which it stood, near the houses of Ballaholly. It was one of the places from which Jurby people watched the famous sea battle of 1760, when the British commander Elliott defeated Thurot. A hundred years later it saw sailing vessels hove to off Jurby Head, to take on board some of the most virile members of the Jurby and Ballaugh community on their way to the New World.

The Cronk Moar, a historic landmark which had outlasted 'the drums and tramplings' of a thousand years, a post where so many generations of Jurby men had stood on watch and ward, was levelled in 1939, on the requirement of the Air Ministry, which found that it obstructed the full view from a coast observation tower.

The Manx Museum authorities who had previously arranged for examination of the mound, obtained permission to remove it themselves. This was done carefully, section by section, and the Cronk was found to consist entirely of sand, from which worked flints were obtained. Further digging disclosed supposed remains of a ship— bottom strakes, stern post and part of the keel.

At that point work was stopped by the outbreak of war, and the excavation covered up. In 1946 Dr. Bersu, the noted archaeologist, completed the work. He found that the tumulus had covered a late ninth century Viking burial in a wooden coffin, and not a ship burial as surmised.

In the same year the Doctor excavated Cronk Carlane or Keilleig near the old Ballateare house which was damaged by a Scottish tenant of the farm in the nineteenth century. It was said that when he began to cart it away the sleep of his family in the dwelling near by was disturbed by such blood-freezing noises that even the matter-of-fact Scot was forced to stop digging and cover up again the burial-urns he had exposed. The cronk was now found to be a pagan Viking burial mound raised over a Neolithic cremation-cemetery.

One of the tumuli of Knock-y-Dowan (Ballachrink) was broken into fifty or sixty years ago, and Viking weapons discovered. The fine companion tumulus has suffered damage from cattle, but now has a protecting fence.

Cronk-y-Cliwe (Hill of the Sword) and Cronk-y-Scoltee (Hill of the Cleft) have been opened, and the Cronk Breck (Speckled Hill) also appears to have been disturbed, for it has greatly diminished in size during the last fifty years. A field-name reveals that there was once a mound called Cronk-ny-Holloe on Sartfield Mooar, and 'the Hill of Ballameanagh' is mentioned in a will of 1699. These two, like the Cronk Mwyllin, near Ballakneale, have been levelled. The tumulus in the churchyard, it has been suggested, is accountable for the name Nappin (Hillock) the farm-land in the middle of which the church stands.

KIRK OOSLAN

In the early times the chief parochial centre appears to have been in north-east Jurby. The Charter confirmed to the Manx Church in 1505 specifically mentions 'the churches of St. Patrick of Jourby', and it is probable that one of these stood on Ballaconly and was the first parish church. It is still known by the suggestive name of *Kirk* Ooslan.

With its excellent glebes for vicar and clerk it stood in the centre of lands called Particles originally granted to the church for the maintenance of scholars, but seized upon in 1429 by the grasping Lord of the Isle. The Particles in their turn were surrounded by the farms of the Bishop's Barony.

The presence of so important an ecclesiastical settlement no doubt arose from the fact that in the valley below the church the Lough, now silted and clogged with reeds and water plants, extended farther up the Lhen depression, and in early times warboats and traders must have found there one of the most secure anchorages between the Ayre and Peel.

The site of the church has never been satisfactorily explored. An eighteenth century tradition relating to Ballaconly says that interference with the church remains resulted in the death, one after another, of seven brothers, leaving their sister, Mary Conoly, heiress to the property. In 1751 she married John Callister and their descendant now holds the estate. According to report uncanny noises have been heard in the Ballaconly house and apparitions seen in the orchard. These have been attributed to the use of church stones in the building and the inadvertent disturbance of an ancient place of burial when alterations were made in the road near the house.

The most important find at Kirk Ooslan was a Scandinavian cross on which scenes from the Sigurd epic are engraved. In addition a smaller cross and a hollowed-out block of sandstone were found. The block is to be seen in the garden of Loughan-y-Shuin. In it are round white stones from a lintel grave examined by Canon Quine in 1916. A portion of a slate slab of poor quality and much flaked was turned up by the plough. On one surface are five small crosses rudely incised, and it has been conjectured that it was used as an altar stone. In a field on the Clerk's Glebe close by the church site is the Cronk-y-Vargee where annual fairs were held on the patronal Saint's day.

THE BISHOP'S BARONY

The meaning of the name 'Jurby' is uncertain. A. W. Moore suggested its derivation from *Dirabyr*, the animals' farm, J. J. Kneen gives *Ivarbyr*, Ivar's farm. Canon Quine considered that it came from *Djorabyr*, the farm of the *Djora* or steward of ecclesiastical lands, which in early times he estimated to cover 1,100 acres of the parish.

Of this area the farms of the Bishop's Barony—eight and a quarter quarterlands in extent—were an important part and included Bretney (Mooar and Beg), Ballaghaie, Ballagarraghyn, the Loughan, the Cooildhoo, Ballig, Ballachristory, the Rhendhoo, and the Kerroo-croie. With the glebes and Particles they formed a compact community known in modern times as 'Jurby East'.

The earliest information concerning the Barony is to be found in the manuscript volumes of the Liber Episcopi, the earliest date being 1580. These books give an account year by year of the administration of the lands in question, the meetings of the Barony Courts, the settings and customs of the farms, and the trials of disputes between tenants, and of offenders against the Bishop as Baronial Lord. The Courts were held twice a year under the presidency of the Bishop's Steward, though in special circumstances one or more of the high officers of the temporal power might be called in to assist.

The executive officer of the Barony of Jurby was the Serjeant, chosen from among the tenants. He saw to it that the customs were paid and summoned the jurymen liable for service at the Barony Court where he presented defaulters and cases for trial. He carried a staff of office called the Rod, and for emolument received his farm rent free during his term of service.

The largest holding was Bretney Mooar (probably the 'Bretby' of the 1505 Charter) which yearly paid a rent of twelve shillings and the following customs:

1 ferlot (= 3 bushels) of barley, 1 bushel of rye, 2 muttons, 2 lambs, 2 geese, 2 hens, and 33 cars of turf, the standard car load being equal to 50 black turves one cubit long by four inches broad. In addition the tenant had to give carriage service and boon-days for shearing.

None of the Bishop's tenants living on his temporal lands could be displaced while able to pay his rent and customs.

An extraordinary payment was demanded on the accession of a new Bishop, when the tenants contributed at the rate of one ox a quarterland. It was a levy which created much grumbling and resentment, particularly when there were frequent changes in the Episcopacy; and even an unpopular Bishop, when sick, had always the consolation that fervent prayers were being offered up for his recovery by the Barony tenants.

In the eighteenth century payment of rents in kind was commuted for money—an arrangement which must have been much more satisfactory for the long-suffering Bishops, who in any case had difficulty in extracting their dues from the tenants.

> 'Mr. Steward,' wrote Bishop Wilson in 1709, 'I am forced to complain of several matters relating to my tenants. . . . The tenants of Jurby have of late neglected to cutt my Turf and begin to think themselves obliged only to carry it for me, notwithstanding the express words of the Records and their former usage.
>
> 'Lastly I have often complained of the evil practice of paying their customes in the very worst grain and goods that they can get, so that I am forced to return it or fling it away . . . the Sergeant of the Southside declaring to me that some of the tenants having not given Bad enough as they thought, borrowed worse than their own to pay in.'

To the Baron Court the tenants brought the differences and quarrels which disturbed their little world, and twice a year juries of six from Jurby travelled to the court which was held at one or another of a dozen places in the diocese—among them, Bishopscourt, Peel, Castletown and Kirk Arbory. This constant juridical experience, which, of course, was shared by the Lord's tenants in the Temporal Courts, must have had a considerable formative effect upon Manx character.

In the seventeenth century a large proportion of the causes tried in Barony Courts sprang from the bad feeling engendered by trespass and damage to crops. In Jurby this was due to the fact that it was one of the last of the parishes to be completely enclosed.

Vindictive people sometimes found in the hedgeless fields an opportunity to gratify their spite. In 1675, for example,

> 'the servant to Thomas Teare took cattle of John Christian out of his fould and drove them into his corne; in respect he is a servant and perhaps of no abbilitie to pay my Lord soe considerable a fine as such a villinous act demerritteth [he] is ordered to be brought by the Lockman of the parish to the Tynwald fayre on Midsomer day next and there in the height of the markett to be whipped before the assembly for exemplary punishment that other such like notorious offenders in that nature may take warning thereby.'

With the gradual extension of enclosures the Court cases correspondingly decreased.

THE BISHOP'S JUSTICE

The Bishop's justice was milder than that of the Lord, and both compare favourably with decisions of much later times. In 1602, for example, John McNidderagh of Jurby was tried for stealing nine shillings and sixpence worth of silver from a companion. He was first committed to Castle Rushen, but as he was domiciled on the barony he had the right to be tried by the Bishop's Court, which found him not culpable of felony because he was under age. He was therefore whipped and allowed to go.

This sentence puts to shame the barbarous punishment of which the Court of General Gaol Delivery was guilty over two hundred years later. In 1838 three boys—one thirteen years of age, the others a year older—were tried at Castletown for larceny. Influenced by the spirit of the English penal code, with its convenient apparatus of punishment, the Court gave one unhappy boy the frightful sentence of seven years in Millbank prison, London, and the others seven years' transportation to Botany Bay.

When a tenant brought charges against his neighbour the latter, following the most approved military traditions, almost invariably made a counter-attack. The benevolent Court then proceeded to reduce the inflated charges to their proper proportion. A typical case came before the Baron Court held at the Nunnery in 1603, when Finlo Bodough was at variance with Patrick Kewin of Bretny and his son William.

Firstly, Bodough said that Kewin entered upon his ground and ploughed it against his will, whence there were damages of 100 shillings. The plaintiff obtained 6d.

Kewin countered with the charge that Finlo had broken pact with him about the labouring of his ground for which he paid part of the customs, and claimed 100 shillings. Kewin received 6d.

Kewin also said that Bodough's cattle had trespassed and eaten his pastures, doing 40 shillings damage. He received 6d.

Finlo Bodough then accused him of making a highway with his horses through his ground, and claimed 40 shillings. The court reduced this amount to 8d.

Patrick Kewin returned to the attack with the assertion that Bodough's sheep, one hundred in number, had eaten his fitches. He asked for 40 shillings and received 6d.

Thereupon Finlo Bodough charged William Kewin with trespass. He said William had ploughed his ground against his will and sown corn therein. He demanded 100 shillings damage. The verdict was that he receive 6d., and that the crop of corn was to be reaped half and half between them.

It was then William's turn. He said that Bodough had pastured his cattle on his fitches and asked for 40 shillings damages. He received 6d.

Finlo had the last word and accused William Kewin of pasturing his horses on *his* fitches and also doing damage to the value of 40 shillings. He received 6d.

Thus the Kewins paid a total of three shillings and twopence in damages, their opponent three shillings, and so Finlo returned triumphant to Jurby with twopence to the good.

Rights of way, at a time when the bridle-paths were unfenced, were a fruitful source of trouble. In 1697 William Vondy of Ballig stated before a Great Enquest that for forty years he had been travelling from his own house through the highway that passed by the Rhendhoo, after which he had free passage to Ramsey, the mountains, and the other market towns. He complained that the farmer of the Rhendhoo was trying to stop the way, whilst his wife had made the sinister statement that she would use her hands and see men's blood.

Neighbouring farmers—John Clucas, John Christory, and Thomas Vondy—gave evidence regarding the right of way, but when questioned further they displayed the caution required by men who lived near so redoubtable a woman as the mistress of the Rhendhoo. 'For the stoppage and the blood', says the record, 'they say nothing.' The jury, drawn from the Southside Barony, could afford to disregard local reactions to their verdict and found in favour of William Vondy.

Apparently the Amazon of the Rhendhoo was not the only masterful woman of whom the parish could boast at the end of the seventeenth century. In 1721 a young farmer from another part of Jurby made a pitiful plaint to Bishop Wilson. 'The Petitioner's grandmother', he writes, 'is very uneasy with his servants after an unchristian manner so that he cannot get his servants to do his work as he ought.' The petition is signed by the servants who promise to work faithfully in the future if the grandmother is duly attended to.

Seven years after the Rhendhoo dispute William Vondy died tragically on his way to a Barony Court, and a jury was appointed to discover whether his sudden end justified the application of the feudal custom called Deodand by which an animal or other chattel causing its owner's death was forfeited to the Lord. The jury returned their verdict as follows:

> 'We whose names are subscribed being sworne in a jury to examine how Wm. Vondy of Jurby dyed by the way comeing to the bishop's court at Peeletown 26 May 1703, and having sworn ... seven men that were in company with the said Vondy when he fell off his horse find that they have not brought nor declared anything that might be the occasion of his death either by the horse's stumbling or any other way whatsoever. And therefore we do really believe that the aforesaid William Vondy was struck dead by God Almighty's hand and then did immediately fall off his horse.'

The horse was thus declared innocent of Vondy's death and the Lord did not obtain his perquisite.

The link between Bishop and Barony was broken in 1908, when his tenants were freed from their obligations by the payment of a commutation.

THE CHURCH OF ST. PATRICK

The present Parish Church of St. Patrick was built in 1813. Architecturally unprepossessing, it was for long the object of very unflattering criticism, and its attractive interior today owes much to the enthusiasm of the late Deemster Farrant, many of whose ancestors rest in the churchyard.

Its predecessor occupied the middle of the churchyard. According to Feltham it was sixty feet long and fourteen feet broad, and, like the vicarage near by, was of a primitive simplicity. A tradition set down by the Rev. J. T. Clarke was to the effect that in 1213 a site was chosen for a parish church in West Jurby, the West Nappin contributing four acres for church and burial ground, and the East Nappin two acres for the vicarage. The date of erection, he says, was shown upon a stone set in an external wall of the six hundred-year-old church, whilst a slate box discovered in the foundations contained proof of its antiquity. But the fate of these material pieces of evidence is not known.

The building was reported to be in a decayed condition in the middle of the eighteenth century. In 1757, Bishop Hildesley re-slated the chancel and improved the poor lighting at the west end, whilst the rest of the church was repaired by the parishioners. But it was much too small to accommodate the rapidly increasing population, and in 1806 the vicar, John Nelson, read a notice to the congregation in Manx and English summoning a parish meeting to consider the provision of a new building.

At this meeting it was resolved to petition Tynwald for a new church which was built seven years later. The chancel was erected by the Bishop, the nave with money obtained by an assessment on the parish. Material from the old church was incorporated in the body of the new.

Jurby Cross, of which there is now no trace, stood outside the churchyard and below the stile, to which the ground rose so steeply that parishioners found it a very inconvenient entrance and not without its dangers in frosty weather. The approach was improved and a gateway made in 1757.

At the Cross the Sumner gave out the parish notices, and the Moar of the year summoned offenders in assault cases on the Sunday preceding the court. The unconsecrated area around the spot was used as a place of interment for suicides. In 1690 the Register records that: 'William Calow murdthered himself the 5th of February and was buried below the churchyard hedge the same day at even near the Cross.'

A sundial bearing on its face of slate the neatly cut inscription, 'A gift by Patt Brew [of Ballavarran] to Jurby Church 1757,' and set in a cylindrical piece of red sandstone, stands by the stile. At equidistant points in the circumference of the drum there are the remains of six iron pins set in the stone.

PENANCE

One of the most dramatic episodes ever witnessed in a Manx church was acted in old St. Patrick of Jurby in November, 1661. The vicar, Sir William Crowe, had been found guilty of going to England and leaving the church serviceless, of slandering the parishioners and of other grave misconduct—one unusual charge being that he had sung 'a psalm of destruction' against John Teare of Ballateare. In addition he had antagonised the temporal power by giving indiscreet expression to his unorthodox opinions regarding the Lord of the Isle and the Monarchy.

He was reported to have said that the Earl of Derby was the greatest plunderer in England. When William Teare of Sartfield drank a toast to King Charles the Second who had been restored to the throne a few months before, Sir William refused to pledge him and said, 'Drink to the Lord Fairfax, for he is the best Lord that ever came over to the Island or ever shall come.'

He was suspended and, chastened by deprivation of the fruits of his benefice, in due time presented an appeal for mercy. A few months later the Bishop, being assured that his repentance was genuine, removed his suspension, conditional on the performance of penance. This consisted of confession in Jurby Church, in the presence of Vicar-General Sir Robert Parr and Ewan Curghey.

The vicar knelt humbly before his parishioners and, addressing them in Manx and English, begged them to grant him forgiveness for his flagrant misbehaviour. The assembly of decent country people sitting on their benches in the dimly lit old church must have listened with mixed feelings to the wayward shepherd on his knees at the chancel steps—at once embarrassed at the spectacle of his abasement, and yet gratified, in the way of human nature, that retribution had fallen on one who had neglected and illtreated them. But they displayed the magnanimity of spirit which the occasion demanded and agreed to overlook his past misdeeds. When the Vicar-General and his colleagues reported to Bishop Rutter that the vicar had purged his offence they added that all the congregation were well pleased.

There are instances of more protracted penances. In 1713 William Macnameer had moved to Ballaugh where he had made himself notorious by his gross misbehaviour. He was sentenced to forty days in St. German's dungeon and to stand at Jurby Church door during service time every Sunday and holy day for a whole year, clad in the white sheet.

SCHOOLMASTERS

On a well known stone in the churchyard is inscribed a long epitaph in Latin to the memory of William Teare who was schoolmaster in Peel for fifty-two years and died in 1756. On one occasion in 1753 he fell from grace, and, having been suspended, asked the Ecclesiastical Court for restoration, with much more dignity than was usually displayed in the abject petitions which were considered essential to gain the sympathetic attention of the Bishop and his officials.

The document runs:

> 'The Answer of Wm. Tear schoolmaster in Peeltown to a Presentment lodged against him:
>
> 'That some matters in the informations or complaint are utterly false and untrue as shall be proved.
>
> 'That some things proceeded from a supposition or presumption that he was disordered by drinking when indeed it was the effect

of a qualm and faintness of Spirits that frequently seize him of late without Drinking or Dramming but in sober sadness, as is known to some of his neighbours, as well as his own Family.

'That not withstanding he does not pretend an exemption from failings or slips of infirmity or surprize, though not frequent or customary, but matter of regret when reflected on and against which he will, and is resolved by Divine assistance, to guard more cautiously hereafter. His request is that the matter of the said Presentment proceeding thereupon may be suspended to further consideration of the merits of the cause and to the expectation and Tryal of the Issue of things for the future. . . .'

The churchwardens of St. Peter's reported favourably on his conduct later and he returned to his school but did not long survive his reinstatement.

Andrew Joughin who kept school near Jurby Church had an even longer career as teacher. He was licensed by the Bishop in 1783 and died in 1838 after having been parochial schoolmaster for nearly fifty-six years. It was in the house of his descendant and namesake that on July 11th, 1897, T. E. Brown had what he called a delightful rencontre, on what proved to be his last excursion into Jurby.

The records of Education in Jurby in the seventeenth and eighteenth centuries are as depressing as those of the other parishes of the diocese. In 1741 and for some years later no regular school was kept, the clerk-schoolmaster did not fulfil his obligations, came to loggerheads with parishioners, and was presented for unbecoming conduct. In 1749, in response to an appeal from the landowners of the west of the parish, Thomas Clarke of the Nappin agreed to keep school in the ancient chapel (variously known at St. Patrick's, St. Columba's, and St. Keyll's) on his farm. It was repaired for the purpose, but the arrangement apparently did not last long, for in 1765 it is stated, 'No school is taught nor has been for some years past.' A new schoolmaster was licensed, however, to teach in the parish. But in 1781 the old conditions recurred and Adam McBooy, the parochial schoolmaster, was presented for negligence in attending and keeping the school.

Stories still live of the sometimes remarkable characters who obtained a scanty livelihood as schoolmasters before the educational changes of 1870. One, a cripple whom his pupils knew as 'Dan the Mastha', had his school in east Jurby and was supposed, probably because of his name, to have been the original of the poet's 'Danny Bewildther'.

Another, Abner Kerruish, a man of considerable natural ability, kept school at Sandygate. He came from Kirk Maughold and lived for forty years in the loft of a farm building at Berrag. He, too, was

Q

a cripple and walked with difficulty. A skilful man with his hands he mended or 'spanked' broken earthenware, made straw plaited hats, and repaired fishing nets—often earning his dinner in this way. Like so many masters of his time he taught mensuration, navigation, and land surveying, and used the old chapel at Sandygate as his school. The improvised desks were loose boards which the boys arranged on trestles. The master sat by the fire, which was kept going by the weekly turves contributed by his pupils. He brought the children to it in relays with a battle-cry of 'Come say! come say!' In cold weather the chance of approaching the smouldering hearth was eagerly sought by the youngsters. But Kerruish carefully apportioned the time for sitting there by using a pendulum consisting of a long string weighted with lead. This was set swinging, its coming to rest being the signal for the call of 'Come say!' and the arrival of a new party eager for the warmth of the fire. A strict disciplinarian, he was guilty of the practice of rapping stupid boys on the head with a ruler, and also did execution on other and safer areas of their anatomy with a carefully trimmed cherry-stick. According to one of his pupils the only text books used were the Bible, Testament, and Hymn Book.

He died in 1874 and his modest gravestone stands near the gable of the church.

THE PARISH MILITIA

The Jurby militia figured prominently in the rising of 1651. The Captain of the Parish, John Teare of Ballateare, his Lieutenant, Dollin Clarke of the Nappin and William Teare of Sartfield, commander of the watch on the Cronk Moar, were among the most active leaders of the Northern Companies. The Jurby men took part in the reduction of the Loyal Fort which stood close to the church of Kirk Andreas, and later in the temporarily successful attack on Peel Castle. Dollin Clarke, who was of an active and combative temper, also led a party of musqueteers from Peel to Ronaldsway, where a sortie was expected from the Countess's forces in Castle Rushen.

His zeal in the popular cause was remembered against him, and at the time of the trial of Illiam Dhone he was one of the seven participants in the rising who were removed from the body of the Keys.

The new Lord of Man might have forgiven Dollin for the sake of his brother Thomas Clarke, who had responded to Earl James's appeal for help in 1649. It was a time of dreadful famine and the Island had been bled white to provide for military activities which were to be ended by the headsman's axe at Bolton two years later. Thomas Clarke was among those landowners who received copies of a letter written by the Earl in which he asked for further financial assistance, the amount varying according to the standing of the farmer. In this case it was the then substantial sum of twenty nobles, and both the circular with its unredeemed promises of future benefits and the receipt for the money still exist, having strayed into the Ecclesiastical records.

Among Dollin Clarke's descendants were the late Speaker of the Keys, Sir Frederick Clucas, and Daniel Clarke the last of his name to occupy the West Nappin. He was renowned for a remarkable natural ability in manipulative surgery—an aptitude fostered in him by his grandmother Radcliffe of Farrants Fort, Kirk Andreas, who was equally gifted and whose passing was mourned by the poor whom she had befriended.

THE CAINES

The family, now extinct in the male line, whose connection with Jurby goes farthest back in written record was that of the Caines, whose farm of Balycane is mentioned in a Bull of Pope Gregory in 1231. According to tradition they added the East Nappin to their original holding by a judicious marriage and were in possession of both in the fifteenth century. John McCayne was warden of the Watch and Ward on the coast in 1497, but the most notable member of the family, in a modest way, was Dollin, who was a member of the Keys and assisted in the election of a Deemster in 1605. He managed to obtain a small portion of the Jurby barony and so qualified for the position of Serjeant which he held for a number of years.

One day in 1603 Dollin received an agreeable surprise when a horn fell from the Nappin roof and was found to contain eleven gold pieces. The story of the horn of gold soon spread, and the coroner laid claim to the money on the ground that it was treasure trove, and therefore the Lord's prerogative. Dollin was, however, able to prove that his wife, before her death, had hidden it in the thatch for her children. He was consequently allowed to keep it for the use of himself and family.

He appears to have made a favourable impression upon Bishop Phillips, to judge from a curious fragment detached from its context and preserved in the Liber Episcopi. It runs,

> 'The Bishop himself sitting by, who then liking well of the man said to the Lieutenant [i.e. the Governor], "I wonder how your worship did so well know him to be an honest man." '

Research made by Mr. W. Cubbon into Manx port records reveals that there was constant direct communication between Jurby and Ireland in the sixteenth century and later. Dollin Caine owned a boat which made use of the Carlane mouth and the creek under

Jurby Head. In 1582 it brought in oak and alder poles and horses, whilst other traders landed cargoes of horses, Irish cloth and timber.

In 1610 Dollin's absence from Tynwald was excused on the ground that he had gone on a trading expedition to Ireland.

WILLIAM CHRISTIAN OF BALLAMOAR

Probably the two most notable Jurby men of the eighteenth century were William Christian (1685–1753) and John Lace of Sartfield.

Christian belonged to the family of Ballamoar, whose position in Jurby for many generations is indicated by the fact that in the last three centuries at least seven of its members have held the commission of Captain of the Parish. He was prominent in the struggle between the temporal power and the Bishop's party which enlivened Insular politics in the eighteenth century.

In 1727 the Lord of the Isle granted him the General-Sumnership on a lease of twenty-one years—an act which denied Bishop Wilson's claim, based on custom, to appoint the chief executive officer of the ecclesiastical courts. Later he was made Attorney-General and finally Receiver-General. The Museum Library possesses his manuscript book of precedents extracted from the court records, which bears testimony to the conscientious spirit in which he carried out his duties.

William Farrant, who played so large a part in public affairs and in the life of Jurby during the latter part of the nineteenth century, was the last of his descendants to hold the estate of Ballamoar.

DEEMSTER JOHN LACE

Deemster John Lace was the son of John Lace of Ballavoddan, in Kirk Andreas, who married the heiress of Sartfield and later became Captain of Jurby. Like most of his predecessors the Deemster was not law bred. In 1791 Lieut.-Governor Shaw recommended him for the vacant Deemstership, saying that he was a senior counsel and the fittest person in the Island for the office, in spite of the defect of a violent and bearish temper.

According to the Governor, Lace was of the 'Patriot' party in the Keys and in certain matters had supported the 'Patriots' in their opposition to the Duke of Atholl. But they were uncertain of his ultimate intentions and feared his masterful temperament. They therefore gladly supported the Governor's recommendation, which, if successful, would remove from the Keys a forceful and incalculable personality.

He became Deemster in 1793 and First Deemster the following year, when J. F. Crellin joined him on the Bench. In advocating

these appointments the Duke of Atholl wrote, 'As almost all the proceedings carried on before the two Deemsters of the Island are in the
Manx language it becomes almost indispensable that Persons who
understand that Tongue should fill these situations.'

In 1806 the Deemsters came into collision with Lieut.-Governor
Smelt in a forgery case, when they refused to issue warrants without
being informed of the specific reason. The angry Governor addressed
interrogatories to the senior Deemster, who declared that he and his
colleague were the sole judges under the Act, in which there was no
reference to the Governor whatever. 'This', he said, 'is the first
instance of one of the Judges of the King's Court being interrogated
or catechised upon any matter depending on or to depend before
him, and I must pronounce it a most dangerous attempt. . . .'

He therefore refused to reply to the interrogatories or any other
interrogatories in writing, without consultation with his brother
Deemster—'not barely to say yes or no, but in the first place to
decide upon their propriety.'

Four years later Col. Smelt complained to London, apparently
without result, that 'Worshipful', the customary title of respect given
to Deemsters Lace and Crellin as well as to the Water Bailiff and
the Clerk of the Rolls, was being dropped in favour of 'Honourable',
a title which should be reserved for the Lieut.-Governor.

In spite of his lack of formal legal training Deemster Lace was an
acknowledged authority on the Common Law. One of his judgments
which has the flavour of a bygone age was remembered in Cregneish.
A certain Karran and his sons were very big men and noted for their
unusual strength.

> 'Once', said Edward Faragher, 'one of the big Karrans was not
> able to go to sea with their boat, and they got another man in his
> place, and they had a good haul of herrings that night. When they
> came to divide the money they gave the strange man only half a
> share, for they reckoned him only half a man. And he summoned
> big Karran before Deemster Lace, and the Deemster asked in
> Manx, *Row uss son gymmyrt noi gheay as roayrt rish Karran mooar
> Crenaish*? "Wert thou able to row against wind and tide like big
> Karran of Cregneish?" And he had to acknowledge that he could
> not, so the Deemster told him to be thankful for what he had got.'

Deemster Lace died in 1812.

MANX GAELIC

Jurby played an important part in the rescue of Manx Gaelic from
extinction. J. E. Harrison, who was a good Manx scholar, was vicar
from 1818 to 1858 and considerably enlarged his Gaelic vocabulary
by his long contact with his parishioners, who lived in a part of the

Island comparatively remote from the steadily growing holiday traffic, and who were among the last to forget their language and traditions. When Prince Lucien Bonaparte, a noted linguist, visited Man in the eighteen-fifties he made frequent journeys to Jurby to interview native speakers.

To Jurby also came Archibald Cregeen to consult the vicar in the making of his famous dictionary, whilst the Rev. J. T. Clarke, of the Nappin, was responsible for the English-Manx section of Kelly's work (published by the Manx Society in 1866). In 1859 the unfortunate J. Ivor Mosley, the compiler of a Manx vocabulary used by the editors of Kelly, was taught Gaelic by Daniel Teare, a member of the Loughcroute family, who had gone to live at Ballaskilly in Kirk Bride.

The Rev. J. T. Clarke was responsible in part for some tracts in Manx and a number of his sermons in Manx are preserved in the Museum Library. A second Jurby author in that language was the remarkable Juan Lewin who was Parish Sumner in the first half of the nineteenth century, though this office did not debar him from being a Methodist preacher.

A native of Lonan, he settled in Jurby at the end of the eighteenth century and resided there until his death at the age of eighty-nine in 1857. For many years he lived alone in a cottage at the Lheeanee Vooar on the Summerhill road, and nearly opposite a dwelling occupied at a later period by John Kissack, a shoemaker, who provided the folk-tune collectors with the air of 'Ramsey Town'. These clay built cottages have now vanished.

Juan was a tailor, but his undisciplined temperament could not accommodate itself to continuous application. His mind wandered from his humdrum work, and his customers were sometimes more surprised than gratified with the eccentricities which appeared in their garments.

Miss Christian Callister, who made a number of Jurby figures of the nineteenth century the subject of her sympathetic pen, has drawn a graphic picture of the Sumner in old age—a tall gaunt man, his long hair falling on bent shoulders, and from under shaggy brows, when the mood was upon him, his eyes gleaming with fanatical fire. At such times he strode along the country roads striking the ground with the staff which was the symbol of his office—a prophet of woe, tormented by dark visions of a sinful world slipping to perdition. He heard the warning voice of God in wind and storm, and strongly moved at such times he knocked at the doors of startled cottagers with the cry, 'Who has sinned and come short of the glory of God?' and called upon men to repent.

The rhyming comments on aspects of life in Jurby for which he was noted and which gave great entertainment to his fellow parishioners have perished. They were scribbled on odd scraps of paper when his fancy was stimulated by some story or subject met with on his journeys through the parish.

Like a number of other Manx writers he was credited with the authorship of the famous *Carval ny Drogh Vraane*. What is more certain is that he was part translator of several temperance tracts into Manx and wrote two ballads: *Arrane er Ineeyn Irrinee* (A Song on Farmers' Daughters) and *Yn Chenn Dolphin* (The Old Dolphin) which are included in A. W. Moore's collection.

HOUSES

The first Methodist meeting place in Jurby was the eighteenth century farmhouse of Ballachrink Kaighin, later a stable. It was built of puddled clay mixed with straw, and shore stones. Clay with straw was often used in the construction of pre-nineteenth century farmhouses and cottages in the parts of the parish where the required material was available. In the first half of the nineteenth century shore stones were largely used in new construction, but were said to make damp interior walls owing to their impregnation with salt.

The Loughcroute house, which became ruinous and was demolished twenty or thirty years ago, was of the puddled clay type, with shore stone foundations. According to tradition it was of great age, and the first two storied dwelling in Jurby. The slated stone house on Ballateare in which lived Captain John Teare who led the Jurby men in 1651, still existed in recent years, shored up against collapse, and was used as a barn. Its successor stands on a terrace above the Carlane Water, facing one of the loveliest visions of land and sea in the Isle of Man.

XVII

P. M. C. KERMODE

Address delivered at the unveiling of a memorial tablet at P.M.C. Kermode's birthplace, Parliament Street, Ramsey, October 5th, 1950.

Philip Kermode was born in this house ninety-five years ago, and spent the most impressionable and formative period of his life in Ramsey and Kirk Maughold. His father, the Rev. William Kermode, was the son of Thomas and Margaret Kermode, of Claughbane, and was for twenty-eight years Chaplain of St. Paul's. Later he became Vicar of Kirk Maughold, and finally Rector of Ballaugh, where he died in 1890.

A man of scholarly tastes he was greatly attracted to history and archaeology, and many members of his large family had literary and artistic gifts—notably Josephine, whose volumes of delightful verse, written over the pen-name of 'Cushag', occupy a permanent place in Manx literature.

In this intellectually stimulating family atmosphere Philip developed many interests, and at first was most strongly drawn to the study of natural history. He appears to have been influenced by the example of the famous Manxman, Professor Edward Forbes, the friend of Huxley and one of the foremost scientists of the nineteenth century, who in his youth studied plants and living creatures in the Curragh and on the seabanks of Ballaugh. He died untimely the year before before Philip's birth.

Kermode, as he himself said, walked humbly in the steps of the great naturalist, and made many valuable contributions to knowledge. Among them he discovered a new species of fossil shell in the sea-brows of Kirk Bride which was named after him, and his list of Manx birds, printed in 1883, was the most complete that had been published up to that time.

It was when engaged in observing birds in 1876 that young Kermode came upon disaster. Searching among the rocks in Kirk Lonan for nests of falcons he fell a hundred and twenty feet into the sea. His close friend and companion, Alfred Rudd, pulled him, severely bruised, into safety, and went for help. He, too, slipped and was killed—a tragedy which cast its dark shadow for the rest of Kermode's life.

By an ironic coincidence, on the day of Kermode's own death more than fifty years later, when the flame of life was flickering to its end, a message came to his house announcing that the Government of Iceland had made him a Knight of the Order of the Falcon.

Although he retained his affection for his early studies it was in the field of archaeology that he found his most engrossing and fruitful work. In the churchyard of Kirk Maughold to which parish his father had been appointed Vicar in 1871 he became familiar with the numerous ancient crosses it contained—mainly Celtic and Norse, and dating from early Christian times to the Middle Ages.

These sacred relics, survivals from remote periods of Manx history, fired his imagination.

'Upon these rude and weathered stones', he once cried, 'we are able to see and to touch the very handwork of those whose skilful fingers crumbled into dust a thousand years ago!'

He saw in them the symbols of that long continuity of a Christian faith which had existed here in Man from, or even before, the time of St. Patrick, and he called upon his fellow countrymen to protect memorials which had been created by the patient skill and devotion of their Manx ancestors twenty, thirty or forty generations before.

As early as 1884, he is found advocating that they should be taken into Government care, and for the next twenty years he set himself to the task of recording and studying them. With enormous industry he examined and described, pictorially and in words, every known ancient cross in the Island; and in addition, had casts made of them. His faithful drawings are a testimony not only to his brilliant draughtsmanship but to the long years of patient application which he devoted to the truthful delineation of his subject.

It is a good thing for the social health of a modern community when from time to time it produces a figure passionately devoted to some worthy cause and following its aims without thought of personal aggrandisement. His was a single-minded enthusiasm divorced from the idea of financial gain; and indeed, as in other cases of a virtue pushed to its extreme, it had its drawbacks; for his lack of interest in the bread and butter necessities of life sometimes brought embarrassment both to himself and to his friends.

His discovery that on Manx stones are carved some of the earliest known illustrations of scenes from the Icelandic sagas, and in particular, the finest of all, the story of Sigurd, made a stir in the Universities of Northern Europe.

The interest which had been aroused was intensified in 1907 with the publication of his book on Manx Crosses, incorporating his written studies and drawings, and revealing for the first time in its fullness the unique treasure the Isle of Man possesses in its ancient monuments. This splendid volume was Kermode's greatest achievement, and once and for all established his reputation as a scholar of eminence.

Closely allied to his work on the Crosses, and as arduous, was his recording of the numerous early keeills or chapels. Of this and of the many other subjects upon which he wrote there is no time to speak, but two Manx institutions will always be associated with his name— the Natural History and Antiquarian Society and the Manx National Museum.

The Antiquarian Society was founded by him in 1879, and for fifty years he was a powerful influence in its activities.

From the beginning he and his fellow members had envisaged the creation of a National Museum and Library, and when after years of agitation, the dream became a reality he was made its first Curator, and the Society's collections formed its first exhibits. From its inception in 1922 the Museum under Kermode's direction and that of his able successors, Messrs. Cubbon and Megaw, has grown more and more important as a centre of Manx national culture.

For Ramsey he had a great affection, and never forgot the obligation of a good citizen to serve the place from which he derived his roots. He was proud of the part his father had played in the affairs of the town; and he himself sat on the Town Board, was its chairman for a time, and fought, unsuccessfully, two elections for the House of Keys.

To Ramsey, too, he bequeathed the most cherished of his possessions, his valuable collection of books, in the hope that one day it would be the nucleus of a library worthy of the town.

The memorial tablet which has been unveiled to-day commemorates a distinguished son of Ramsey who was a great scholar and a great lover of his country.

INDEX

Abjuration, 37, 38
Academic School, 125, 128, 146
Alehouses, 82, 83, 144, 224
Allens of Maughold, The, 127
Allen, Henry (–1746), 139
Allen, Robert (–1663), 114
Allen, Thomas (–1726), 114
Amusements, 144–6
Antidotes to Witchcraft, 25
Archdeacon, 75, 105, 131
Ardrenk, 228, 229
Ashole (The Mount), 154
Aston, Sir Arthur, 67–9
Atholl, 2nd D. of, 128, 177
Atholl, 3rd D. of, 190–3
Atholl, 4th D. of, 61, 173, 196, 198

Baldwin Mill, 164
Ballarragh, Lonan, 51, 52
Ballaughton Mill, 18
Ballabeg, Arbory, 27
Ballacallow, Bride, 66, 86
Ballacregga, Michael, 53
Ballakeoig, 52, 132
Ballamaddrell, 20, 163, 197
Ballamoar, Ballaugh, 16
Ballamoore, Patrick, 186, 187
Ballanorris, 20, 169
Ballateare, 70
Ballaugh, 210
Ballawhane, 28
Bangor and Sabal Abbeys, 104
Banishment, 37, 38
Barbados, Manx in, 49–52, 187
Barbers, 144
Bar, Manx, 201, 208
Bare Broom, The, 23
Barony, The Bishop's, 42, 212, 234
Barony, Serjeant of the, 234
Barrow, Bishop, 88, 117, 124, 131, 132, 217
Bell, Death, 107
Bells, The Three, 122
Bible, Manx, 115, 116, 125
Bishop Mark (1291), 105
Black Hill, 37
Black, John, of Ramsey, 88, 89
Blackbird of Baldwin, The, 164
Blessing, 21, 220
Blood-drawing, 25, 58
Blood-letting, 33

Boat-drawing, 136
Bollan Bane, The, 28
Bonaparte, Prince Lucien, 246
Books, 120, 121
Booming Trade, The, 143
Boundaries, 150, 154, 161
Breach of Promise (1729), 39
Brewing, 85, 145, 224
Bridgman, Bishop, 42, 136
Bridge and Staff, 126
Bridle, The, 135, 136, 142, 147
Bridson, Capt, Paul, 92, 93
Bulwark, The Douglas, 33, 67
Burial in Church, 111, 220
Buchan, Lady, 224

Caesar, Jane, 16, 17
Caines of Jurby, The, 60, 243
Calcot, Major R., 32, 73, 138
Calcott, Dr. R., 34
Calcott of Ballalough, 20, 97
Callister, Christian, 246
Cammag (Hockey), 134, 145
Callow, Ballafayle, 130
Camps, Militia, 70, 75
Cannell, Sir Hugh, 108
Captain of Parish, 63–83, 92, 200
Captain of Town, 41, 67, 84, 93
Captains' Revolt, 65, 72
Carlane, The, 230
Carrasdhoo Men, The, 231
Charming, 15, 28–30
Chapter Court, 131
Chaloner, Gov., 117
Choice Child, 47
Christian, Wm., Jurby, 132, 244
Christians of Milntown, 94
Christian, Edward, 94
Christian, W. (Illiam), *see Illiam Dhone*
Christian, Ewan, Deems., 96, 97, 100
Christian, Dr. P., 35
Christian, B'yonaige, 74, 79
Christian, Deems. J. (–1852), 98, 201, 203
Church Courts, 38, 130, 131
Church Discipline, 130
Church, Head of the, 41
Church Sites, 109, 110
Church Records, 138
Church Stile, 26
Churchyard, 118, 119

Civil War (1642–1651), 69, 112
Clarke, Daniel, 121
Clarke, Dollin, 72, 74
Clarke, Rev. J. T., 238, 246
Clergy, The, 104
Clergy, Character of, 112–118
Clergy, Stipends of, 104, 124
Clergy, Wives of, 122, 123
Clerk, Parish, 106–109
Clocks, 121
Coinage, Manx, 80
Combinations, 199, 200
Commuted Tithes, 209
Commuted Penance, 137
Compurgation, 141, 142
Contraband Trade, 143, 182, 184
Convocation of 1703, 38, 137
Coroner, 14, 37, 43, 57–62
Corpse Lodging, 219
Cosnahan, Sir W., 113
Cosnahans, The, 127
Counterfeit Money, 81, 82
Countess of Derby, C., 72, 73
Cranstal, Christian of, 70, 79
Cregeen, Archibald, 203, 204, 246
Crellin, Vicar J., Arbory, 118, 197
Crellin, Thos., Peel, 43
Crigan, Bishop, 42, 153
Cronk Lheannag, 73
Cross, Mustering, 65, 72
Cross, Parish, 109
Crosses, Manx, 249
Crowe, Sir Wm., 117, 239
Crypt of St. German's, 15, 129
Curghie, Deems. John, 45
Curghie Ewan, 79
Curghie, Rev. M., 115, 139
Curragh Glass, The, 14
Curses, The, 22–5
Curwen, John C., 98
Cutlar, McCulloch, 66

Death Bell, The, 107
Deer, The Lord's, 160, 161
Defence of the Isle, 75–8
Deodand, 39, 238
Derby Fort, 45
Derby, James 7th Earl, 69–72, 96, 97
Derby, James 9th Earl, 76
Dew, Magic, 19
Dhoo, The river, 41, 61, 109
Divorce, 140
Dollagh, The, 222, 223
Doctors, 31–5
Dogs in Church, 133
Domestic Workers, 126
Douglas Fort, 90
Drawing Blood, 25, 58
Druids in Man, 13

Dowry, 219
Duckenfield, Col., 73
Dues, Bishop's Barony, 235
Duck-baiting, 146
Duchess of Gloucester, 16
Dungeon of St. German's, 129, 148
Duntulm Castle, Skye, 14
Dust, Magical, 19, 21, 27, 134

Ealish Vrian, Witch, 15
Eary Beg, 100
Eary Kelly, 171
Education, 115, 117, 125
Elf-shots, 29
Emigration, 46, 49
Enquest, Great, 149–73
Evil Eye, The, 21, 27
Excommunication, 88, 136

Fairfax, Lord, 73, 240
Fairies, 29
Fairs, 80
Fargher of Skibrick, 130
Farm Workers, 126, 127
Farrant, Robert, 198
Farrant, William, 199
Farrant, Deems. R., 238
Felons, 40
Fencibles, 78
Fire, 26–8
Fish Tithe, 116, 117, 198, 202
Flexney, William, 33, 43
Forbes, Edward, 211, 248
Forester's Lodge, 228, 229
Fort Loyal, 242
Four Horsemen, The, 78, 79
Free Quartering, 71
Friary, Tyldesley of the, 20, 25, 27
Funerals, 107, 111
Furniture, House, 88, 120, 121

Gaelic, Manx, 101, 115, 245
Gaut, The Sculptor, 214
Gell, Rev. John, 178
Gellin (Gelling), Capt. Paul, 75, 76
General Sumner, 14, 131, 132, 213
Glebe, 106, 109, 119
Glen Dhoo, 226
Godred Crovan, 94
Gordon, Radcliffe of, 70, 74
Governor's Pass, 45
Greenhalghe, Gov., 68, 69, 70
Grenanes, The, 151, 172
Groat, Ploughman's, 107, 133

Halsall, Rev. Anthony, 183
Handfasting, 140, 141
Hand-mills, 165
Hand-suit, 149

Hango Hill, 74
Hare, Witch into, 20
Hedges, 152
Hendricks, Mary, 136
Heywood, Capt. Thos., 91, 93
Highways, 155, 156
Hildesley, Bishop, 120, 125, 142
Horne, Governor, 76
Horses, Scabbed, 58
House, Surgeon to the, 31, 32
Household Troops, 42–5
Houses, Jurby, 247
Howard, Rev. Thos., 105, 214
Huddleston, Sir J., 119, 120

Ill Hour, An, 23, 103
Illiam Dhone, 34, 72–5, 94, 97, 153
Increase, The, 17–18, 58
Iron, Magical use of, 26

Jacobite Risings, 92, 93
Juan Lewin, 199, 246, 247
Jony, Witch of Braddan, 15, 17, 18
Jurby, Kirk Patrick of, 230–47
Jury, Fodder, 160
Jury of the House, 44
Jury of Life and Death, 14, 150
Jury, Market, 85, 86, 89, 167
Justices of the Peace, 208

Kaighin of Camden, N. J., 53–6
Keeills, 104, 110, 111
Kella Mill, 162
Kermode, P. M. C., 248–50
Kerruish, Abner, 241, 242
Keys, The, 53, 56, 69, 75–7, 168, 194, 195
Keys, Dismissal of, 74
Killing of Mac a Faille, 100
King Orry, 94, 230
Kirby, Braddan, 37
Kishan Measure, 57, 163
Kneeling, 24
Knock Rushen, 20, 25
Kyteler, Dame Alice, 19

Laa Boaldyn, (May Day), 26
Lace, Lieut., John, 73, 74
Lace, Danold, 54, 56
Lace, Deemster John, 244, 245
Lamothe, Dominique de, 31
Landmarks, 152, 153
Land Workers' Wages, 46, 47
Language, Manx, 101, 115, 245
Lawyers, 24, 208
Lilly, The Snow, 178–80
Lloyd, Bishop, 115
Lhen Mooar Mill, 165, 166
Lockman, The, 43, 59, 60

Lodgings, 85, 87, 88
Loghtan Sheep, 177
Lord of the Isle, 36
Lord's Licence, The, 45
Lord's Prerogative, The, 36
Lord's Profit, The, 36, 37
Lord's Forest, The, 150, 228
Lord's Soldiers, The, 42, 45
Lord's Warren, The, 40
Losta Lome, 24, 109
Lucy, Wreck of the, 168
Lutwidge, Receiver Gen., 191

McCrone, James, 201–3
Magic, Imitative, 16
Manannan, 13
Manannan's Chair and Road, 171
Manslaughter, 59
Markets, 85, 86, 89, 167
Marriage, 140–1
May Day, 18, 26, 27, 28
Measures, Official, 57
Mellia, The, 27, 127
Memorial, Keys', 190, 191
Methodist Movement, 221
Meyrick, Bishop, 42
Mills, 163–6
Mills, Hand, 165
Milntown, 94–100
'Mischief' Bill, 190
Moar, Parish, 43, 57, 58
Montpelier, 172
Money, Counterfeit, 81, 82
Moore, Sir Geo., 174–96
Moore, Rev. Edward, 125, 127
Moore, Rev. Philip, 125
Moryson, Dr. Dan, 31
Mulcture, 163–5
Murray, Bishop, 198, 200–8
Mustering Cross, 65, 72
'Mylecharaine', 231
Muskets, Clergy's, 75

Naturalisation, 64, 88
Nelson, Esther, 231
Nelson, Dr. Samuel, 31
Norris, Deemster, 39
North, Danger from the, 110
Nunnery, The, 34, 74, 154, 161

Oates, Capt. J., Bibaloe, 75, 76
Oates, Sir John, 119
Ogham Inscription, 13
Opprobrium, 147
Orry, King, 94, 230
Oural Losht (Burnt Offering), 26–8

Parishes, Creation of, 104
Parish Captain, 63–83

Parish Clerk, 53, 106–8
Parr, Chas., V. G., 139, 218
Parr, Deemster John, 124, 217
Parr, Sir Robert, 34, 114, 212, 216
Parr, Sir Thos., 18, 116, 123, 124
Pawn (security), 43
Parson; Parson's Clerk, 131
Peel, 32, 68, 85, 174, 176
Peel Castle, 39, 43, 45, 73, 129, 171
Peggy, The Snow, 178, 180, 187, 188
Peggy, The (yacht), 181
Penance, 15, 122, 135, 142, 239
Perambulation, Parish, 18, 153, 154
Phillips, Bishop, 113
Phynnodderree, The, 19
Pinfolds, 160, 161
Ploughman's Blessing, 21
Ploughman's Groat, 107, 133
Ploughman and Driver, 48
Poaching, 40, 41
Points of Refuge, 78
Porridge, Servants', 47
Port, The, Ballaugh, 227, 228
Potato Riots, The, 197–209
Private Vengeance, 58
Pulrose, 23, 37
Privateers, 31, 77, 187

Quaker Rebel, The, 55
Quakers, The, 53, 88, 130–2
Quarter-day, Witches', 19
Quayle, Bridge House, 178, 180

Raiders, Sea, 66, 67
Ramsey: Meaning of Name, 170
Ramsey, Captain of, 86, 89
Ramsey Fence, 87
Radcliffe, Dr. Chas. B., 31
Radcliffe, Dr. John N., 31
Records, Church, 138
Recreations, 144–6
Rectories, Manx, 104, 105, 131
Regaby, John Kneale, 79
Registers, Ballaugh, 217
Revestment, The (1765), 38, 77, 189
Richmond, Bishop, 199
Rights of Way, 157–160
Rising, The (1651), 70, 72
Robinson, Rev. S., 123, 124
Rod, The Coroner's, 60
Roper, William, V. Gen., 201
Rowe, Controller John, 167, 169
Running Trade, The, 90, 176, 182, 184
Rutter, Bishop, 137, 217
Rushen Abbey, 149
Rushen, Castle, 31, 37, 41, 45, 73, 76, 87, 89

Sabbath Breaking, 131, 134, 142–4

Sanctuary, 58, 59
St. Bees, 104, 105, 149
St. Columba, 29
St. German's, 105, 129
St. John's, 28, 143, 156
Sankey, Gov., 84, 152
St. Trinian's, 110, 125, 149
Sayle, Capt. J., the Craige, 73
Scarlett, 43
Schools, 115, 125
Schoolmasters, 109, 125, 240–2
Scrondal Mill, 226
Sea Raiders, 66
Seating, Church, 111, 112
Settlers in Barbados, 49–52
Seven Swearings, 23
Shaw, Dr. Thos., 32, 33
Sheading Courts, 58, 61, 95, 155
Sieve and Shears, 21, 22
Silk, Dr. Abraham, 34
Sites, Church, 109, 110
Skeet, The, 134
Skillicorn, Capt., 51, 52
Skyhill, 94, 99
Slander, 135
Slieau Whallian, 14
Slieau Dhoo, 151
Smelt, Lt. Gov., 200–5, 207, 245
Smith, Gov., 196
Smuggling, 184, 185, 192
Smoke Penny, 107
Soldiers, The Lord's, 42, 45
Sorcery, 13–29
Speaker of Keys, 195
Spiritual Courts, 130, 131, 137
Standish of Ellanbane, 45, 101
Stanlagh Mooar, The, 69
Starvey Road, The, 27
Stephen, Ballavarran, 199
Stevenson, Balladoole, 46, 70, 163, 221
Stool of Correction, 21
Strayed Animals, 39
Sumner, General, 14, 131, 213
Sumner, Parish, 131–135, 137
Surgeon to the House, 31, 32
Swearing, 153
Swearing Stone, 23
Synod at Braddan (1291), 105

Tarra (increase), The, 17, 18, 58
Taubman, J. (1662), 74; (1779), 195
Teare, Capt. John, 242, 247
Teare Ballawhane, 28
Tenure, Customary, 70
Thwaites, Sir T., 21, 115, 144
Three Bells, The, 122
Tithes, Gathering, 133, 197, 199
Tithes, Fish, 116, 117
Tithes, Impropriate, 110

Tobacco Spinning, 181, 182
Tobin, John, 144
Tobin, Caesar, Middle, 198
Tokens, 149, 197, 100
Town Captain, 84–93
Town Markets, 85, 86, 167
Trade, 176, 190, 193
Trading Voyages, 178–80
Traditional Ballad, 171
Trammon Tree, 28, 220
Transport, Means of, 156, 157
Tromode Mill, 152
Tubman, Capt. T., German, 73
Twenty-four, The, *see Keys*
Tynwald, 28, 42, 46, 58, 61, 69, 70, 78, 79, 81, 83, 194
Tynwald Hill, 14, 23, 93

Vicar General, 131, 201
Vicar of Thirds, 104, 105
Vicar of Pension, 104, 105
Vinch (Finch), Robt., 33
Viol, violin, 145

Wages, 46, 126, 127
Waldron, William, 36
Walker, Wm., D. D., 127, 213, 220
Ward, Bishop, 209
Warden of the Watch, 61
Warren, The Lord's, 40, 41
Watch Hill, 64, 65
Watch and Ward, 63, 64, 76–8, 87, 211
Wesley, John, 221
Whithorne Priory, 45, 104
Wigan Lane, Fight at, 72
Wigs, 144
Wilks, Jas., V. G., 119, 127, 190, 215, 224
Wilks, Colonel Mark, 208, 224
Wills, Ballaugh, 218, 219
Wilson, Bishop, 15, 90, 91, 125, 128, 132, 137, 176, 198, 213, 235
Witches, 13
Woods of Balleira, 107, 108
Wreck, 215–16, 168–70

Yard (rod), The, 60
Yarding, 47, 126